THE ANATOMY SERIES OF INTERNATIONAL INSTITUTIONS

The EU Merger Regulation
and the
Anatomy of the Merger Task Force

THE ANATOMY SERIES OF INTERNATIONAL INSTITUTIONS

The EU Merger Regulation and the Anatomy of the Merger Task Force

José Rivas
Head of Competition Law Team,
Hammond Suddards

HAMMOND SUDDARDS
SOLICITORS

KLUWER LAW
INTERNATIONAL

LONDON–THE HAGUE–BOSTON

Published by
Kluwer Law International Ltd
Sterling House
66 Wilton Road
London SWIV IDE
United Kingdom

Kluwer Law International incorporates
the publishing programmes of
Graham & Trotman Ltd,
Kluwer Law & Taxation Publishers
and Martinus Nijhoff Publishers

Sold and distributed in
the USA and Canada by
Kluwer Law International
675 Massachusetts Avenue
Cambridge MA 02139
USA

In all other countries, sold and distributed by
Kluwer Law International
P.O. Box 322
3300 AH Dordrecht
The Netherlands

ISBN 90–411–9767–2
Series ISBN 90–411–0735–5
[CIP 99–00000 if LOC received before printing]
© Kluwer Law International 1999
First Published 1999

British Library Cataloguing in Publication Data
A catalogue record for this book is available from the British Library

Typeset in 10/12 pt Veljovic by Photoprint Typesetters, Torquay, Devon
Printed and bound in Great Britain by MPG Books Ltd, Bodmin, Cornwall

CONTENTS

PREFACE

Hammond Suddards produced this book with the aim of providing a timely, precise and comprehensive guide to the EU Merger Regulation and the Merger Task Force. With the EU progressing ever closer towards the accomplishment of an internal market, it is important that companies understand the effects the Merger Regulation may have on planned transactions and comprehend fully the workings of the Merger Task Force. The book is addressed mainly to business people so that they can act and plan ahead accordingly.

The book marks the third in a series of 'anatomy' books written by Hammond Suddards and the second published by Kluwer Law International. The aim of this series is to cover a wide range of topical legal issues through comprehensive, but user-friendly, legal analysis which will benefit practitioners, businesses and interested parties alike. Other forthcoming 'anatomy' books will continue this tradition by focusing on a variety of European and international legal topics.

Many people have contributed to the completion of this book and the editor is particularly grateful to Francisco-Enrique González Díaz, Unit Head of the Merger Task Force, for his comments and suggestions. I would also like to thank the following individuals: Tom Pick who prepared a comprehensive first draft and was of valuable assistance throughout and Bróna Heenan and Benoît Keane who undertook the research of specific points and helped to prepare the final version.

Anyone wishing further information regarding the Merger Regulation and/or the Merger Task Force should contact:

Mr. José Rivas
Hammond Suddards, Avenue Louise 250, Box 65, 1050 Brussels, Belgium.
Tel: + 32 + 2 + 627 76 76
Fax: + 32 + 2 + 627 76 86
E-Mail: Jose.Rivas@HammondSuddards.co.uk

A. INTRODUCTION

A.1 *Aim of the Book*

The aim of this book is to give a practical overview of the application of the Merger Regulation and the competent bodies working with it. It is intended to provide the reader with all the information necessary to handle the Merger Regulation effectively and correctly. The original Merger Regulation (Council Regulation 4064/89) which came into force on 21 September 1990 was recently amended by Council Regulation 1310/97 (the Amending Regulation) and the amendments made by the Amending Regulation represent some important changes which will be explained in greater detail. In this book the term 'Merger Regulation' refers to the original Merger Regulation as amended by the Amending Regulation. An unofficial consolidated version of the Merger Regulation (including the amendments made by the Amending Regulation) can be found in Annex 1. The amendments introduced by the Amending Regulation came into force on 1 March 1998.

As the aim of this book is to aid the reader in using and implementing effectively the Merger Regulation in his or her business environment, the legal issues involved in the study of the Merger Regulation will be analysed in a less academic fashion and a more practical approach to this study shall be undertaken.

A.2 *Historical Background*

Before the entry into force of the Merger Regulation, no explicit merger control provisions existed in the European Union (EU), with the exception of the Coal and Steel Treaty,[1] and therefore there was not a sufficiently coherent framework of legal rules in place.

---

[1] The Merger Regulation only covers transactions involving products subject to the EC Treaty. Concentrations falling within the scope of the European Coal and Steel Treaty (ECSC Treaty) are subject to the specific provisions of the ECSC Treaty (Article 66). As an attempt at simplification and in view of the forthcoming expiry of the ECSC Treaty

The main legal as well as political reason for establishing the Merger Regulation was the strong need to regulate excessive concentration within the Common Market, which increasingly flourished during the 1980's and thus affected sound competition between undertakings.

Footnote 1 cont.

the Commission has issued a Notice concerning alignment of procedures for processing mergers under the EC and ECSC Treaties (see Annex 7). The most notable features of the Notice are: (1) a statement of objections will be sent to the parties where the Commission plans to subject the authorisation of a concentration to conditions or even to prohibit the transaction; (2) the parties' rights of defence are enhanced as express provision is made for access to the file and the possibility of making oral observations; and (3) provided the transaction is notified using the Form CO, the Commission will endeavour to adopt a decision within one month or five months of notification.

B. **THE SCOPE OF THE MERGER REGULATION**

B.1 *A 'Concentration'*

See Diagram A.

DIAGRAM A   WHAT IS A CONCENTRATION?

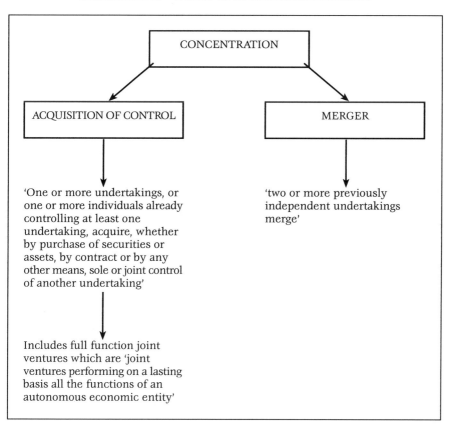

CONCENTRATION

ACQUISITION OF CONTROL

MERGER

'One or more undertakings, or one or more individuals already controlling at least one undertaking, acquire, whether by purchase of securities or assets, by contract or by any other means, sole or joint control of another undertaking'

'two or more previously independent undertakings merge'

Includes full function joint ventures which are 'joint ventures performing on a lasting basis all the functions of an autonomous economic entity'

For a merger or acquisition to be within the scope of the Merger Regulation the transaction itself must satisfy the elements of a *concentration* pursuant to Article 3.

A transaction shall therefore be considered to be a concentration where either of the following requirements are fulfilled[1]

(a) two or more previously independent undertakings merge, or
(b) one or more persons, already controlling at least one undertaking or one or more undertakings, acquire, whether by purchase of securities or assets, by contract or by any other means, direct or indirect control of the whole or parts of one or more other undertakings.

In addition, Article 3(2) states that:

the creation of a joint venture performing on a lasting basis all the functions of an autonomous economic entity shall constitute a concentration within the meaning of paragraph 1(b).

Therefore, there are three methods whereby an operation will be a concentration within the meaning of Article 3 and these are:

- a merger;
- the acquisition of control; and
- a full function joint venture.

A 'merger' is reasonably self-explanatory. However, an acquisition of control can generally be sole or joint. Sole control usually happens where an undertaking acquires a majority of the voting rights of a company. It should be noted that it may arise with a minority shareholding when this leads to a majority of the voting rights. An option to purchase or convert shares cannot in itself confer sole control unless the option is going to be exercised in the near future according to legally binding agreements. Generally speaking, joint control will ensue where two or more undertakings or persons have the possibility of exercising decisive influence over another undertaking. For example, it will exist when there is equality in voting rights or appointment to decision-making bodies between two undertakings.

A full function joint venture is more fully described in the Commission Notice on the concept of full function joint ventures under Council Regulation 4064/89 on the control of concentrations between undertakings (the 'Full Function Joint Venture Notice', see Annex 3). Accordingly:

---

[1] Article 3(1) Regulation 4064/89. Unless otherwise indicated, references to Regulation 4064/89 must be understood as references to Regulation 4064/89 as amended by Regulation 1310/97.

... the joint venture must perform, on a lasting basis, all the functions of an autonomous economic entity. Joint ventures which satisfy this requirement bring about a lasting change in the structure of the undertakings concerned.

The Full Function Joint Venture Notice goes on to explain that a full function joint venture must satisfy the following two requirements to be a concentration within the meaning of Article 3:

- *Joint control.* Control is based on the possibility of exercising decisive influence over an undertaking, which is determined by both legal and factual considerations; and
- *Structural change of the undertakings.* i.e. the joint venture must act as an autonomous economic entity. This means that a joint venture must operate on a market, performing the functions normally carried out by undertakings operating on the same market. One of the elements to be taken into account is whether the joint venture has management which is dedicated to its day to day operations.

Prior to 1 March 1998, the distinction made between 'co-operative' and 'concentrative' joint ventures was very relevant. Co-operative full function joint ventures, being joint ventures where there is an element of 'co-ordination' of competitive behaviour of the undertakings, were previously excluded from the ambit of the Merger Regulation. This distinction has lost its value somewhat, since, as from 1 March 1998, all full function joint ventures which have a 'Community dimension' (see B.2 below) are now brought within the ambit of the Merger Regulation (see B.4.2 below).

B.2 *Community Dimension*

In order to fall within the scope of the Merger Regulation, the concentration has to have a Community dimension pursuant to Article 1 of the Merger Regulation. Such a Community dimension will exist if certain turnover threshold criteria are met. See Diagram B.

There are two sets of turnover threshold criteria set out in Article 1. The criteria set out in Article 1(2) are the original Community dimension criteria that have not been amended by the Amending Regulation. In the event that the turnover figures do not fall within the scope of Article 1(2), the second set of threshold criteria are applied and these are set out in Article 1(3).

DIAGRAM B   COMMUNITY DIMENSION

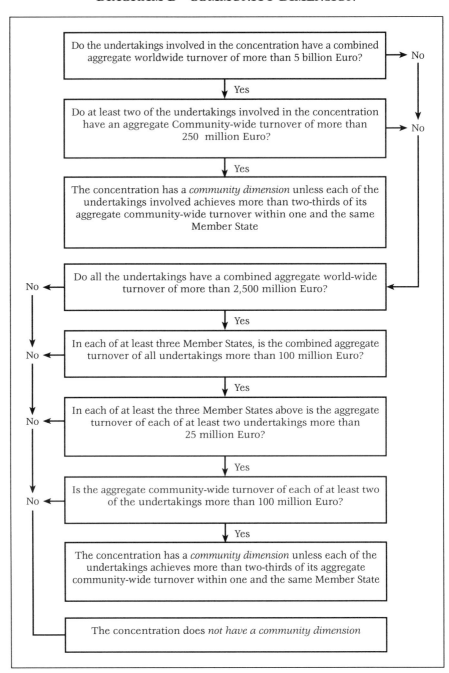

The Article 1(2) criteria, the original threshold criteria, are as follows:

- the combined aggregate worldwide turnover of the undertakings involved in the concentration is more than 5 billion Euro; *and*
- the aggregate Community-wide turnover of each of at least two of the undertakings involved in the concentration is more than 250 million Euro;
- *unless* each of the undertakings concerned achieves more than two-thirds of its aggregate Community-wide turnover within one and the same Member State.

Set out below are two examples of transactions which meet the original turnover threshold criteria (all figures in million Euro):

EXAMPLE 1

	Member State A	Member State B	EU turnover	Worldwide turnover
Company A	1,000	1,501	> 250	2,501
Company B	1,501	1,000	> 250	2,501
				5,002

EXAMPLE 2

	Member State A	Member State B	EU turnover	Third countries turnover	Worldwide turnover
Company A	101	150	> 250	4,500	4,751
Company B	150	101	> 250	—	251
					5,002

Past experience with the application of Community merger control under the original Merger Regulation had shown that at Community level legal uncertainty had increased whenever there were concentrations that had a significant impact in several of the Member States. This meant, for example, that they qualified for examination under national merger control proceedings in each of those Member States and therefore national filings were required, thus showing that these transactions had effect within the Community but fell outside the scope of the Merger Regulation itself. The European Community recognised this and this was the reason for the introduction of the criteria set out in Article 1(3). This amendment to the Merger Regulation ensures that there is a pan-European authority dealing with concentrations that have a significant impact in several of the Member States and therefore the so-called one-stop shop principle is underlined.

The new threshold criteria create benefits all round by cutting legal costs and reducing the administrative burden on the companies concerned.

7

Furthermore, conflicting assessments by the national competition authorities and the Merger Task Force (the MTF) are avoided. As from 1 March 1998, an undertaking is able to file a single notification if the Article 1(3) criteria set out below are met:

(a)   the combined aggregate worldwide turnover of all the undertakings concerned is more than 2500 million Euro; *and*
(b)   in each of at least three Member States, the combined aggregate turnover of all the undertakings concerned is more than 100 million Euro; *and*
(c)   in each of at least three Member States included for the purpose of point (b), the aggregate turnover of each of at least two of the undertakings concerned is more than 25 million Euro; *and*
(d)   the aggregate Community-wide turnover of each of at least two of the undertakings concerned is more than 100 million Euro; *unless* each of the undertakings concerned achieves more than two-thirds of its aggregate Community-wide turnover within one and the same Member State.

Set out below are two examples of transactions which meet the new turnover threshold criteria (all figures in million Euro):

EXAMPLE 3

	Member State A	Member State B	Member State C	Total EC and worldwide turnover
Company A	1,174	51	26	1,251
Company B	26	50	1,174	1,250
	1,200	101	1,200	2,501

EXAMPLE 4

	Member State A	Member State B	Member State C	Third countries turnover	EC turnover	Worldwide turnover
Company A	75	75	51	2,198	201	2,399
Company B	26	26	50	—	102	102
	101	101	101	—	—	2,501

The single notification process that has effectively been brought in by the Merger Regulation increases the transparency of the notification process of large cross-border mergers and acquisitions in the EU as several different complicated filings in various Member States are no longer needed.

It is important to keep in mind that the 'Community dimension' criteria do not necessarily require a concentration of companies within Member States. The Merger Regulation may equally apply to concentrations of companies residing outside the Community if the turnover thresholds criteria laid down in Article 1(2) or 1(3) are satisfied.

The European Commission (the Commission) published a Notice on 2 March 1998 concerning turnover.[2] It is not proposed to deal with the content of this Notice in this book, as the Notice deals in great detail with the calculation of turnover and undertakings from which the turnover figures should be taken.

Finally, it should be mentioned that special criteria for the calculation of turnover of credit institutions, other financial institutions and insurance undertakings are provided for in Article 5 of the Merger Regulation.

B.3 *Extensions and Limitations of Scope*

The Merger Regulation is based on the 'one-stop shop' principle by establishing the Commission as the overall EU competition authority controlling and regulating concentrations that fall within the scope of the Merger Regulation. Article 21 states:

1. Subject to review by the Court of Justice, the Commission shall have sole jurisdiction to take the decisions provided for in this Regulation.
2. No Member State shall apply its national legislation on competition to any concentration that has a Community dimension.

It is further provided by Article 22(1) of the Merger Regulation that:

This Regulation alone shall apply to concentrations as defined in Article 3 and Regulations No. 17, (EEC) No 1017/68, (EEC) No 4056/86 and (EEC) No. 3975/87 shall not apply, except in relation to joint ventures that do not have a Community dimension and which have as their object or effect the co-ordination of the competitive behaviour of undertakings that remain independent.

Accordingly, if a concentration falls within the scope of the Merger Regulation, the procedure under Regulation 17 (and the other Regulations quoted above) is inapplicable. Regulation 17 lays down the procedure applying to cases falling within Articles 81 and 82 (ex Articles 85 and 86) of the EC Treaty. Therefore, these Articles do not need to be looked at in relation to concentrations that fall within the ambit of the Merger Regulation. However, Article 22(1) of the Merger Regulation makes it clear that there is an exception to this general rule, and this is for joint ventures that do not have a Community dimension. In such circumstances, it should be verified whether the transaction might fall within Article 81 (ex Article 85) of the EC Treaty.

Furthermore, three main derogations to the one-stop shop principle exist which are outlined below.

---

[2] The Commission Notice on calculation of turnover under Regulation 4064/89 on the control of concentrations between undertakings, OJ C66/25 of 2 March 1998, see Annex 6.

B.3.1   The 'Distinct Market' Exception[3]

A Member State may request the Commission to refer back to the competent national authorities of that Member State a concentration which (i) threatens to create or strengthen a dominant position or (ii) affects competition in a distinct market within its territory that does not form a substantial part of the Common Market. If the Commission considers that such a distinct market exists as well as a threat that the concentration will create or strengthen a dominant position, it may deal with the case itself. Alternatively, it may refer the whole or part of the case. If a concentration affects competition in a distinct market within the territory of a Member State which does not form a substantial part of the Common Market, the Commission shall refer the whole or part of the case to the relevant national authorities.

This provision has been established because there has been considerable concern by some Member States that the Commission might come to the conclusion that a concentration is innocuous as regards the Common Market yet it still might be harmful if one considers competition at a domestic level. This may be the case even if the 'distinct market' at the domestic level is not a substantial part of the Common Market.

If the Commission agrees with the Member State and a case is totally or partially referred, the Member State will apply its own national competition legislation on the referral by the Commission. However, it should be remembered that the onus is always on the Member State to make an application to refer to the Commission.

B.3.2   The Dutch Clause

An exception exists relating to the investigation of a non-Community dimension concentration by the Commission. This gives the Commission the power, at the request of a Member State or at the joint request of two or more Member States together, to investigate such a concentration.[4]

This mechanism provides for control by the Commission in circumstances where there is no effective review of mergers at a domestic level or the Member States consider the Commission to be better placed to assess the transaction. It applies in cases where, even though the concentration falls below the thresholds, it nevertheless creates or strengthens a dominant position as a result of which effective competition would be significantly

---

[3]   This 'distinct market' exception is laid down in Article 9, Regulation 4064/89.
[4]   Article 22(3) to (5), Regulation 4064/89.

impeded within the territory of a Member State or of the Member State(s) making a joint request.

The suspension provisions[5] also apply to concentrations which are subject to the Dutch clause. However, a concentration under this clause will only be suspended to the extent that it has not been put into effect on the day the parties are informed by the Commission that such a request has been made by one or more Member States. Since the obligation to suspend the concentration is only applicable insofar as it has not been put into effect before the parties have been informed by the Commission of a request by a Member State, there will be transactions that are implemented despite the fact that there has been a request for a referral. This may entail unwelcome bother for the Commission in that it may be obliged to unravel a concentration that has been put into effect.

The Commission, on a referral under the Dutch clause, can only initiate action if it concludes that trade between Member States will be affected as a result of such a concentration.

B.3.3 Legitimate Interest

The 'legitimate interest' exception allows Member States to prohibit a concentration which would otherwise be authorised by the Commission in the interests of public security, plurality of the media and prudential rules in the financial services sector. Any other public legitimate interest alleged by the Member State(s) needs to be approved by the Commission in advance.[6]

This third exception to the one-stop shop principle is quite different from those just dealt with, as it allows a Member State to intervene on non-competition grounds.

B.4 *Assessment Criteria*

If the concentration falls within the scope of the Merger Regulation, the Commission will then investigate whether the concentration is compatible with the Common Market pursuant to Article 2 of the Merger Regulation. See Diagram C.

---

[5] Article 7, Regulation 4064/89.
[6] Article 21(3), Regulation 4064/89.

DIAGRAM C   ASSESSMENT PROCEDURE BY THE COMMISSION

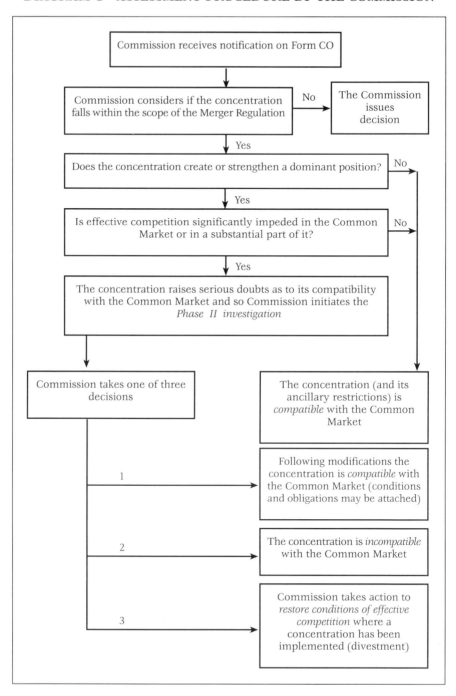

B.4.1 Appraisal of Concentrations

A concentration is deemed to be incompatible within the Common Market if:

- it creates or strengthens a dominant position; and
- as a result of which, effective competition would be significantly impeded in the Common Market or in a substantial part of it.[7]

In reaching its decision of compatibility/incompatibility the Commission will consider the following substantive appraisal criteria:

- the structure of all the markets concerned;
- actual and potential competition from undertakings located either within or outside the Common Market;
- the market position of the undertakings concerned and their economic and financial powers;
- legal and other barriers to entry, supply and demand trends;
- the alternatives available to suppliers and users and their access to supply and markets;
- the interests of intermediate and ultimate consumers; and
- the development of technical and economic progress.[8]

In considering these criteria, the Commission will have to deal with each case of concentration individually and will have to take a closer look at the relevant product or service market and the relevant geographic market, in order to analyse the market power created or reinforced by the proposed concentration.

The issues of both dominance and market definition go hand in hand with the investigation of the proposed concentration and its possible implications on competition in the Common Market. Once the relevant product and geographic markets have been defined, the investigation of the dominant position of the proposed concentration will have to concentrate on those markets and scrutinise the effects the concentration might inflict on competition.

A dominant position arises if, as a result of the concentration, a company or a group of companies is in a position to behave to an appreciable extent independently of their competitors, customers and consumers. There is an indication that a concentration may not create or strengthen a dominant position where the market share of the undertakings concerned does not

---

[7]   Article 2(3), Regulation 4064/89.
[8]   Article 2(1)(a) and (b), Regulation 4064/89.

exceed 25 per cent either in the Common Market or in a substantial part of it.[9]

B.4.2 The Distinction between Concentrative and Co-operative Joint Ventures

Since the entry into force of the Amending Regulation on 1 March 1998, all full-function joint ventures, whether concentrative or co-operative, provided they meet the turnover threshold criteria, are considered to be a concentration and therefore to be examined within the procedure and deadlines of the Merger Regulation.

If the full-function joint venture created is of such nature that its parent companies withdraw totally and definitely from the sphere of activities of the joint venture and thus leave behind a full function autonomous economic entity which has all the characteristics of a concentrative joint venture, then the full force of the Merger Regulation will apply and it will be appraised in accordance with the dominance test (described in B.4.1. above).

If creation of the joint venture has as its object or effect the co-ordination of the competitive behaviour of undertakings that remain independent then, in addition to the dominance test, the principles of Article 81(1) and 81(3) (ex Article 85(1) and 85(3)) of the EC Treaty will be applied to the co-operative aspects. In connection with the co-operative aspects, the following will be considered by the Commission:

- whether two or more parent companies retain to a significant extent activities in the same market as the joint venture or in a market which is downstream or upstream from that of the joint venture or in a neighbouring market that is closely related to this market
- whether the co-ordination which is the direct consequence of the creation of the joint venture affords the undertakings concerned the possibility of eliminating competition in respect of a substantial part of the products or services in question.[10]

Little guidance exists as to who makes the decision at the outset as to whether the concentration has co-operative effects or not. It appears that the MTF must decide in the initial stages whether the full-function joint venture has any co-operative elements. The relevant Directorate within DG IV dealing with Article 81 and 82 (ex Article 85 and 86) matters is involved in this decision from the very beginning. If the full-function joint-

---

[9]   Recital 15, Preamble, Regulation 4064/89.
[10]   Article 2(4), Regulation 4064/89.

DIAGRAM D   ASSESSMENT OF JOINT VENTURES BY THE COMMISSION

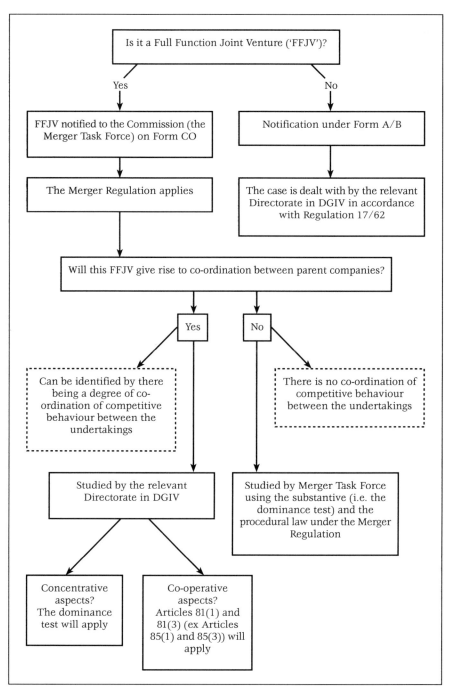

venture has co-operative aspects, the MTF will not deal with the case and the whole case will be transferred to the relevant Directorate within DG IV, who then apply the dominance test to the concentration aspects of the full-function joint venture and Article 81(1) and 81(3) (ex Article 85(1) and 85(3)) to its co-operative aspects. If there is no co-operative element in the full-function joint venture, and it appears that it is in fact purely concentrative, the MTF does have jurisdiction to look into the joint venture and does so using the dominance test. (See Diagram D).

The identification of co-operative aspects in a given transaction may be a difficult task. This is particularly so in high tech and/or rapidly evolving sectors, such as the telecoms sector where the dividing line between markets is constantly changing.

It would appear that rather than making rash decisions based on a pre-determined policy, the MTF analyses transactions in these sectors on a case by case basis. It is to be assumed that in the near future, once these markets have matured, the identification of co-operative elements in these markets will be more straightforward.

Finally, it is worth noting that the concentrative aspects of full-function joint ventures below the turnover thresholds fall within the competence of the Member States and, therefore, are subject to their relevant national competition laws. As regards the co-operative aspects of such joint ventures, the previous situation applies; that is to say, they are subject to the application of Articles 81 and 82 (ex Articles 85 and 86) of the EC Treaty by the Commission within the procedural framework of Regulation 17 ('Information on the assessment of full-function joint ventures pursuant to the competition rules of the European Commission', see Annex 8).

C. PROCEDURE

C.1 *Informal Contacts*

Large companies, because of their likelihood of being involved in transactions caught by the Merger Regulation and who think that they may need to make a notification, tend to start building contacts on an informal basis within the Commission and in the Member States. Member States' competition authorities should not be forgotten as they can influence the Commission's final decision through the Advisory Committee. Equally, the national authorities may have an informal say in the decision as many former MTF personnel return to their own country to work. It is a good idea to equate senior Commission officials with high level management of the companies involved as Commission officials will not appreciate meeting with junior staff who do not have a good grasp of the issues. The ease of contact that results will help to make officials who may be involved in future decisions more co-operative.

C.2 *Briefing Paper to be Submitted to the MTF*

Given the demanding nature of the notification exercise and the complexity of some of the legal questions, it is prudent for the undertakings concerned to have a pre-notification meeting with the relevant Commission officials. In this context, it is advisable to provide the officials with a briefing paper some weeks before the expected date of notification.

The submission of such a briefing paper is a good way of informing the MTF of a proposed concentration at an early stage. It can therefore give the MTF the possibility to consider the concentration in the light of the Merger Regulation.

Ideally, the briefing paper itself should be followed by a first draft of the Form CO and should contain all the information necessary for the MTF to obtain a preliminary view of the intended transaction. In order to serve this purpose, the briefing paper should contain all relevant information about the parties themselves and their field of commercial activities in addition to as much information about their proposed transaction as is possible to collect at that stage. This includes draft documentation, for example: all corporate governance documentation; any joint venture agreement with the parent company; supply and distribution agreements with the parent company, etc. This of course requires co-operation between the members of the undertakings concerned and the lawyers dealing with the case as well as knowledge of the markets and products. To achieve this task in the best possible way, it is necessary to identify the competent members of each undertaking involved who are able to supply the information. A well-defined strategic network should therefore be set up in order to co-ordinate the work between the undertakings and the lawyers and to source the information needed.

C.3 *Pre-notification Meetings*

In Recital 10 of Commission Regulation 447/98 on notifications, time limits and hearings provided for in Council Regulation 4064/89 on the control of concentrations between undertakings (the Implementing Regulation), it is stated:

Whereas the Commission should give the notifying parties and other parties involved, if they so request, an opportunity before notification to discuss the intended concentration informally and in strict confidence . . .

The procedure under the Merger Regulation is very complex and follows very strict time limits (which will be dealt with at a later stage). It must therefore be in the interests of all parties to be aware of the particular impact the individual case in question might have when being dealt with under the Merger Regulation. This is even more relevant in the case of the undertakings concerned, because concentrations are particularly sensitive to any delays.

The MTF works with the presumption of innocence, at least during Phase I investigations. Notifying parties should not hesitate to work with the MTF in a climate of co-operation. However, it should not be forgotten that Phase II is more akin to litigation.

A pre-notification meeting is important for many reasons. For example, first, it serves the need for the undertakings concerned to obtain a preliminary sense of the MTF's thinking and its possible approach in handling the case, as well as guidance on the notification procedure itself. At this stage, it can be ascertained whether the Merger Regulation applies, and whether the transaction raises any co-operative issues which would entail the transfer of the case to the relevant Directorate of DG IV.

Secondly, it gives the MTF the opportunity to advise the parties to dispense with supplying unnecessary information at the time of the formal notification or, in the alternative, to advise them to supply more information on certain relevant matters. Information waivers (see C.4.3.3 below) should be discussed at this stage as opposed to later when work may have already been done on irrelevant matters. There may be parts of Form CO which do not need to be completed. It is especially important that these issues are ironed out at an early stage as notification needs to be completed in the short space of a week from the conclusion of the agreement. It is also possible that the MTF may grant an extension of time for filing Form CO.

Thirdly, in cases which entail difficult assessment of the relevant market(s) or of the structure of the deal or involve a complex and rapidly changing sector, the pre-notification meeting is of vital importance to avoid a declaration that the notification is incomplete[1] or a decision to enter into Phase II. In such complex cases, which will require more man hours, the more time the MTF has to consider the documentation the better. With a view to covering as much ground as possible at pre-notification stage, nothing prevents notifying parties from authorising the MTF to contact third parties at this stage. Equally, notifying parties should consider the pre-notification meeting as an opportunity for submitting their draft proposed undertakings to the MTF. This will allow the MTF to consider from the very beginning the impact of the transaction in the market in the light of the proposed undertaking without the parties yet being bound by the undertakings.

Preliminary contacts on a confidential basis with the MTF should therefore be seen as an essential step for all parties to diminish uncertainties and to 'co-operate' in a way so that a possible investigation under the Merger Regulation runs as smoothly as possible. The early meetings should be planned and prepared for carefully. For example, when choosing representatives to attend meetings, the importance of making a good first impression on the MTF staff should be borne in mind. If suitable people attend, this will ease communication and go towards ensuring that all sides get the most out of the pre-notification meeting. It is advisable that the following people attend on behalf of the notifying parties: (i) specialist competition lawyers; (ii) representatives of high level management within the companies, who are responsible for the industrial and business activities; (iii) the individual(s) responsible for the deal itself and to whom the merger team ultimately reports. This is to ensure that the MTF is working with a team of representatives. It will serve no purpose if the MTF officials, whose time is valuable, are faced with a team of people who do not have a

---

[1] It has been reported that in 1997, 17 declarations of incompleteness were made out of a total of 172 notifications. From 1 January 1998 to 13 November 1998 17 declarations of incompleteness were made out of 196 notifications. (See Merger: Best Practice Guidelines (www.europa.eu.int) Annex 10).

19

full understanding either of competition law or of the commercial realities of the transaction.

In summary, the pre-notification meetings can be regarded as a trial run, without the pressure of time constraints which inevitably follow after notification. As the MTF is accessible and approachable, informal discussions (whether by telephone or face to face) are a good means of securing contact with the relevant officials. It is advisable to allow some weeks for pre-notification meetings to follow their natural course before the notification has to be made. Although in general pre-notification discussions last approximately one month, it has been known for them to continue for up to one year. The fact that the Preamble of the Merger Regulation itself and even Form CO refers to such meetings reflects the MTF's keenness that such a process is used. Form CO states in the opening paragraph A:

Experience has shown that pre-notification meetings are extremely valuable to both the notifying parties and the Commission in determining the precise amount of information required in a notification and, in the large majority of cases, will result in a significant reduction of the information required. Accordingly, notifying parties are encouraged to consult the Commission regarding the possibility of dispensing with the obligation to provide certain information . . .[2]

Some practitioners recommend that the applicant identifies and contacts the preferred person for dealing with the case during pre-notification discussions. Although the MTF is not entirely in favour of this, external lawyers and advisers may be able to suggest particular officers who would be more suited to one case than another, based either on linguistic grounds or on their expertise in a certain field. The sooner they are involved, the more likely they are to be assigned to the case. It should be borne in mind however that the MTF does not necessarily favour this degree of case management planning and that such steps should be undertaken with appropriate subtlety.

In summary, topics for discussion at the pre-notification meeting might include:

- confirmation as to whether the Merger Regulation applies to the transaction;
- if the Merger Regulation does apply, whether Article 81 (ex Article 85) of the EC Treaty issues are also involved;
- a request for exemption from the obligation to suspend the transaction;
- whether Form CO must be completed in full, or whether the MTF would accept a partial waiver, i.e. a more limited notification. Form

---

[2] Form CO OJ L377/9.

CO is extensive and its completion time consuming. It is also possible, where a party does not have certain information, or is unable to give complete information, for that information to be omitted, providing that 'good reasons' are provided;[3]

- the extent of supporting documentation required by the MTF. It is wise to identify what information you have available, and what may need to be prepared, so that resources can be employed as efficiently as possible;
- potentially affected product and geographic markets;
- other foreseeable difficulties, whether relating to the provision of information, or otherwise.

C.4   *Notification Procedure*

See Diagram E: an overview of the notification procedure.

C.4.1   Timetable

Within seven days from the making of the relevant agreement or acquisition of a controlling interest or the announcement of a public bid, a notification has to be made to the MTF.[4]

The Implementing Regulation specifies in more detail the rules relating to time limits which are applicable to notification. Notification must be either delivered to the Commission by hand at the address indicated on Form CO or have been dispatched by registered letter to that same address.[5]

In dealing with the timetable of pre-notification, two factors have to be clarified: first, from when the one-week deadline effectively starts to run in relation to the conclusion of an agreement; and secondly, how this one-week period is then calculated.

Concerning the first question it must be stressed that only a legally binding agreement concerning a concentration is able to trigger the one-week deadline. This includes agreements in the form of a definitive document, and heads of agreement and similar documents, as long as they have a legally binding character. In order to fulfil this legal requirement a concluded agreement must have as its purpose the creation of legally binding

---

[3]   Article 3(2), Regulation 447/98.
[4]   Article 4(1), Regulation 4064/89.
[5]   Article 20, Regulation 447/98.

DIAGRAM E   DO THE PARTIES HAVE TO NOTIFY?

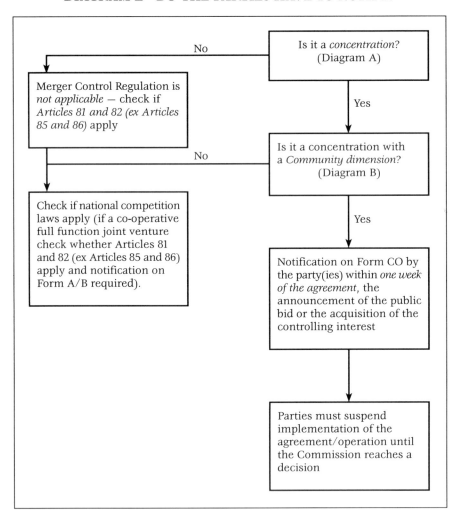

relations on which each party can rely and must not include the possibility of unilateral rescission by one of the parties.

In fixing the time limits, account has to be taken of working days. 'Working days' means all days other than Saturdays, Sundays, public holidays and other holidays as determined by the Commission and which are published in the Official Journal. If the last day of the seven-day deadline coincides with a 'non-working day' in the country of dispatch, the deadline expires on the following working day. The month of August is generally the big holiday period for the European Institutions. Officially, notifications can be made in this month but it is advisable, if at all possible, not to notify during this month.

Once the notification arrives, copies are sent to the following bodies and departments:

- The Merger Task Force
- The Member States
- The Legal Service of the Commission
- Directorate A in DG IV
- The relevant sectoral unit in DG IV
- Associated Directorates General

C.4.2 Notifying Parties

Notification should be made by the person or undertaking acquiring control of the whole or part of one or more undertakings.[6]

The fact that only the acquiring undertaking is obliged to make the notification does not free it from the burden of providing information concerning the target company. This information may prove difficult to obtain from the target company at a stage where it is not absolutely certain that the transaction will be accomplished. Nevertheless the sole undertaking responsible for an eventual incomplete notification is the acquiring company.

If however the concentration consists of a merger or in the acquisition of joint control, both parties are under an obligation to notify. Where a situation of *de facto* joint control arises from the acquisition of a significant minority shareholding in another undertaking by a new investor, a joint notification is required.

In practical terms a joint notification should be submitted by a joint representative of the concerned undertakings who is authorised to transmit and receive documents on behalf of all the notifying parties.

C.4.3 Form CO

Form CO is the form which must be used in relation to the notification of a concentration. The original Form CO has been modified several times and the present version has only been in use since the entering into force of the Implementing Regulation on 1 March 1998.

---

[6] Articles 4(2) and 3(1)(b), Regulation 4064/89.

Form CO requires a complex set of information as regards the parties, the nature of the transaction and the markets affected. This information has to be supported by considerable economic analysis including not only information on general conditions in the potentially affected markets, but also, information on the economic effects the proposed concentration might inflict if concluded.

Notification on Form CO should be done in the intended language of the proceedings. Any supporting information which is in a non-official EU language will need to be translated, and this factor needs to be worked into the already tight timetable. An important issue is that the MTF's official exchange rate tables must be used when calculating turnover. These can be obtained from DG IV's website on the Internet (www.europa.eu.int).

The colossal amount of work involved in preparing and completing a Form CO can only be done with the help of specialist competition lawyers. Their advice, together with skilled advice from economists, must be seen as an essential part of the legal procedure under the Merger Regulation. In order to highlight the legal and economic implications of the proposed concentration, the consultation of lawyers and economists should be made well in advance of the notification procedure and thus at a time when the parties' plan to merge arises and should be maintained during the various procedural stages.

C.4.3.1   *Copies to be submitted*

In Section E of the introduction to the Form CO on 'How to notify' it is stipulated that one original and 23 copies of Form CO and all supporting documentation must be submitted to the MTF. Exactly what the 'supporting information' consists of is dealt with in Section 5 of Form CO. This includes relevant annual reports and accounts, the offer document in the case of a public bid (if applicable) and any other 'documents bringing about the concentration'. In addition, where at least one affected market is identified, the completed notification must also contain as supporting documentation copies of analyses, reports, studies and surveys that have been prepared for the purposes of assessing or analysing the concentration with respect to competitive conditions, actual or potential competitors and market conditions.

It is important to understand clearly what information the Commission requires by way of supporting documentation. If the content of the information is incorrect or the number of copies submitted (for example) is not right, the notification will be deemed to be incomplete.[7] This in turn

---

[7]   Article 4(4), Regulation 447/98.

may delay the date of when the notification becomes effective. In other words, this gives the Commission a reason to delay its decision on the concentration.[8]

C.4.3.2 *Information to be submitted*

Any notification must contain the information requested by Form CO and this can broadly be divided into two parts.[9]

First, the Introduction to Form CO basically gives guiding information on how to complete Form CO correctly. The Introduction should therefore be read carefully. Amongst other things, the Introduction addresses questions on how to notify, the need to submit a correct and complete notification, the possibility to submit a notification in short form in the case of the creation of a joint venture with minor Community importance, and questions on the handling of confidential information.

Secondly, the next part of Form CO is divided into 12 sections. Sections 1 to 5 of Form CO are quite straightforward and oblige the parties to provide information covering essential facts and figures concerning:

- the notifying party (or parties);
- details of the concentration such as the legal nature of the concentration, turnover figures for the last financial year;
- ownership and control issues with respect to the concerned undertakings;
- personal and financial links and previous acquisitions; and
- the 'supporting documentation' that should accompany the Form CO.

It is the information provided in these sections that determines the critical legal question of whether the concentration qualifies for investigation under the Merger Regulation.

Sections 6 to 9 get to the heart of the economic analysis in requiring the parties to:

- identify the relevant product and geographic markets and the markets affected by the notified concentration;
- provide information on product markets affected for each of the last three financial years;

---

[8] Section B(c) of the Introduction to the Form CO.
[9] Article 3, Regulation 447/98.

- provide information on the structure of supply and demand, details of market entry, the importance of research and development, the available systems of distribution and servicing, details of major suppliers and customers, the relevance of co-operation agreements, the trade associations presently active in the market; and
- provide information on any conglomerate aspects of the proposed concentration where any of the parties holds a market share of 25 per cent or more in any product market in which there is no horizontal or vertical relationship, the worldwide context in which the concentration is taking place, justification and identification of any ancillary restraints.

The grounds outlined above are the ones that have not been modified by the Amending Regulation and can be considered to be the grounds on which the Commission will assess whether a purely concentrative full function joint venture is compatible with the Common Market and does not impede effective competition.

Section 10 lists the additional grounds brought in by the Amending Regulation and can be said to be the grounds on which the Commission will assess the compatibility with the Common Market of full function joint ventures which have co-operative aspects. These further grounds require the parties to explain the extent to which the parent companies are active in the same market as the joint venture or in related markets, and to what extent, if any, there is co-ordination between the parent undertakings and the joint venture and therefore to justify and explain how the criteria of Article 81(3) (ex Article 85(3)) of the EC Treaty apply.

Section 11 requests the parties to:

- explain any ancillary restraints which are related to the implementation of the concentration;
- decide whether the operation should be treated as an application either for negative clearance or for individual exemption under Article 81(3) (ex Article 85(3)) of the EC Treaty in the event that the MTF finds that the transaction does not constitute a concentration.

Section 12 of Form CO requires the parties to declare that the information given to the Commission is correct to the best of the knowledge and belief of those who sign the notification, that all estimates are identified as such and are the best estimates of the underlying facts, and that all opinions expressed are sincere.

In general, any assumptions made by the applicant should be clearly identified as assumptions. If certain items of information which are required by Form CO are not available, the reason for this should be stated. Estimates, which are identified as such, should be inserted in the place of the missing information. In addition, any inaccuracies in the information provided may render the notification ineffective until rectified. The accuracy of information should therefore be thoroughly checked. It should also be mentioned that the applicant must consider whether any of the supporting information submitted is likely to damage their case. Memoranda, for example, stating that the particular company is 'dominant', or the 'absolute leader' in its market and other like phrases, will not aid the applicant in satisfying the MTF that the transaction in question should be cleared. The applicant should be prepared to explain the document to the MTF in the best possible light.

C.4.3.3 *Information waivers*

Section A of the Introduction to Form CO pays tribute to the extent of the burden of information that has to be provided by the parties. Whenever a party is unable to provide a response to a question or can only respond to a limited extent on the basis of available information, the party is supposed to indicate this fact and give accompanying reasons.

If a party considers some of the information required as unnecessary for the Commission's investigation of the case, it may ask the Commission to dispense with the obligation to provide that information.[10] The Commission is empowered to dispense with the obligation where it considers that such information is not necessary for the examination of the case. However, it is suggested that waivers of information should be discussed at a very early stage, in order that unnecessary work and time is not wasted (see C.3 above).

The Commission tends to make wide use of this waiver procedure, however the information required is significant and therefore it is most useful for companies whose proposed concentration is likely to fall within the scope of the Merger Regulation to keep a continuously updated set of relevant data.

Depending on the nature of the transaction, it is possible to agree with the MTF that either a short-form Form CO or even a partially completed Form CO be submitted in place of the full Form CO.

Notification in short form is possible where joint control is acquired by two or more undertakings and:

---

[10]   Article 3(2), Regulation 447/98.

(i) the turnover of the joint venture and/or the turnover of the contributed activities, is less that ECU 100 million in the EEA territory; and
(ii) the total value of assets transferred to the joint venture is less than ECU 100 million in the EEA territory.

All information on Form CO must be correct, complete and not misleading, otherwise it will be considered to be incomplete. A party wishing to limit the amount of information provided, should consider broaching the subject at the informal discussion stage. In this way time will not be wasted in collecting information which was unnecessary. Clarifying what information is needed will also reduce the risk of the notification being rejected as incomplete, which may lead to the imposition of a fine for late notification. It may be that the MTF itself considers some information to be irrelevant to the transaction and they should therefore be addressed directly on this point.

The notification only becomes effective once complete and accurate information is received by the Commission. Although it is desirable to limit the information to be submitted, care should still be taken that the MTF has sufficient information. A party will be liable to a fine of up to ECU 50,000 if incorrect or misleading information is supplied intentionally or negligently.[11] Further, a decision on the compatibility of a notified concentration can be revoked where it transpires that the decision was based on incorrect information for which one of the undertakings is responsible.[12]

The potential psychological impact of an incomplete notification should not be underestimated. It should be pointed out, however, that Form CO may be returned for a number of reasons. It may be for example, that the industry sector is so complex that a party may in good faith have omitted to refer to a relevant sector which can later transpire to be important. It is preferable for the Form CO to be returned incomplete, and for additional time to be won, than for the case to proceed to Phase II through sheer lack of information. The return of an incomplete Form CO can also have negative indirect results due to damaging press coverage.

Notifying parties should inform the MTF immediately if any important changes occur after submitting Form CO.

C.4.3.4 *Confidentiality*

The MTF is well-known and trusted for keeping business secrets. Nevertheless, it is advisable to submit confidential information separately,

---

[11] Article 14(1)(b), Regulation 4064/89.
[12] Article 8(5), Regulation 4064/89.

clearly marked as 'Business Secrets'. Note in particular that third parties may be granted access to the Commission's non-confidential files if they have an interest in the case. It is therefore even more important to submit confidential information marked as such.

C.4.4 Failure to Notify and Consequences

Besides the possibility of fines being levied (see C.9 below) a concentration caught by the Merger Regulation which has not been notified cannot legally be put into effect.

C.4.5 Publication of Notification

The Commission is required to publish the fact of the notification,[13] which is done in the Official Journal of the European Communities (C series), whenever the Commission finds that a concentration falls within the scope of the Merger Regulation. In practice the publication contains a summary of the notification on a preliminary basis and the statement that a final decision on the notification is reserved. The publication also contains the date of the notification, the names of the parties, the nature of the concentration as well as the economic sectors involved.

Interested third parties are invited to submit their possible observations on the proposed concentration, normally no later than 10 days following the date of the publication. These observations can either be faxed or sent by post under a reference number to the MTF.

C.5 *Phase I Investigation*

Once a notification is received, the Commission is required to examine this notification in due process.[14] This first period of assessment is commonly called the 'Phase I investigation' and entails procedural implications for both the Commission as well as the parties to the transaction.

It should be remembered that discussions between the applicant(s) and the MTF should not cease as soon as the notification has been made. The subsequent proceedings should be seen as a mutual exchange of information between the MTF and the applicant and possibly even other Directorates of DG IV if the concentration has co-operative aspects. The

---

[13] Article 4(3), Regulation 4064/89.
[14] Article 6(1), Regulation 4064/89.

applicant(s) should have an idea what its bottom line is – if the MTF is not happy with this or that part of a transaction, will the applicant be happy to relinquish a certain point in favour of retaining something which is more important to it? Knowing what are the essential points to the transaction may help to avoid a Phase II investigation.

C.5.1 One-month Deadline

There is a tight one-month time limit within which the Commission has to examine the notification and adopt a decision,[15] however, such a decision can be reached in less than a month. In most cases, because of the complexity of the cases and strict internal procedural deadlines the one month deadline will most probably be fully exploited. This one-month deadline begins to run from the day following the effective date of the notification (i.e. the day following that of the receipt of the notification[16] or, if the information to be supplied with the notification is incomplete, on the day following that of the receipt of the complete information. Where the Commission finds that not all the necessary information is provided, it will normally exercise the powers to request further information).[17] As a result, the one-month deadline will start under the rules laid down above when those requirements are then satisfied.

The time period for adopting the decision ends with the expiry of the day which in the following month falls on the same date as the day from which the period runs.[18] For example, if a notification is filed on 15 January the deadline for adopting the decision will end on 16 February. In the exceptional circumstances that the last day for the Commission adopting its decision does not exist in that month, the period expires with the last day of that month. For example, if notification is submitted on 30 January the period expires on 28 February or 29 February in a leap year (see C.8 below).

However, there are two possibilities under which the one month time limit can be extended.

The first consists of an extension to six weeks.[19] This usually applies in cases where the Commission receives a request from a Member State in accordance with the 'Distinct Market' exception or where the parties concerned submit undertakings (obligations *vis-à-vis* the Commission), by

---

[15]   Article 10(1), Regulation 4064/89.
[16]   Article 10(1), Regulation 4064/89 and Article 6(4), Regulation 447/98.
[17]   Article 4(2), Regulation 447/98 and further specified in Form CO.
[18]   Article 7(4), Regulation 447/98.
[19]   Article 10(1), Regulation 4064/89.

virtue of which the parties intend to allow the Commission to adopt a decision authorising the transaction. The time period will end with the expiry of the day which, in the sixth week following that in which the period began, is the same day of the week as the day from which the period runs.[20]

There is a second exception[21] whereby under certain exceptional circumstances the one-month period can be suspended where, owing to circumstances for which one of the parties involved in the concentration is responsible, the Commission has had to request information by decision[22] or to order an investigation by decision.[23] The suspension of the time limit will begin on the day following that on which the event causing the suspension occurred[24] and it will end with the expiry of the day on which the reason for suspension is removed.

C.5.2 Procedural Role of the Parties

The Phase I investigation of a concentration requires the parties to strictly follow certain procedural rules and obligations. They have the possibility to actively take part in the proceedings and strengthen their position as to the desired compatibility of the proposed concentration or, alternatively, have little contact with the MTF. The main procedural requirements are laid down below.

C.5.2.1 *Suspension of concentration*

A concentration with a Community dimension may not be put into effect[25] either before its notification to the Commission or until it has been declared compatible with the Common Market pursuant to a Phase I decision or final decision,[26] or on the basis of a fictitious decision of compatibility (see C.7 below).[27]

Strict penalties for breach of this provision are provided.[28] The fine imposed can be up to 10 per cent of the aggregate worldwide turnover of the undertakings concerned.

---

[20] Article 7(5), Regulation 447/98.
[21] Article 10(4), Regulation 4064/89.
[22] Article 11, Regulation 4064/89.
[23] Article 13, Regulation 4064/89.
[24] Article 9(3), Regulation 447/98.
[25] Article 7(1), Regulation 4064/89.
[26] Article 6(1)(b) or Article 8(2), Regulation 4064/89.
[27] Presumption according to Article 10(6), Regulation 4064/89.
[28] Article 14, Regulation 4064/89.

It is expressly provided that the Commission can, upon request, exempt a transaction from the rules relating to suspension. This power of derogation is given to the Commission to enable it to take appropriate action to prevent the rules operating so as to cause serious damage to one or more of the undertakings involved in the transaction. The request by the undertaking for such a derogation from the obligation to suspend the concentration must be reasoned and, in deciding upon the request, the Commission shall take into account, *inter alia*, the effects of granting the request on the parties or even on a third party, and the threat to competition posed by the concentration.

It should finally be noted that in granting a derogation, it is possible for the Commission to impose conditions and obligations to ensure conditions of effective competition are maintained.[29]

C.5.2.2 *Undertakings*

The original Merger Regulation did not expressly provide that the Commission could accept undertakings/commitments submitted by the notifying parties in Phase I. However the practice of the MTF was to accept modifications, undertakings, and conditions in Phase I subject to hearing interested parties and consulting with Member States. The Amending Regulation expressly provides that a notified concentration may be modified in accordance with undertakings submitted by the notifying Parties during Phase I so that it no longer raises serious doubts as to its compatibility under the Common Market. Accordingly, the MTF as a result of such undertakings may decide in its Phase I to declare the concentration compatible with the Common Market.[30] It should be noted however, that an undertaking is never actively solicited by the MTF. Undertakings are compromises offered unilaterally by the parties.

Recital 8 of the Amending Regulation states that the acceptance of commitments in Phase I should be limited to cases 'where the competition problem is readily identifiable and can be easily remedied'. The suitability of a commitment is an issue that can be discussed at pre-notification meetings. The MTF are always willing to enter pre-notification investigations if the parties are willing to do so, even far in advance of notification. The MTF would then be able to begin their investigations even before the timetable was officially open, thus easing time pressures later.

The timing of a proposed undertaking can be important. Phase I undertakings must be submitted to the MTF within three weeks from the date of

---

[29] Article 7(4), Regulation 4064/89.
[30] Article 6(2), Regulation 4064/89.

receipt of the notification. If the parties know, for example following pre-notification discussions, that their proposed remedy is acceptable to the MTF, then they could include the proposed remedy with the actual notification itself. In accordance with the text of the Merger Regulation, if submitted together with the notification, the commitment will be considered simply as part of the notification, and not as an undertaking 'changing the initial structure of the deal'. However, if offered *after* the notification, it will be considered as an undertaking which 'changes the initial structure of the deal' and will trigger an extension of the time limits of Phase I investigation from four to six weeks.[31] The MTF will then have six weeks in total within which to reach a decision in Phase I. It could be argued therefore that, provided a proposal is acceptable to the MTF, the parties can time the submission of the 'undertaking' accordingly, depending on whether they want the matter to be concluded within four weeks or are happy for it to be delayed. However, such a strict interpretation of the text of the Merger Regulation would appear to contradict its spirit.

Undertakings, to be acceptable to the Commission, must be clear-cut and remove all the competition concerns identified by the MTF. Otherwise, Phase II investigation will be initiated.

In summary, in the interests of reducing the risk of having to re-notify a modified concentration or face Phase II proceedings, parties should strive, particularly during the pre-notification stage but also following notification, to anticipate any problems that may arise and discuss them with the case handlers within the MTF at the earliest possible stage.

C.5.2.3 *Withdrawal of notification*

The parties are free to halt the transaction and withdraw its notification at any stage of the proceedings.

C.5.3 **Procedural Role of the Merger Task Force**

There are few formal rules for the MTF governing the examination procedure at this stage in the proceedings. At the outset the MTF will check that the notification is complete and submitted by the proper parties. If it is incomplete, the MTF is obliged to inform the parties without delay and fix a date by which the omission or defect can be made good.[32]

---

[31] Article 10(1) second paragraph, Regulation 4064/89.
[32] Article 4(2), Regulation 447/98.

However, far more important at this stage of the proceedings are the rules governing the fact finding powers of the MTF and the close contact with the concerned parties and even third parties and Member States that takes place before any Phase I decision is made. The use of these rules is not limited to Phase I or Phase II proceedings, although in practice, because of the time restraints, their use in the Phase I is less likely. However, the following rules may play an important role even during Phase I investigations.

C.5.3.1 *Request for information*

The MTF is empowered to obtain all necessary information from Member State governments, and competent authorities as well as from undertakings, associations of undertakings and individuals. The timetable for a Phase I decision is very tight and in practice the MTF may be inclined to use its formal powers to request information (i.e. by decision) as this extends the time period for giving a Phase I decision (see C.8.4 below). However, in practice this is difficult because the adoption of the formal decision by the Commission requesting information will not be possible due to time constraints. In any event, a request for information by decision can only be made after an unsuccessful informal request.

Copies of requests for information sent to individuals, undertakings or associations of undertakings concerned, must be sent to the competent authorities of the Member State where they are resident or have their base at the same time.[33] The request for information must state the legal basis on which it is made, its purpose and the possible penalties that may be imposed for supplying incorrect information.[34] The information must be provided by the owners or representatives of the undertakings, or, in the case of legal persons, companies or firms or associations having no legal personality, by the persons authorised to represent them by law or by their statutes. If the MTF issues a decision requesting information it shall fix an appropriate deadline and state the penalties if the complete information requested is not supplied within the period.[35] This decision shall also set out the parties' right to have the decision reviewed by the Court of Justice.

The MTF does have the power to conduct 'dawn raids' in order to collect information. It has exercised this power only once to date. The more usual method of obtaining information is through requests and meetings with third parties.

---

[33] Article 11(2), Regulation 4064/89.
[34] Article 14(1)(c), Regulation 4064/89.
[35] Articles 14(1)(c) and 15(1)(a), Regulation 4064/89.

C.5.3.2 *Liaison with national authorities*

The MTF is required to stay in close and constant liaison with the competent authorities of the Member States,[36] which may express their opinions throughout the proceedings. The MTF accordingly gives the national authority access to the file. However, during a Phase I investigation and prior to a Phase I decision being taken, there is no obligation for the MTF to consult with the Advisory Committee.

C.5.3.3 *Referral to Member States*

As stated above (B.3.1), it is possible for the Commission to refer a notified concentration to the competent authorities of the Member States concerned.

The MTF must always transmit to the competent authorities of the Member States copies of notifications within three working days and copies of the most important documents lodged with or issued by the Commission under the Merger Regulation pursuant to Article 19(1). These 'most important documents' also include undertakings which are intended by the parties to form the basis for a decision authorising the transaction.

A Member State may then inform the MTF within three weeks of receipt of the notification by that Member State, that a proposed concentration threatens to create or to strengthen a dominant position as a result of which effective competition would be significantly impeded on a market within that Member State which presents all the characteristics of a distinct market.[37] The same counts for the situation where a proposed concentration may affect competition on a market within that Member State, which presents all the characteristics of a distinct market and which does not constitute a substantial part of the Common Market.[38] In the event that the MTF is so informed, the period of time in which the preliminary examination must be completed is extended from one month to six weeks.

C.5.3.4 *Third parties*

As already mentioned (see C.4.5 above), third parties are invited to submit any observations on the proposed concentration which they may have, normally no later than ten days following the date of the publication in the

---

[36] Article 19(2),Regulation 4064/89.
[37] Article 9(2)(a), Regulation 4064/89.
[38] Article 9(2)(b), Regulation 4064/89.

Official Journal of the European Communities. They can therefore approach the MTF and are, due to the fact of the publication in the Official Journal, promptly alerted to the existence of a concentration and can therefore comment on the proposal and intervene in the proceedings.[39] Although the timetable during Phase I investigations is short, the MTF tries to seek out third parties' views, most notably customers and suppliers, especially on specific issues of the proposed concentration.

C.5.3.5 *Phase I decisions*

Of the following three types of decision, one must be taken before the end of the Phase I investigation.

- Where the Commission concludes that the notified concentration does not fall within the scope of the Merger Regulation, either because the concentration has no Community dimension (i.e. turnover threshold criteria are not met), or because the operation does not constitute a concentration, it shall record that finding by means of a decision. This is commonly called a '6(1)(a) decision'.
- Where the Commission concludes that the notified concentration, although falling within the scope of the Merger Regulation, does not raise serious doubts as to its compatibility with the Common Market, it shall decide not to oppose it and shall declare it compatible with the Common Market. This decision declaring the concentration compatible with the Common Market shall also cover restrictions directly related and necessary to the implementation of the concentration (i.e. ancillary restrictions, see C.10). This is commonly called a '6(1)(b) decision'.
- Where the Commission concludes that the notified concentration raises serious doubts as to its compatibility with the Common Market, it shall decide to initiate proceedings. This decision will take the form of an initiation of the Phase II investigation. This is commonly called a '6(1)(c) decision'.

The wording of 'serious doubts' in the above context is not defined in the Merger Regulation, but the Commission normally takes the view that no 'serious doubts' arise in cases where on the basis of the information available concerning the undertakings, there are no clear indications that the notified concentration will eventually lead to the creation or strengthening of a dominant position which will significantly impede effective competition in the Common Market or in a substantial part of it.

---

[39]   Article 4(3), Regulation 4064/89.

Where the Commission comes to the conclusion that, following modification by the concerned undertakings, a notified concentration no longer raises serious doubts as to its compatibility, it shall decide to declare the concentration compatible with the Common Market.

If the Commission comes to the conclusion that the Phase I decision is based on incorrect information for which one of the concerned undertakings is responsible, or where it has been obtained by deceit, or the undertakings are in breach of an obligation attached to such decision, it may revoke its decision.

There exists no obligation for the Commission to publish Phase I decisions. However, the Commission must notify such decisions to the undertakings concerned and the competent authorities of the Member States without delay.[40] Phase I decisions are now available through the Internet at the website of the European Commission (www. europa.eu.int).

C.6 *Phase II Investigation*

Following the adoption of the decision initiating proceedings, the MTF will continue its analysis of the effects of the proposed concentration on market conditions in order to confirm or, as the case may be, change its preliminary finding that the concentration would create or strengthen a dominant position. This is done during the so-called Phase II investigation provided for by the Merger Regulation. It is the Competition Commissioner who is responsible for deciding whether to clear the transaction at the end of Phase I. A decision to open a Phase II investigation is taken by the Competition Commissioner in liaison with the President of the Commission.

C.6.1 Four-month Deadline

The final decision on the compatibility/incompatibility of a concentration must be taken within four months of the date of initiation of proceedings (see C.10 below).

C.6.2 Fact-finding Powers

During Phase II investigations the fact-finding powers of the Commission play an even more important role than during the Phase I investigation

---

40   Article 6(5), Regulation 4064/89.

due to the fact that the Commission is able to operate within a more flexible timetable of at least four months.

In addition to the already mentioned power of the Commission to request information from the parties of the proposed concentration, governments and competent authorities of the Member States and individuals (see C.5.3.1 above), the Commission's power also includes carrying out all necessary investigations into undertakings and associations of undertakings such as:[41]

- examining the books and other business records;
- taking or demanding copies of or extracts from the books and business records;
- asking for an oral explanation on the spot; and
- entering any premises, land and means of transport of undertakings.

In exercising these powers the Commission officials must produce an authorisation in writing specifying the subject-matter and purpose of the investigation and the penalties which apply if incomplete information is provided by the parties.[42] A failure by the parties to co-operate can result in the payment of fines from 1,000 Euro to 50,000 Euro if the failure is intentional or negligent. Before the investigation takes place, the Commission shall inform in writing the competent authority of the Member State within the territory of which the investigation is to be carried out, of the fact of the investigation and the identity of the authorised officials carrying out the investigation. Officials of the competition authority of a Member State where the investigation is to be carried out may, at the request of the Commission or of that authority, assist the officials of the Commission in carrying out their duties.

C.6.3   Statement of Objections

According to the Merger Regulation, the undertakings concerned in the concentration must be given the opportunity to make known their views on the objections against them at every stage of the procedure up to the consultation of the Advisory Committee.[43] In practice, the opportunity is given when the Commission is proposing to adopt a decision, especially a final decision on the compatibility of the proposed concentration with the Common Market. The Commission must inform the notifying parties

---

[41]   Article 13, Regulation 4064/89.
[42]   Article 13(2), Regulation 4064/89.
[43]   Article 18(1), Regulation 4064/89.

concerned in writing of its objections concerning the proposed concentration.[44] This document is commonly called the 'Statement of Objections' and tends to be delivered by the Commission about two months after the initiation of Phase II. It is the Competition Commissioner who adopts the Statement of Objections.

At the same time the Statement of Objections must fix a time limit for the parties' response to those objections (the 'Reply to the Statement of Objections') and this time limit is in general quite short and normally in the region of two weeks. Significant amounts of management time should be set aside for the lawyers and the companies concerned to prepare the reply to the Statement of Objections (see C.6.5 below) and the oral hearing which will ensue immediately after the Reply to the Statement of Objections has been delivered.

The Commission can base its decision only on objections on which the parties have been able to submit their observations as their rights of defence must be fully respected during the proceedings. Other parties involved must be informed of the objections and a time limit fixed for them to give their written views. It is increasingly common to grant them an oral hearing. Access to the file is open to at least the parties directly involved.

C.6.4 Access to the File and Business Secrets

It is expressly provided that the parties involved in the concentration must be given access to the Commission's file,[45] subject to the legitimate interest of undertakings in the protection of their business secrets. That right serves the need for the parties to be in a position to properly prepare their defence.

Once the parties have received the Commission's Statement of Objections, they can in so far as evidence and other documentation has not already been supplied with that statement, request access to the file. Up until this point there is no express provision allowing the parties to have access to the file. The reason for this is that no objections have been raised against the parties. In addition, the Commission provides the parties with a list of documents in the Commission's file together with a short description of each document. It is advisable that the parties scrutinise the list very carefully as there may be other documents relevant to the parties rights of defence which have not been extracted and appended to the Statement of Objections. The Commission will only annex certain documents to the

---

[44] Article 13(2), Regulation 447/98.
[45] Article 18(3), Regulation 4064/89.

Statement of Objections, not all the documents which are present in the file. The parties are entitled to consult the originals of the documents directly and obtain photocopies.

The Commission is only required to give access to the file to the parties 'directly involved' in the transaction. However, other parties involved who have been informed of the Commission's objections are to be given access in so far as it is necessary for them to submit their observations.[46] The Commission is therefore not obliged to give automatic access to the file to any third party heard during the administrative procedure.

The access to the file procedure is supervised by the Hearing Officer. By his terms of reference he is in a position to rule on any discrepancy between the Commission and the parties as to whether access to particular documents should be given.

No access will be given to documents containing business secrets of other parties concerned or of third parties, or to other confidential information, which includes no access to internal papers of the Commission or documents between the Commission and other authorities. However, any party which indicates that certain material is confidential, shall give reasons to the Commission and provide a separate non-confidential version in the time limit set by the Commission.[47]

C.6.5 Reply to the Statement of Objections

As already mentioned (see C.6.3 above), the Merger Regulation refers to the parties' right to submit their observations on the Commission's objections. This is primarily done in writing and commonly referred to as the 'Reply to the Statement of Objections'. In their written response the parties can set out all matters relevant to their case and may attach any relevant documents as proof of the facts set out. Further, the parties may propose that the Commission hears persons who may corroborate those facts. The parties must submit one original and 29 copies of their response to the Commission.[48]

The Reply to the Statement of Objections is an important tool in the Phase II procedure as it gives the concerned parties the possibility and the right to address any legal, economic or other arguments to the Commission. It therefore gives the parties the chance to challenge not only the factual but

---

[46] Article 13(3), Regulation 447/98.
[47] Article 17, Regulation 447/98.
[48] Article 13(4), Regulation 447/98.

also the legal and economic basis of the Commision's observations. Legal and economic advice at this stage of the procedure is therefore of vital importance.

C.6.6 Oral Hearings

Oral hearings are provided to supplement the written procedure.[49] The Commission must grant a formal hearing to (i) the notifying parties, and (ii) other parties involved provided that first, they request to be heard in their written comments and second they show a sufficient interest. All parties on whom the Commission proposes imposing a fine or periodic penalty payment must be heard by the Commission provided they request to be heard in their written comments (without the need for such parties to show sufficient interest). In any event, the Commission is free to grant a hearing to the above parties even if they do not meet the stated requirements, however, the Commission is under no obligation to do so.

The Commission will summon the persons to be heard to attend on a fixed date. Normally the hearing takes place shortly after the date fixed for the delivery of the Reply to the Statement of Objections. Individuals may appear in person or by a legal or authorised representative and undertakings and associations of undertakings may be represented by a duly authorised agent appointed from among their permanent staff.[50] The persons heard have the right to ask for assistance by lawyers or other authorised persons admitted by the Hearing Officer (e.g. university professors, economic advisers) during the hearings.[51] However, it is for the parties to take the initiative in this respect.

The oral hearing itself is conducted by the so-called Hearing Officer, an independent Commission official who is specifically appointed for the task.[52] The hearings are not public and persons are heard separately or in the presence of other persons summoned to attend. The arrangements are flexible but business secrets must be protected. A party should therefore advise the Hearing Officer in advance if and when business secrets and other confidential information are to be presented, so that suitable arrangements can be made for the party to be heard separately for the whole or part of the hearing. Finally the statement made by each party is recorded in the language in which the statement is made and although automatic interpretation is available no translation of the minutes of the hearing is made.

---

[49] Articles 14, 15, 16, Regulation 447/98.
[50] Article 15(2), Regulation 447/98.
[51] Article 15(3), Regulation 447/98.
[52] Article 15(1), Regulation 447/98.

C.6.7 Hearing of Third Parties

Especially during Phase II investigations the right to be heard becomes important for third parties if the Commission or the competent authorities of the concerned Member States deem it necessary.[53] Those showing sufficient interest, especially members of the administrative or management bodies of the undertakings concerned or the recognised representatives of their employees are entitled, on application to the Commission, to be informed in writing of the nature and the subject matter of the procedure. The Commission must then fix a time limit within which they make known their views. Third parties must make known their views in writing or orally within the time limit fixed. They may confirm their oral statements in writing. The Commission may then, where appropriate, afford the parties who have so requested in their written comments, the opportunity to participate in a formal hearing.

It is important to know that third parties that are granted the right to be heard are not automatically entitled to see the objections sent to the parties concerned or otherwise learn of the Commission's intentions regarding the proposed concentration. However, as already stated, 'other parties involved' are informed of the objections.

C.6.8 Consultation of the Advisory Committee

The Merger Regulation contemplates that an Advisory Committee on concentrations must be consulted before any final decision is taken or a decision imposing a fine or periodic penalty payment is made.[54] The Advisory Committee consists of representatives of the Member States and is chaired by a Commission official.[55] One or two representatives may be appointed but at least one must be competent in competition matters. The existence of the Advisory Committee emphasises the importance of making early contact with the competition officials in the Member States (see C.1 above).

A summary of the case, together with an indication of the most important documents and a preliminary draft of the decision to be taken for each case considered, must be sent with the invitation to attend the meeting of the Advisory Committee to the national authorities. The meeting shall take place not less than 14 days after the invitation has been sent although the Commission may in exceptional cases shorten that period as appropriate in

---

[53] Article 14(4), Regulation 447/98.
[54] Article 19(3), Regulation 4064/89.
[55] Article 19(4), Regulation 4064/89.

order to avoid serious harm to one or more of the undertakings concerned by a concentration.

The Advisory Committee shall deliver an opinion on the Commission's draft, if necessary by taking a vote, and even if some members are absent. The Commission is meant to take the utmost account of the opinion delivered by the Advisory Committee and shall inform it of the manner in which its opinion has been taken into account. However, the Commission is not legally bound by the Advisory Committee's opinion. The opinions of the Advisory Committee are frequently published in the Official Journal.

C.6.9 Undertakings

As already mentioned above in connection with the Phase I investigation, the parties of the proposed concentration are also free during Phase II investigations to modify their concentration plans.

The Phase II investigation itself must be terminated by a formal decision as to the compatibility or incompatibility of the concentration concerned and the Commission has in fact no power to authorise a concentration which is incompatible with the Common Market. A finding of compatibility may follow the modification of a concentration by the parties made after discussions with the Commission in the light of the Commission's objections to the concentration in its original form. The Commission may attach to its decision conditions and obligations intended to ensure that the undertakings concerned comply with the commitments they have entered into *vis-à-vis* the Commission with a view to rendering the concentration compatible with the Common Market.[56]

Such modifications can be of a structural kind, usually in the form of a disposal of part of the business being acquired or certain of its assets in order to lead to a reduction of market shares to a level at which there can be no question of dominance being created or enhanced. Furthermore, the Commission has been prepared to accept more complex remedies which affect other changes in structural conditions in the market concerned, particularly by attempting to introduce a new or strengthened competitor.

Any modifications to the original concentration plan made by the undertakings must be submitted to the Commission within no more than three months from the date on which proceedings were initiated.[57] However, the

---

[56]   Article 8(2), Regulation 4064/89.
[57]   Article 18(2), Regulation 447/98.

Commission may in exceptional circumstances extend that period. Having said that, it becomes clear that one of the most important considerations for the parties concerned in the Phase II investigation is the informal discussion with the MTF. Those discussions may relate to undertakings or commitments being offered to the Commission and the consequent agreement or rejection of obligations and conditions which the Commission could accept in order to authorise the transaction.

C.6.10 Final Decisions

When the Phase II has been initiated it must be closed by one of the three following decisions (i.e. compatibility with or without conditions, incompatibility or divestment) which are published in the Official Journal, in the C series.[58] A final decision on the merits can only be reached by the full Commission.

C.6.10.1 *Compatibility*

Where a concentration does not create or strengthen a dominant position as a result of which effective competition would be significantly impeded in the Common Market, or in the case of full function joint ventures having co-operative aspects that fulfil the criteria laid down in Article 81(3) (ex Article 85(3)) of the EC Treaty, the Commission must issue a decision declaring the concentration compatible with the Common Market.[59] Where modifications have been made to achieve this result, the Commission may impose conditions and obligations to ensure the fulfilment of the parties' undertakings. Failure of a party to comply with an obligation imposed by the Commission renders that party liable to a fine[60] and revocation of the declaration of compatibility.[61] The Commission may also impose a periodic penalty payment to secure performance of an obligation.

C.6.10.2 *Incompatibility*

Where the Commission finds that the proposed concentration creates or strengthens a dominant position as a result of which effective competition would be significantly impeded in the Common Market or a substantial part of it or, in the case of a full function joint venture having co-operative

---

[58]   Article 8(2)–(5), Regulation 4064/89.
[59]   Article 8(2), Regulation 4064/89.
[60]   Article 14(2), Regulation 4064/89.
[61]   Article 8(5)(b), Regulation 4064/89.

aspects[62] which does not fulfil the criteria laid down in Article 81(3) (ex Article 85(3)) of the EC Treaty, it must issue a decision declaring the concentration incompatible.[63] Putting into effect a concentration declared incompatible by such decision renders the parties liable to a fine (see C.9 below) and exposes the parties to the risk of having the transaction declared null and void.[64]

C.6.10.3 *Divestment decision*

Where a concentration has already been implemented, the Commission may by decision take any action that it considers appropriate to restore conditions of effective competition.[65] It may in particular require the undertakings or assets brought together to be separated or require the cessation of joint control. In practice, the Commission may order the sale of shares or the divestiture of assets to restore the previous status quo. A failure to take measures so ordered by the Commission renders a party liable to a fine. A periodic penalty payment may also be imposed.[66]

A decision requiring divestiture, or the imposition of a similar remedy, may form part of a decision prohibiting a concentration[67] or be a separate decision. It should be noted that the four-month time limit that applies to Phase II decisions of compatibility and incompatibility, does not apply to a decision requiring divestment. Therefore, as far as the modalities of implementation of the divestment are concerned, the parties and the Commission have a longer period for negotiation.

C.7   *The Fictitious Decision of Compatibility*

A concentration is deemed to have been declared compatible if either:

- no Phase I decision is issued by the Commission within one month; or
- no final decision is taken by the Commission within four months.[68]

---

62 Article 2(4), Regulation 4064/89.
63 Article 8(3), Regulation 4064/89.
64 Article 7(5), Regulation 4064/89.
65 Article 8(4), Regulation 4064/89.
66 Article 15(2)(b), Regulation 4064/89.
67 Article 8(3), Regulation 4064/89.
68 Article 10(6), Regulation 4064/89.

c.8　*Calculation of Time Limits*

C.8.1　Beginning and End of Periods Referred to in Months

Such periods are, for example, the periods in which the Commission has to adopt a Phase I decision and a Phase II decision.

These periods are calculated as follows:

- Phase I decision: This period begins at the start of the working day which follows the date the notification is received at the Commission. The period expires on the day in the following month which has the same number as the date when the period began;
- Phase II decision: This period begins at the start of the working day after the day on which proceedings were initiated. It expires on the day in the following fourth month which has the same number as the date when the period began.

However, and this applies to the calculation of all the above time periods, if there is no same numbered day in the relevant month, the period in question expires on the last day of that month. Also note the comments below in relation to working days and public holidays (see C.8.3 below).

EXAMPLE 5

A concentration is notified on 17 January, the period in which the Commission has to take its Phase I decision ends on 18 February.

The Commission decides to initiate Phase II proceedings on 29 October and the period in which it has to take its final decision ends on 28 February, or 29 February if it is a leap year (i.e. the last day of February).

C.8.2　Beginning and End of Periods Referred to in Weeks

These periods relate both to the distinct market exceptions and to undertakings in Phase I. So far as the distinct market exceptions is concerned two situations can be distinguished. The first is the amount of time in which a Member State has to inform the Commission that a distinct market is in issue. The second is the amount of time that the Commission has to take a decision when a Member State has informed it that a distinct market is in issue.

These periods are calculated as follows:

- The period which a Member State has in order to inform the Commission that a distinct market is in issue: This period begins on

46

the working day following the receipt of the notification by the Member State and expires on the same day three weeks after the period began.

- The period in which the Commission has to adopt its first decision when a Member State has informed the Commission that a distinct market is in issue: This period begins on the working day following the receipt of the notification by the Commission and expires on the same day six weeks after the period began.

The comments below (at C.8.3) should be noted in relation to working days and public holidays.

EXAMPLE 6

A concentration is notified on Tuesday 1 September. The notification was received by the Member State concerned on Friday 4 September. The period that the Member State has in order to inform the Commission that a distinct market is in issue expires on Monday 28 September. Given that the Member State does so inform the Commission, it then has until Wednesday 14 October to adopt its Phase I decision.

C.8.3 Working Days and Public Holidays

C.8.3.1 *Working days*

If the last day of any of the periods as calculated above falls on a non-working day, the period then expires on the following working day. Note that a non-working day can be a Saturday or a Sunday, or any Public Holiday (including holidays of the Commission).

EXAMPLE 7

A concentration is notified on Thursday 3 September. The time limit for the Commission to adopt its Phase I decision expires on Monday 5 October, as 4 October is a Sunday.

C.8.3.2 *Recovery of Public Holidays*

Once the question of working days has been looked at, the recovery of Public Holidays needs to be considered. If Public Holidays or other holidays of the Commission (as published annually in the Official Journal) occur during any of the time periods referred to in C.8.1 or C.8.2 above, then a corresponding number of working days is added to the period.

EXAMPLE 8

Using the example above, if two bank holidays occur during the time period for the Commission to give its Phase I decision, two days need to be added after 5 October, i.e. the period expires on Wednesday 7 October.

C.8.4 Suspension of Time Limits

The time limits in which the Commission has to render either a Phase I or a Phase II decision can be suspended. This happens when:

- information which has been requested either from a notifying party, or another party involved, or a third party is not provided during the time limit set by the Commission; or
- one of the notifying parties or another party involved refuses to submit to an investigation or to co-operate in such an investigation; or
- the notifying parties do not inform the Commission that there have been material changes in the notification.

The suspension period lasts for as long as the event causing the suspension lasts, e.g. if a notifying party does not provide information for 13 days after the time limit set by the Commission has expired, its decision will be suspended for the same amount of time.

As a final comment, it is advisable to request the MTF to confirm when the time limits in question expire or begin so that the parties are certain when to expect decisions from the Commission.

C.9 *Fines*

The Commission has wide powers within the Merger Regulation to impose fines and periodic penalty payments on infringing companies. Failure to notify a merger or acquisition can result in a fine of between 1,000 Euro and 50,000 Euro.

A fine up to 10 per cent of the aggregate turnover of the companies involved can be imposed in any of the following three cases:

- putting into effect a merger or acquisition which has not been notified or which, although notified, has been put into effect before it has been declared compatible with the Common Market;
- putting into effect a merger or acquisition which has been declared incompatible with the Common Market; and

- non-compliance with a decision ordering divestiture of a merger or acquisition declared incompatible with the Common Market.

A periodic penalty payment of up to 100,000 Euro can be imposed for each day of delay in complying with a decision requiring the undertakings to comply with certain commitments or ordering that assets brought together be separated, or the cessation of joint control or any other measure taken in order to restore effective competition.

If the parties supply incorrect or misleading information in a notification, fines between 1,000 Euro and 50,000 Euro can be imposed. If the Commission sends a request for information (and no decision is issued), undertakings and individuals can refrain from supplying such information. However, the supply of incorrect information may be punished by fines of between 1,000 Euro and 50,000 Euro.

If a person or undertaking does not provide the information requested, the Commission can issue a decision requesting the information: the fine for not supplying the information requested by a decision can be between 1,000 Euro and 50,000 Euro.

A refusal to submit to an investigation or supplying incomplete information during an investigation ordered by decision can lead to a fine of between 1,000 Euro and 50,000 Euro. Furthermore, each day of delay in allowing the investigation to proceed or in providing complete and correct information where the investigation and/or the request for information have been ordered by decision can be fined with a periodic penalty payment of up to 25,000 Euro.

C.10   *Ancillary Restrictions*

Ancillary restrictions are restrictions which are 'directly related' to a concentration and are 'necessary to its implementation' (See Annex 9 and F.1 below). These two conditions are discussed in detail below. They are agreed on between the parties to the concentration and limit the parties freedom of action in the market. They do not include restrictions that affect third parties. They will be covered by a decision which declares the concentration compatible with the Common Market and therefore do not require separate individual scrutiny under Articles 81 and 82 (ex Articles 85 and 86) of the EC Treaty. The Commission is empowered to deal with ancillary restraints in Phase I proceedings.

'Directly related' means that the restrictions are ancillary to the implementation of the concentration – they must be subordinate to the main object of the concentration. Restrictions agreed at the same time as the concentration, which have no actual link with the concentration, are not ancillary restrictions and therefore are not covered by decisions of compatibility.

'Necessary to the implementation of the concentration' means that without such restrictions, the concentration either could not be put in place or, if it was, it would be implemented under less certain conditions, at greater expense, over a longer period of time, or would be likely to have less success. In making a judgement as to whether the restrictions in question are necessary to the implementation of the concentration, any alternative restriction that is less restrictive of competition should be chosen by the parties.

Examples of ancillary restrictions include non-compete clauses on the vendor. These exist because the acquirer of the business must be able to benefit from some protection against competitive acts of the vendor in order to gain the loyalty of customers and therefore acquire the full value of the assets transferred. Contractual prohibitions are therefore imposed on the vendor in the context of a concentration achieved by the transfer of an undertaking or part of an undertaking. However, these prohibitions on competition are acceptable when their duration, geographical field of application and subject matter do not exceed what is reasonably necessary for the successful implementation of the concentration.

As regards duration, a period of five years[69] is admissible when the transfer of the company includes the goodwill and know-how, and a period of two years when it includes only the goodwill. As regards geographical scope, such a clause must be limited to the area where the vendor established the products or services before the transfer. Finally, as regards subject matter, such clauses must be limited to the products and services in the economic activity of the undertaking transferred. A non-compete obligation on the acquirer is not normally considered to be an ancillary restriction and therefore it has to be examined under Articles 81 and 82 (ex Articles 85 and 86) of the EC Treaty.

Another example of an ancillary restriction is a licence of industrial and commercial property rights and of know-how. Under certain circumstances, the vendor and owner of such rights may wish to keep such rights outright in order that it can exploit them for activities other than the activities which have been transferred by virtue of the transaction. Therefore, licences will need to be put in place so that the acquirer will have the full use of the assets that it needs in the exploitation of the business acquired.

---

[69] A proposal to reduce it to three years is under discussion. See F.1.2.2 below.

A final example is purchase and supply agreements. These are often necessary for the continuation of the business that the vendor has transferred to the acquirer. Without such agreements being put in place, the acquirer will not have a guaranteed source of supply of products which are necessary to the business. Accordingly such contracts which are ancillary to the main purpose of the concentration and which concern these products are concluded.

In the light of the Commission's experience in merger control to date, several draft Notices are under discussion, one of which is the draft Notice on Restrictions Directly Related and Necessary to Concentrations which will, if adopted, replace the existing Notice on Ancillary Restraints. For a detailed description of this draft Notice, see F.1 below.

D. STRUCTURE OF THE MTF

D.1 *MTF–Directorate-General IV/B (DG IV/B)*

The MTF is the competent body within the Commission's DG IV dealing with concentration cases that fall within the scope of the Merger Regulation and that therefore may have an impact on competition within the Common Market.

The contact details of the MTF are as follows:
Commission of the European Communities
Directorate-General for Competition (DG IV)
Merger Task Force
150 Avenue de Cortenberg
B-1049 Brussels
Belgium
Telephone: (00 32 2) 295 8681 (Mr Götz Drauz)
Fax: (00 32 2) 296 4301

The current Heads of the Unit are:
Claude Rakovsky
Francisco Enrique González-Díaz
Wolfgang Mederer
Paul Malric-Smith

D.1.1 Organisation and Personnel

The MTF, which is a separate Directorate (Directorate B) of DG IV, was established in 1990 and is generally seen as the shining example of DG IV. It is headed by a Director, currently Mr Götz Drauz, a competition lawyer from Germany. It consists of four units, each of which is headed by a Unit Head and containing approximately eight to nine case handlers plus support staff. Case handlers are selected according to their availability and language skills rather than any sectorial allocation of case and this flexibility permits members of one unit to work on a case with members of another unit. A hearing officer is responsible for confidentiality of information received.

The MTF comprises some 35–40 staff, (excluding support staff). This allows cases to be handled efficiently and the necessary fact-finding to be carried out within the short time limits imposed by the Merger Regulation. Approximately one-third of the staff is made up of secondees from national competition authorities (such as the German Bundeskartellamt, the French Ministère d'Economie or the UK Office of Fair Trading).

The MTF is frequently praised for its efficiency and approachability and therefore it can only benefit other Directorates if Commission officials gain experience of the MTF and export ideas elsewhere. The MTF is appreciated for its understanding of companies and industry – the other Directorates in DG IV do not enjoy such a reputation.

It is recognised that lack of resources is a 'major problem' for the MTF. Case handlers risk having more work than they can deal with. Cases have doubled but this has not been equalled by the number of staff taken on, which has increased by 10 per cent in the same period of time. It is estimated that the lowering of the thresholds in the Merger Regulation will increase the workload of case handlers by 20–25 per cent. Deals are inevitably becoming more complex and more 'European' as the Single Market gathers speed. The MTF has groups of case handlers arguing each side of a case, which weeds out the weaknesses of the applicants' arguments. Furthermore, it intends and does at present refer as many cases as possible back to the national competition authorities.

D.1.2 Timing the Notification

It is useful to know when the regular meetings take place. There are weekly departmental meetings every Wednesday morning in the MTF and Mr Schaub, the Director General of DG IV, also holds weekly meetings every Monday with all the Directors to discuss any difficult cases. The Commissioner responsible for competition matters, currently Mr Mario Monti, usually holds weekly meetings; tricky cases will be on this agenda. Armed with this knowledge, it is feasible for an applicant to time the notification just right so it gets onto one of these important agendas, to be discussed without delay.

D.1.3 Handling of Cases

The MTF has prepared its own manual of procedure. Much of the internal work is done by meetings rather than written procedure. The informal weekly meeting referred to above is where current cases as well as general issues and problems of interpretation are discussed.

Cases are normally allocated to a Unit on the basis of availability as well as possession of relevant language skills. The 'Management', i.e. the Director and the Unit Heads decide which team of two or more case-handlers will deal with the case. It is the Director who has final say. The case will ultimately be subject to the control of the case manager who will normally be one of the four Unit Heads. Where practical, at least one member of the case-handler team will be selected for his knowledge of the sector of the industry concerned. These details are often settled before notification, having been ironed out during pre-notification meetings.

D.1.4 Decision-Making

There are several different types of decisions under the Merger Regulation which may be adopted by the Commission. The decisions are ultimately taken not by officials but by the Commission itself, which means either by all the Commissioners together (the so-called 'College of Commissioners'), or by an individual Commissioner under delegated authority. An example of the latter would be in the case of the scrutiny of concentrations, the Commissioner for Competition, currently Mr Mario Monti. In EC jargon the decision-making by an individual Commissioner under delegated authority is called 'habilitation'. As a result, the Competition Commissioner has the power to take clearance decisions at the end of the Phase I investigation alone as well as decisions initiating the Phase II investigation, although he must consult the President of the Commission, currently Mr Romano Prodi, before taking this step. However, all decisions taken at the end of the Phase II investigation must be taken by the full College of Commissioners.

In accordance with Article 253 (ex Article 190) of the EC Treaty, decisions must give the reasons on which they are based and, in accordance with the Merger Regulation[1], must only be based on objections on which the parties have been given the opportunity to defend themselves by reply to those objections. These provisions, however, do not allow the Commission to discuss all the arguments put forward by the parties in response to the Statement of Objections but reasons given by the Commission in its decision must be sufficient to justify the decision. The reasons must be sufficiently stated and provide the party concerned with the information necessary to ascertain whether the decision is justified and allow the Court of First Instance to check the legality of the decision.

---

[1] Article 18(3), Regulation 4064/89.

54

During the decision making process, the case team works together with other parts of DG IV. This is particularly the case following the changes brought about by the Amending Regulation which brings all full function joint ventures within the scope of the Merger Regulation. As stated above in B.4.2, the MTF will direct its thoughts as to whether the full function joint venture has any element of co-ordination and if so, will invite an official from the relevant Directorate, dealing with Articles 81 and 82 (ex Articles 85 and 86), to give their view. If the official does indeed think that the concentration has co-operative aspects, then his Directorate will take over the investigation of the transaction.

The MTF liaises with other departments of DG IV, in addition to the example given above. In particular the operational Directorates in the industrial or commercial sector that is affected by the operation and the co-ordination Directorate (Directorate A of DG IV) are involved. The MTF is also able to call on outside experts and specialists if necessary. Most importantly the MTF will consult other Directorates of the Commission depending on the subject matter of the case, and therefore Directorates within, e.g., DG VII (transport), DG XIII (telecommunications), DG XV (internal market and financial services) may be involved. The Legal Service of the Commission will also be involved throughout and its opinion will be sought at key stages of the proceedings.

D.1.5 Publication of Notifications and Decisions

D.1.5.1 *Phase I decision*

An announcement of a Phase I decision is published in the Official Journal in all 11 Community Languages. The Phase I decision itself will only be available in the language in which the parties notified.

D.1.5.2 *Phase II decision*

Phase II decisions are published in all Community languages in the Official Journal series.

Paper versions of Phase I decisions are available through:

- sales agents of EUR–OP, the official Publications of the European Community
- EUDOR service (European Union Document Delivery Service)

55

TABLE A   NUMBER OF PHASE II DECISIONS ISSUED BY THE MTF FROM 1990 TO 31 DECEMBER 1999

Decision and Article	1990	1991	1992	1993	1994	1995	1996	1997	1998	31 Dec 1999	Total
Compatible with common market (8.2)		1	1	1	2	2	1	1	2	0	11
Compatible with undertakings (8.2)		3	3	2	2	3	3	7	5	8	36
Prohibition (8.3)		1			1	2	3	1	2	1	11
Restore effective competition (8.4)									2	0	0	2

TABLE B   NUMBER OF PHASE II DECISIONS FROM 1990 TO 31 DECEMBER 1999

Decision	1990	1991	1992	1993	1994	1995	1996	1997	1998	31 Dec 1999	Total
Phase II		5	4	3	5	7	7	11	9	9	60

An annual subscription to the paper version is also available for ECU 300 (subscription code 'VMG'). Decisions will be posted to the subscriber every two months.

Decisions are available in full text on the Internet for a limited period through the web site of DG IV (www.europa.eu.int). Phase II decisions are published in the C series of the Official Journal. See further Diagram F.

TABLE C   NUMBER OF PHASE I DECISIONS ISSUED BY THE MTF FROM 1990 TO 31 DECEMBER 1999

Decision and Article	1990	1991	1992	1993	1994	1995	1996	1997	1998	31 Dec 1999	Total
Out of scope of merger Regulation (6.1(a))	2	5	9	4	5	9	6	4	6	1	51
Compatible with common market (6.1(b))	5	47	43	49	78	90	109	118	207	236	982
Compatible with undertakings (6.1(b))		3	4		2	3		2	12	19	45
Partial referral to member states			1		1			6	3	1	12
Full referral to member states				1			3	1	1	3	9

TABLE D   TOTAL NUMBER OF OTHER DECISIONS ISSUED BY THE MTF

Decision and Article	1990	1991	1992	1993	1994	1995	1996	1997	1998	31 Dec 1999	Total
Decisions imposing fines									1	4	5
Derogation from suspension (7.4)	1	1	2	3	1	2	3	5	13	7	38
Phase II proceedings opened (6.1(c))		6	4	4	6	7	6	11	12	20	76

Further the MTF publishes Phase I decisions on the Internet and final phase decisions appear in the C series of the Official Journal.

TABLE E   INCREASE IN THE NUMBER OF NOTIFICATIONS SINCE 1990

Notifications received	1990	1991	1992	1993	1994	1995	1996	1997	1998	31 Dec 1999	Total
	12	63	60	58	95	110	131	172	235	292	1228

E   COURT ACTIONS AGAINST FINAL DECISIONS

Any merger control decision of the Commission can be annulled under proceedings by the Court of First Instance, if the action is brought by the addressees of the decision, or by the European Court of Justice, if the action is brought by a Member State. The European Courts have unlimited jurisdiction to review Commission decisions imposing fines or periodic penalty payments for failures to comply with the Merger Regulation.

Legal actions must be instituted within two months of publication of the Commission final decision or notification of the decision to the plaintiff, or two months from the day on which the decision became known to the plaintiff, whichever applies.

There have been few opportunities for parties to transactions to appeal Commission decisions, due to the limited number of prohibitions issued. Third parties, such as shareholders, competitors, employees, etc., have to show that they are directly and individually concerned by the decision in order to bring an action to the Court of First Instance.

F.   DRAFT NOTICES ON MERGER CONTROL

DGIV has just released three draft Notices dealing with important areas of practice under the Merger Regulation regarding the treatment of (1) restrictions directly related and necessary to the implementation of concentrations,[1] (2) commitments[2] and (3) routine cases, respectively.[3] These draft notices reflect the Commission's recent experience in merger control. This chapter will outline the new developments which would be introduced by the draft Notices should they be approved by the Council, as expected.

F.1   *Draft Commission Notice on Restrictions Directly Related and Necessary to Concentrations*

The draft Commission Notice on Restrictions Directly Related and Necessary to Concentrations ('the new Notice') will replace the existing Notice on Ancillary Restraints which is almost nine years old. An updated version reflecting the Commission's extensive experience during this period is therefore overdue in order to present the Commission's current practice in this field. In addition, the new Notice is accompanied by a draft Memorandum which both outlines the Commission's practical experiences in the past and its interpretation of the new Notice in this field. It provides an invaluable guide to the Commission's future merger control policy.

The first change to be aware of is that the term 'ancillary restraints' has been replaced with the phrase 'restrictions directly related and necessary to the implementation of concentrations'. The reason for this is that the

---

[1]   Draft Commission Notice on Restrictions Directly Related and Necessary to Concentrations reviewing the Commission Notice regarding Restrictions Ancillary to Concentrations OJ of 14 August 1990, p.5. The new draft is accompanied by an Explanatory Memorandum.

[2]   Draft Commission Notice on Commitments submitted to the Commission under Council Regulation 4064/89 and under Commission Regulation 447/98.

[3]   Draft Commission Notice on a Simplified Procedure for Processing Certain Concentrations under Council Regulation 4164/89.

phrase 'ancillary restraints' has a specific meaning in competition law, which is not used in the Merger Regulation.

This first section will concentrate on outlining the future new rules as provided for in the new Notice, outlining changes in the practice of the Commission from that under the present Notice.

F.1.1 Principles of Evaluation and Definitions

As is clear from the new phrase used in the draft Notice, restrictions must first be 'directly related' to the concentration and secondly they must be 'necessary', in order to be examined under the Merger Regulation.

F.1.1.1 *'Directly related'*

In order that the clause is examined together with the concentration it must first be directly related to the concentration in that it is 'subordinate in importance to the main object of the concentration'.[4]

F.1.1.2 *'Necessary'*

To determine whether or not the restriction is necessary, the Commission will take account of the clause's (1) nature, (2) duration, (3) subject matter and (4) geographical field of application.[5] Finally there must be no other justifiable alternative or 'less restrictive clauses' that could not achieve the same aims of the restrictive clause without causing similar restrictions on competition.

F.1.2 Common Clauses in the Acquisition of an Undertaking

As a general rule, the needs of the buyer to benefit from certain protection are more compelling than the corresponding needs of the vendor. It is the buyer who needs to be assured he will be able to run the acquired business so as to recoup the investment made. Restrictions benefiting the vendor either are not directly related to the concentration or, where they are, they are unlikely to need to go as far in scope and/or duration as those that benefit the acquirer. These are words of warning and illustrate the Com-

---

[4] Draft Memorandum: Treatment of Ancillary Restraints.
[5] Para. 7, Draft Commission Notice on Restrictions Directly Related and Necessary to Concentrations.

mission's reluctance to accept non-competition clauses in favour of the seller.

F.1.2.1 *Non-competition clauses: general*

The new Notice introduces some very important changes from the Commission's former practice under the old Notice as regards non-competition clauses.

The Commission advises parties always to provide an explanation of the rationale underlying non-competition restrictions and justify fully their request for them to be viewed as directly related and necessary to the concentration. The parties should highlight that the non-competition clause may be necessary for the purchaser to recoup his investment and to gain experience before the seller can re-enter the market.

F.1.2.2 *Acquisition of an undertaking*

In acquisitions of an undertaking, non-competition clauses imposed on the seller which are reasonably limited in duration, geographic scope and subject matter are classic restrictions directly related to and necessary to the completion of a concentration.

Where the transfer of the undertaking includes both goodwill and know-how, there is a presumption that non-competition clauses up to the duration of three years are justifiable.[6] This is a dramatic reduction from the previously acceptable period of five years. Where only goodwill is involved, the duration of two years for the non-competition clause remains unchanged by the new Notice. A longer duration will need to be justified by the parties.

The presumption concerning the geographic and product scope of a non-competition clause is that the restriction should be limited to those products and services and geographical areas where the vendor had established the product before the transfer. Any extension of this principle must be justified by the parties.[7]

---

[6] Para. 13, Draft Notice on Restrictions Directly Related and Necessary to Concentrations.
[7] Paras 14 and 15, Draft Commission Notice on Restrictions Directly Related and Necessary to Concentrations.

F.1.2.3 *Joint ventures*

The same presumptions as those regarding the transfer of an undertaking generally apply to joint ventures. In addition, however, the Commission accepts in the draft Memorandum[8] that the parties to a joint venture (i.e. the parents) may agree a non-competition clause whose duration is longer, even up to the joint venture's lifetime. The parties will need to justify that the non-competition clauses are necessary and directly related on grounds such as the expression of the parents' lasting withdrawal from the market, the need to protect the joint venture's start-up, to ensure that the parents utilise fully their assets, or to protect the joint venture from free-riding by the parents.

The most important change is the absolute rejection in the new Notice of clauses preventing a parent from competing with the joint venture or the other parents *after the duration of the lifetime* of the joint venture.[9] This contrasts with the previous practice of the Commission to accept such non-competition clauses whose terms were equivalent to the duration of the joint venture's existence plus a short duration (usually one or two years) thereafter.

F.1.2.4 *Non-solicitation and confidentiality clauses*

The new Notice includes provisions on non-solicitation and confidentiality clauses[10] which will be evaluated in the same way as non-competition clauses. The Commission has adopted a tolerant attitude to such clauses over the years and recognises the importance they play in ensuring the implementation of a concentration.

F.1.3   Licence Agreements

Patents and know-how licensing agreements, within the meaning of the block exemption on Technology Transfer,[11] fall under the new Notice, as do trade marks and related rights such as copyright, design rights and business names. All will be assessed under the same criteria.

---

[8]   Para. 8, Draft Memorandum: Treatment of Ancillary Restraints.
[9]   Para. 40, Draft Commission Notice on Restrictions Directly Related and Necessary to Concentrations (author's emphasis).
[10]   Para. 17, Draft Commission Notice on Restrictions Directly Related and Necessary to Concentrations.
[11]   Technology Transfer Regulation 240/96, OJ 1996 L 31/2.

F.1.3.1 *Transfer of undertaking or acquisition of an undertaking*

No substantial changes have been made in the text of the new Notice other than to add a provision which recognises that where a licence is granted from the seller of a business to the buyer, the seller can be made subject to a territorial restriction similar to a non-competition clause in the context of a sale of a business.[12]

F.1.3.2 *Joint ventures*

The Notice is more lenient towards the transfer of licences of property rights that are collateral to a full-function joint venture. Joint ventures usually involve the transfer of technology necessary for the carrying out of the activities assigned to it. If the parents want to remain the owners of the property rights in order to exploit them for other activities, they will license the technology to the joint venture. Such licences may serve as a substitute for the transfer of property rights. Consequently the licence may be considered to be an integral part of the operation. This applies regardless of the nature of the licence.

If the scope of the licence is wider than that of the activities of the joint venture, while it is not necessarily anti-competitive, it may be difficult to argue that it is necessary to the implementation of the joint venture.

Licence agreements can of course always rely on an automatic exemption from Article 81 (ex Article 85) if they fall within the scope of the block exemption on Technology Transfer.

F.1.4 Purchase and Supply Agreements

The draft Notice provides that purchase and supply agreements between the vendor and the acquirer or between a parent and its joint venture may be considered directly related and necessary to the implementation of the concentration for a transitional period. In the case of a complete transfer of an undertaking this may be necessary to facilitate the break up of economic unity of the vendor and the partial transfer of the assets to the acquirer.[13] The aim of such agreements is to prevent any disruption in the break up of previously integrated activities[14] and to provide continuity of

---

[12] Para. 18, Draft Commission Notice on Restrictions Directly Related and Necessary to Concentrations.

[13] Para. 22, Draft Commission Notice on Restrictions Directly Related and Necessary to Concentrations.

[14] Para. 17, Memorandum on Draft Commission Notice on Restrictions Directly Related and Necessary to Concentrations.

purchases for the vendor or the acquirer as they were previously assured as a single economic entity.[15]

The draft Notice requires that such agreements are limited to pre-existing purchase and supply relationships within the integrated seller and their duration must be limited to a period objectively necessary for the replacement of the relationship of dependency by autonomy in the market.

F.1.4.1 *Most common purchase/supply clauses*

The most common clauses are:

- obligations to purchase/supply a given quantity;
- obligations to purchase/supply without limitation;
- preferred supplier/preferred customer status; and
- exclusive purchase/supply arrangements.[16]

Provisions regarding services and outsourcing generally also fall under the same analysis, as do distribution agreements. In any event distribution agreements may fall within the scope of the relevant Block Exemption.[17]

It should be noted that the new Notice states that supply obligations which benefit the vendor or the supplier, will require 'particularly careful justification by the parties'.[18]

F.1.4.2 *Types of acceptable obligations*

The Memorandum offers insight as to which types of obligations the Commission will favour. As a general rule, agreements providing obligations to supply/purchase given *quantities* are preferred over obligations where there are no quantitative limitations or which provide for exclusivity arrangements. Indeed 'there should be a negative presumption against such form of non-limitation and against exclusivity'.[19] The parties may rebut this presumption but the reasons must be compelling.

---

[15] Para. 24, Draft Commission Notice on Restrictions Directly Related and Necessary to Concentrations.
[16] Para. 19, Memorandum on Draft Commission Notice on Restrictions Directly Related and Necessary to Concentrations.
[17] Paras 30 and 31, Draft Commission Notice on Restrictions Directly Related and Necessary to Concentrations.
[18] Para. 25, Draft Commission Notice on Restrictions Directly Related and Necessary to Concentrations.
[19] Para. 23, Memorandum on Draft Commission Notice on Restrictions Directly Related and Necessary to Concentrations.

F.1.4.3 *Acceptable duration*

Given the wide variety of supply arrangements it is impossible for the Commission to have a general presumption in relation to the duration of purchase/supply obligations, which would apply across the whole range of options. However the large number of case specific and sector specific concerns do provide a basis for the Commission to give a precise guide. Therefore it is advisable to make the Commission aware of comparable commercial practice in the sector, as this becomes an important reference for the Commission when making its analysis and decision.

The Commission has conceded that for complex intermediate products three years are normally viewed as an acceptable period of duration.[20] In the case of specific market conditions such as limited sources of supply, this duration can be extended up to a maximum of five years. A longer period would only be acceptable in exceptional circumstances.[21]

F.1.5 **Other Agreements**

There are some types of agreements which do not easily lend themselves to categorisation within the existing categories of the Notice. These may nevertheless be treated within the existing categories. Agreements relating to use of trade marks and business names can be dealt with together with the transfer of licence of such trade marks to the extent they constitute an additional guarantee for the acquirer. Outsourcing agreements can be subsumed into the category of purchase and supply agreements and distribution agreements can be treated as supply agreements. However, agreements relating to the lease of premises or utilities and to assets not transferred but which relate to the business are to be considered as part of the notified concentration and thus do not constitute restrictions directly related and necessary to a concentration.

F.1.6 **Procedural Issues**

When notifying a concentration, each restriction should be individually identified. The parties should explain why these are directly related and necessary to the implementation of the concentration by reference to

---

[20] Para. 24, Memorandum on Draft Commission Notice on Restrictions Directly Related and Necessary to Concentrations.

[21] In the past this has occurred primarily in the chemical industry either because other suppliers were unavailable or difficult to access or where the supply arrangements prior to the transaction were highly integrated and economically interdependent within one group.

precise clauses and not merely to complete agreements. The Commission refuses to consider non-binding agreements or simple declarations of intention as eligible for scrutiny as ancillary restraints. The penalty for the absence of sufficient reasoning is that the agreement will not be covered by the final decision.

F.2   Draft Notice on Commitments submitted to the Commission under Regulation 4064/89 and under Regulation 447/98

This draft Notice on Commitments sets out the general principles for designing commitments that are suitable for resolving competition concerns in proceedings under the Merger Regulation. The Notice reflects the Commission's experience to date regarding the assessment, acceptance and implementation of commitments.

F.2.1   General Principles

The parties may seek to resolve the competition problem by modifying the original notified concentration or by committing to modify the originally notified concentration within a specific period after the clearance of the merger.

The Commission's approach is that commitments should be made to reduce market power and restore competition where a proposed concentration will create or strengthen a dominant position. The Commission considers the capacity of a commitment to remedy a competition problem on a case by case basis. It takes into account the specific characteristics of the relevant market under scrutiny. Clearly, this does not make it easy to determine in advance what the appropriate remedy should be in order to satisfy the Commission.

The Commission may accept commitments in both phases of the investigation procedure. In order to be effective, commitments must be capable of being implemented speedily and effectively within a short time period. Commitments offered in Phase I must resolve uncomplicated competition problems with clear cut remedies. In Phase II[22] the Commission has to take a clearance decision as soon as serious doubts are removed as a result of commitments submitted by the parties.

Divestiture is not always a plausible solution as competition problems may arise from other factors such as the combination of key patents, the

---

[22]   Pursuant to Article 10(2) of the Merger Regulation.

existence of exclusive agreements or existing structural links between the parties and other market players. In such circumstances, the remedy must aim at off-setting the increase in market share to such an extent that the competitive concerns no longer arise (e.g. a licence, removal of exclusivity etc.).

Commitments must provide a lasting solution to the competition problem. The Commission will not entertain 'commitments' that would amount merely to a promise not to abuse a dominant position. The Commission has not ruled out other types of commitments such as (1) not to use a trade mark for a certain period, or (2) to make part of the production capacity of the entity arising from the concentration available to third party competitors, or more generally (3) to grant access to essential facilities on non-discriminatory terms. These alternative commitments may be capable of preventing the emergence or strengthening of a dominant position.

Joint ventures will be subject to scrutiny under both Article 2(3) and Article 2(4) of the Merger Regulation by the Commission. Essentially where a joint venture will lead to a co-ordination of its parent companies which constitutes an appreciable restriction of competition within the meaning of Article 81(1) EC, commitments have to prevent the elimination of competition if requirements of an exemption under Article 81(3) are not met. As above, commitments should provide a lasting solution.

While the formulation and offer of remedies lies with the parties, the Commission's assessment of the problem will be the decisive factor in the determination of what the parameters of the remedy should be. The enforcement of the commitments is guaranteed in an attachment of obligations in the Commission clearance decision. Non-fulfilment of the commitments results in fines as outlined in Article 14(2)(a) of the Merger Regulation.

F.2.2 Commitments Accepted by the Commission

There are three main types of commitments.

F.2.2.1 *Divestiture*

According to the Commission Notice on Commitments, divestment is 'the most effective way to preserve competition apart from prohibition'.[23] Divestiture creates the conditions necessary for the emergence of a new

---

[23] Para. 19, Draft Notice on Commitments.

competitive entity or alternatively allows third party competitors on the market to strengthen their position. In areas of competitive overlap this remedy should be seen as a principal way to satisfy the Commission.

The most common circumstances in which the option to divest arises is in multi-product transactions involving several markets where the competitive concerns raised by the given merger are limited to specific products or geographical markets. An offer by the parties to divest, which will solve these competition problems, will give rise to a clearance of the transaction as a whole, subject to the condition that the commitments to divest are enforced.

Where the competition problem arises due to a horizontal overlap in the same market, a divestiture of the overlapping business activities of the target company have typically been the most common solution adopted by the Commission. The Commission also recognises that a divestiture package of overlapping assets from the acquirer and the target which includes brands and supporting production assets can amount to a business and may be sufficient to create the conditions necessary for the emergence of a new competitor.

Divestiture is not limited by any means to overlapping businesses. Indeed the doctrine extends to joint ventures whereby a cut in structural links with another major competitor may be necessary to facilitate competition in a market with the newly merged entity.

F.2.2.2 *Termination of exclusive agreements*

This commitment becomes attractive for the Commission where a merged entity has a considerable market share and there are foreclosure effects resulting from existing exclusive agreements which may contribute towards the creation or strengthening of a dominant position. The termination of such exclusive agreements may be considered appropriate to eliminate the competitive concerns.

F.2.2.3 *Access to infrastructure and key technology*

Control over infrastructure and access to key technology such as patents, know-how and other intellectual property rights can also amount to serious barriers to entry. Commitments facilitating access to the necessary infrastructure or licence agreements may be regarded by the Commission as an adequate remedy, particularly where divestiture is not feasible.

F.2.2.4 *Commitment packages*

Commitments may be part of a package containing similar or mixed commitments such as divestiture and/or licensing agreements. The combination of commitments will 'differ' depending on the specific competition problem to be resolved.

F.2.3 Situations where Remedies are Difficult

Generally speaking, the Commission does seek to accommodate merging parties and is willing to explore proposed solutions in order to resolve competition concerns raised. There are, however, concentrations where no adequate remedies can be found. In such circumstances, the Commission will seek the only remedy available: prohibition.

F.2.4 Specific Requirements for Submission of Commitments in Phase I

The deadlines, for the submission of commitments in Phase I, are laid down in Article 18 (1) of Commission Regulation 447/98 and they must be submitted no later than three weeks after the date of receipt of the notification. In order to meet the necessary criteria of acceptance, Phase I commitments must:

- be submitted in due time, at the latest on the last day of the three week period;
- specify the commitments in sufficient detail to allow full assessment to be carried out by the Commission.

The Commission will then consult the authorities of the Member States on the proposed commitments and, where appropriate, the market participants, in particular those competitors and customers who raised concerns during the initial investigation.

Following this assessment, the Commission may clear the concentration if it is satisfied that the commitments remove the grounds for serious concern. If, on assessment, the commitments are not sufficient to remove the competition concerns, the Commission will proceed to an Article 6(1)(c) decision and open a Phase II investigation.

F.2.5 Specific Requirements for Submission of Commitments in Phase II

Article 8(2) of the Merger Regulation requires the Commission to declare a concentration compatible with the Common Market where, following

69

modification, a notified concentration no longer creates or strengthens a dominant position within the meaning of Article 2(3) of the Regulation.

The deadlines for submission of commitments in Phase II are laid down in Article 18(2) of Regulation 447/98. Such commitments should be submitted not more than three months from the day on which proceedings were initiated. Two points must be made in this regard. First, ambushing the Commission with last minute commitments is less likely to lead to success, particularly where little effort has been made to resolve areas of dispute. Another disadvantage of offering commitments at a later stage is that the Commission may, by then, have established that the concentration will create or strengthen a dominant position, and any commitments offered will have to eliminate such a position.

Proposals for commitments submitted in order to form the basis for a decision pursuant to Article 8(2) must meet the following requirements:

- they must be submitted on time, at the latest on the last day of the three-month period;
- they must address all the competition problems raised in the Statement of Objections and not subsequently abandoned by the Commission. In this respect the obligations entered into by the parties must be specified to a sufficient degree of detail in order to enable a full assessment to be carried out.

The Commission will first assess commitments itself and, if satisfied that they remove competition concerns, consult the national authorities involved as well as third parties affected by the concentration. If the commitments are deemed insufficient to resolve the concerns by the Commission, it will inform the parties accordingly.

Secondly, in exceptional circumstances, the Commission may be willing to extend the three-month period.[24] The extension will only be granted if the Commission recognises such exceptional circumstances and if it considers that there would be sufficient time to make a full assessment of the modifications. Moreover, the Commission will consider if there is enough time for further consultation with the Member States national competition authorities as well as concerned third parties affected by the merger. If there is not, then the proposed commitments cannot be taken into account. However, this does not preclude the parties from submitting a new notification designed to meet competition concerns.

---

[24]   Para. 36, Draft Notice on Commitments.

F.2.6 Requirements for Commitments and their Implementation

Commitments may sometimes be implemented before the clearance procedure but more often than not, they are implemented following clearance. Post-clearance commitments require safeguards to ensure they are enforced successfully and in a timely fashion.[25]

F.2.6.1 *Essential features of divestment remedies*

Divestiture usually concerns the tangible and intangible assets of a company or business activity, which previously was incorporated into the business. The parties proposing a divestiture should give a detailed, accurate account of those assets affected by the divestiture.[26] The divestiture should take place in a fixed time limit, agreed between the parties and the Commission, so that there is no doubt about its implementation timetable. This time period remains undisclosed to third parties.

Divestiture is usually subject to the Commission's prior approval of the purchaser. The sale will not be approved if the proposed purchase is likely to give rise to its own competition problems or delay the implementation of the remedy.

F.2.6.2 *Interim preservation*

In order to ensure the viability of the divested interest, interim measures will be put in place to maintain the independence, economic viability, marketability and competitiveness of the divestiture package. The aim of these commitments is also to keep the divestiture package separate and isolated administratively from the business retained.

The parties will be expected to use all reasonable efforts to ensure all relevant assets, both tangible and intangible, of the divestiture package are maintained pursuant to good business practice and in the ordinary course of business. Usual business practice must continue with management functions, sufficient working capital and a line of credit all being maintained. The Commission's aim is to ensure, pending divestiture, that all the assets of the package are managed as a distinct and saleable business with its own management composed of personnel independent from the parties.[27]

---

[25] Para. 38, Draft Notice on Commitments.
[26] Para. 39, Draft Notice on Commitments.
[27] Para. 42, Draft Notice on Commitments.

F.2.6.3 *Implementation*

As it is not practical to have the Commission involved in managing the divestment, its choice is to leave it to the merging parties or to appoint a trustee to effect the divestment.[28] Usually, a trustee is appointed. This role is normally taken on by a financial institution, whose duty it becomes to ensure the divestment takes place in good faith.[29] The role of the trustees will vary from one case to the next. General duties include supervision of the divestment and regular progress reports to the Commission.

F.2.6.4 *Approval of the purchaser*

To ensure that the divestment acts as an effective counter-balance to the competition concerns of the Commission, it is important that the purchaser meets the requirements of the commitments. The burden of proof is upon the seller to convince the Commission that the purchaser does indeed satisfy the aforementioned criteria.

The Commission may conclude that it would create delay in timely implementation, more competition problems or other difficulties. In light of such a conclusion, the Commission will deem the purchaser unacceptable, and inform the parties accordingly.

F.2.7 Final Remarks on the Notice

The draft Notice on Commitments is a useful and practical guide for practitioners to the Commission's approach to solving the various competition problems a concentration may cause. It is to be welcomed for removing the mystery behind satisfying the Commission for those not acquainted with the practices of the Commission, while at the same time providing long-awaited legal certainty for those who are.

F.3 ***Draft Commission Notice on a Simplified Procedure for Processing Certain Concentrations under Council Regulation 4064/89***

The third draft Notice proposed by the Commission marks an important step towards the new approach of the Commission to merger control. This Notice is clear evidence that the Commission now is confident the system

---

[28] Para. 43, Draft Notice on Commitments.
[29] Para. 44, Draft Notice on Commitments.

is so well established that parties can, under certain circumstances, be left to their own devices. This draft Notice shows the merger control policy has come of age.

The draft Notice sets out a simplified procedure for the treatment of certain merger cases that by their nature do not normally raise competition problems. The Notice envisages that in such cases the Commission will refrain from adopting a formal clearance decision, and the mergers in question will thus be approved automatically upon expiry of the Phase I deadline. Various measures are foreseen in order to ensure the transparency and legal certainty of the merger control process.

The Notice is aimed at automatically clearing the types of mergers that normally get clearance without having raised any substantive doubts. This procedure will allow the Commission to concentrate its energy on more difficult cases thereby making its policy more 'focused and effective'.[30] As usual, pre-notification contact between the Commission and the parties is encouraged and plays a very important role in this new procedure. When all the conditions are met, the Commission will abstain from taking a decision, thereby deeming the merger valid. This occurs without the formality of being 'approved and declared compatible with the common market within one month of the notification pursuant to Article 10 paragraphs 1 and 6 of the Merger Regulation'.[31]

F.3.1   Concentrations Eligible for Simplified Procedure

The Notice sets out the following categories of concentrations as eligible for the new procedure:

- where two or more undertakings acquire joint control over a joint venture, provided that the joint venture has no, or negligible, actual or foreseen effects within the EEA territory. Such cases occur where:
  - the turnover of the joint venture and/or of the activities contributed is less than 100m Euro in the EEA territory; and
  - the total value of assets transferred to the joint venture is less than 100m Euro in the EEA;
- where two or more undertakings merge, or one or more undertakings acquire sole rights or joint control over another undertaking, provided that none of the parties to the concentration are engaged in

---

[30]   Para. 2, Commission Draft Notice on a Simplified Procedure for Processing Certain Concentrations under Council Regulation 4064/89.

[31]   Para. 1.3, Commission Draft Notice on a Simplified Procedure for Processing Certain Concentrations under Council Regulation 4064/89.

business activities in the same product and/or geographical market or in the product market which is upstream or downstream of a product market in which any other party to the concentration is engaged;

- where two or more undertakings merge or one of or more undertakings acquire sole or joint control of another undertaking; and two or more of the parties to the concentration are engaged in business activities:
  - in the same product market and geographical market (horizontal relatioships);
  - in a product market which is upstream or downstream of a product market in which any other party to the concentration is engaged (vertical relationships),

provided that their combined market share is not 15 per cent or more for horizontal and 25 per cent or more for vertical relationships.

According to the Commission's experience such concentrations do not give rise to competition concerns save in exceptional circumstances.

Given that market definitions play a crucial role in the assessment of the above, the Commission invites parties to meet with it to clarify market definitions in the pre-notification process. The notifying parties remain however responsible for informing the Commission of all alternative relevant product and geographical markets on which the notified concentration could have an impact.

F.3.2 Procedural Provisions

It is worth repeating that pre-notification discussions play a vital role in this new procedure. Competition problems, especially with regard to market definition, can be clarified at this informal stage. This stage is particularly important where parties are seeking the Commission to waive a full form notification on the grounds that no competition concerns arise.

In addition to the usual publication of the fact of notification of the concentration in the Official Journal of the EC, the Commission will publish the same information in the language of the case on its Internet website upon receipt of the notification with the indication that it may be approved by silence. In this way third parties will be aware and able to submit any objections or bring to the Commission's attention any competition concerns they may have.

If the Commission is satisfied that the concentration qualifies for the simplified procedure it will abstain from adopting a formal decision within one month of the receipt of the notification pursuant to Article 10(1) and (6) of the Merger Regulation. However, at any stage of this period the Commission may decide to revert back to a Phase I merger procedure, including investigations and a written decision. To a certain extent, this amounts to having the cake and eating it.

After the expiry of this term, the Commission will send written notification to the parties that the time has expired. The Commission will publish in the Official Journal the fact that a concentration is deemed to have been declared compatible with the Common Market.

The deemed approval will include ancillary restrictions which are directly related and necessary to the implementation of the concentration without any explicit declaration by the Commission. However restrictions are not ancillary merely because the parties deem them as such. While the draft Notice on restrictions directly related and necessary to concentrations will, no doubt be helpful in this regard, an amount of uncertainty will remain.

ANNEXES: REGULATIONS AND NOTICES

Annex 1A. Council Regulation on the control of concentrations between undertakings (original text)

Annex 1B. Council Regulation 1310/97 amending Council Regulation 4064/89

Annex 1C. Unofficial consolidated text of Council Regulation 4064/89

Annex 2. Commission Regulation 447/98 on the notifications, time limits and hearings provided for in Council Regulation 4064/89 (OJ L61/1 of 2 March 1998)

Annex 3. Commission Notice on the Concept of Full Function Joint Ventures under Council Regulation 4064/89 (OJ C66/1 of 2 March 1998)

Annex 4. Commission Notice on the concept of concentration under Council Regulation 4064/89 (OJ C66/5 of 2 March 1998)

Annex 5. Commission Notice on the concept of undertakings concerned under Council Regulation 4064/89 (OJ C 66/14 of 2 March 1998)

Annex 6. Commission Notice on the calculation of turnover under Council Regulation 4064/89 (OJ C66/25 of 2 March 1998)

Annex 7. Commission Notice concerning alignment of procedures for processing mergers under the ECSC and EC Treaties (OJ C66/36 of 2 March 1998)

Annex 8. Information on the assessment of full function joint ventures pursuant to the competition rules of the European Commission (OJ C66/38 of 2 March 1998)

Annex 9. Commission Notice on ancillary restrictions (OJ C203/5 of 14 August 1990)

Annex 10. Merger: Best Practice Guidelines (www.europa.eu.int)

Annex 11. National Authorities dealing with Mergers

Annex 1A

COUNCIL REGULATION (EEC) NO 4064/89 OF 21 DECEMBER 1989 ON THE CONTROL OF CONCENTRATIONS BETWEEN UNDERTAKINGS

CORRIGENDA: CORRIGENDUM TO COUNCIL REGULATION (EEC) NO 4064/89 OF 21 DECEMBER 1989 ON THE CONTROL OF CONCENTRATIONS BETWEEN UNDERTAKINGS (OFFICIAL JOURNAL OF THE EUROPEAN COMMUNITIES NO L 395 OF 30 DECEMBER 1990

Given that certain errors appear in the various language versions of the abovementioned Regulation, the entire text shall be published as below in the form of a corrected version replacing the version of the Regulation published in *Official Journal of the European Communities* No L 395 of 30 December 1989, page 1.

THE COUNCIL OF THE EUROPEAN COMMUNITIES,

Having regard to the Treaty establishing the European Economic Community, and in particular Articles 87 and 235 thereof,

Having regard to the proposal from the Commission ([1]),

Having regard to the opinion of the European Parliament ([2]),

Having regard to the opinion of the Economic and Social Committee ([3]),

(1) Whereas, for the achievement of the aims of the Treaty establishing the European Economic Community, Article 3 (f) gives the Community the objective of instituting 'a system ensuring that competition in the common market is not distorted';

(2) Whereas this system is essential for the achievement of the internal market by 1992 and its further development;

([1]) OJ No C 130, 19. 5. 1988, p. 4.
([2]) OJ No C 309, 5. 12. 1988, p. 55.
([3]) OJ No C 208, 8. 8. 1988, p. 11.

(3) Whereas the dismantling of internal frontiers is resulting and will continue to result in major corporate reorganizations in the Community, particularly in the form of concentrations;

(4) Whereas such a development must be welcomed as being in line with the requirements of dynamic competition and capable of increasing the competitiveness of European industry, improving the conditions of growth and raising the standard of living in the Community;

(5) Whereas, however, it must be ensured that the process of reorganization does not result in lasting damage to competition; whereas Community law must therefore include provisions governing those concentrations which may significantly impede effective competition in the common market or in a substantial part of it;

(6) Whereas Articles 85 and 86, while applicable, according to the case-law of the Court of Justice, to certain concentrations, are not, however, sufficient to control all operations which may prove to be incompatible with the system of undistorted competition envisaged in the Treaty;

(7) Whereas a new legal instrument should therefore be created in the form of a Regulation to permit effective control of all concentrations from the point of view of their effect on the structure of competition in the Community and to be the only instrument applicable to such concentrations;

(8) Whereas this Regulation should therefore be based not only on Article 87 but, principally, on Article 235 of the Treaty, under which the Community may give itself the additional powers of action necessary for the attainment of its objectives, including with regard to concentrations on the markets for agricultural products listed in Annex II to the Treaty;

(9) Whereas the provisions to be adopted in this Regulation should apply to significant structural changes the impact of which on the market goes beyond the national borders of any one Member State;

(10) Whereas the scope of application of this Regulation should therefore be defined according to the geographical area of activity on the undertakings concerned and be limited by quantitative thresholds in order to cover those concentrations which have a Community dimension; whereas, at the end of an initial phase of the application of this Regulation, these thresholds should be reviewed in the light of the experience gained;

(11) Whereas a concentration with a Community dimension exists where the combined aggregate turnover of the undertakings concerned exceeds given levels worldwide and within the Community and where at least two of the undertakings concerned have their sole or main fields of activities in different Member States or where, although the undertakings in question act mainly in one and the same Member State, at least one of them has substantial operations in at last one other Member State; whereas that is also the case where the concentrations are effected by undertakings which do not have their principal fields of activities in the Community but which have substantial operations there;

(12) Whereas the arrangements be introduced for the control of concentrations should, without prejudice to Article 90(2) of the Treaty, respect the principle of non-discrimination between the public and the private sectors; whereas, in the public sector, calculation of the turnover of an undertaking concerned in a concentration needs, therefore, to take account of undertakings making up an economic unit with an independent power of decision, irrespective of the way in which their capital is held or of the rules of administrative supervision applicable to them;

(13) Whereas it is necessary to establish whether concentrations with a Community dimension are compatible or not with the common market from the point of view of the need to maintain and develop effective competition in the common market; whereas, in so doing, the Commission must place its appraisal within

the general framework of the achievement of the fundamental objectives referred to in Article 2 of the Treaty, including that of strengthening the Community's economic and social cohesion, referred to in Article 130a;

(14) Whereas this Regulation should establish the principle that a concentration with a Community dimension which creates or strengthens a position as a result of which effective competition in the common market or in a substantial part of it is significantly impeded is to be declared incompatible with the common market;

(15) Whereas concentrations which, by reason of the limited market share of the undertakings concerned, are not liable to impede effective competition may be presumed to be compatible with the common market; whereas, without prejudice to Articles 85 and 86 of the Treaty, an indication to this effect exists, in particular, where the market share of the undertakings concerned does not exceed 25% either in the common market or in a substantial part of it;

(16) Whereas the Commission should have the task of taking all the decisions necessary to establish whether or not concentrations with a Community dimension are compatible with the common market, as well as decisions designed to restore effective competition;

(17) Whereas to ensure effective control undertakings should be obliged to give prior notification of concentrations with a Community dimension and provisions should be made for the suspension of concentrations for a limited period, and for the possibility of extending or waiving a suspension where necessary; whereas in the interests of legal certainty the validity of transactions must nevertheless be protected as much as necessary;

(18) Whereas a period within which the Commission must initiate proceedings in respect of a notified concentration and periods within which it must give a final decision on the compatibility or incompatibility with the common market of a notified concentration should be laid down;

(19) Whereas the undertakings concerned must be afforded the right to be heard by the Commission when proceedings have been initiated; whereas the members of the management and supervisory bodies and the recognized representatives of the employees of the undertakings concerned, and third parties showing a legitimate interest, must also be given the opportunity to be heard;

(20) Whereas the Commission should act in close and constant liaison with the competent authorities of the Member States from which it obtains comments and information;

(21) Whereas, for the purposes of this Regulation, and in accordance with the case-law of the Court of Justice, the Commission must be afforded the assistance of the Member States and must also be empowered to require information to be given and to carry out the necessary investigations in order to appraise concentrations;

(22) Whereas compliance with this Regulation must be enforceable by means of fines and periodic penalty payments; whereas the Court of Justice should be given unlimited jurisdiction in that regard pursuant to Article 172 of the Treaty;

(23) Whereas it is appropriate to define the concept of concentration in such a manner as to cover only operations bringing about a lasting change in the structure of the undertakings concerned; whereas it is therefore necessary to exclude from the scope of this Regulation those operations which we have as their object or effect the coordination of the competitive behaviour of undertakings which remain independent, since such operations fall to be examined under the appropriate provisions of the Regulations implementing Articles 85 and 86 of the Treaty; whereas it is appropriate to make this distinction specifically in the case of the creation of joint ventures;

(24) Whereas there is no coordination of competitive behaviour within the meaning of this Regulation where two or more undertakings agree to acquire jointly

81

control of one or more other undertakings with the object and effect of sharing amongst themselves such undertakings or their assets;

(25) Whereas this Regulation should still apply where the undertakings concerned accept restrictions directly related and necessary to the implementation of the concentration;

(26) Whereas the Commission should be given exclusive competence to apply this Regulation, subject to review by the Court of Justice;

(27) Whereas the Member States may not apply their national legislation on competition to concentrations with a Community dimension, unless this Regulation makes provision therefor; whereas the relevant powers of national authorities should be limited to cases where, failing intervention by the Commission, effective competition is likely to be significantly impeded within the territory of a Member State and where the competition interests of that Member State cannot be sufficiently protected otherwise by this Regulation; whereas the Member States concerned must act promptly in such cases; whereas this Regulation cannot, because of the diversity of national law, fix a single deadline for the adoption of remedies;

(28) Whereas, furthermore, the exclusive application of this Regulation to concentrations with a Community dimension is without prejudice to Article 223 of the Treaty, and does not prevent the Member States from taking appropriate measures to protect legitimate interests other than those pursued by this Regulation, provided that such measures are compatible with the general principles and other provisions of Community law;

(29) Whereas concentrations not covered by this Regulation come, in principle, within the jurisdiction of the Member States; whereas, however, the Commission should have the power to act, at the request of a Member State concerned, in cases where effective competition could be significantly impeded within that Member State's territory;

(30) Whereas the conditions in which concentrations involving Community undertakings are carried out in non-member countries should be observed, and provision should be made for the possibility of the Council giving the Commission an appropriate mandate for negotiation with a view to obtaining non-discriminatory treatment for Community undertakings;

(31) Whereas this Regulation in no way detracts from the collective rights of employees as recognized in the undertakings concerned,

HAS ADOPTED THIS REGULATION:

Article 1   Scope

1.   Without prejudice to Article 22 this Regulation shall apply to all concentrations with a Community dimension as defined in paragraph 2.

2.   For the purposes of this Regulation, a concentration has a Community dimension where:

(a)   the combined aggregate worldwide turnover of all the undertakings concerned is more than ECU 5 000 million; and

(b)   the aggregate Community-wide turnover of each of at least two of the undertakings concerned is more than ECU 250 million,

unless each of the undertakings concerned achieves more than two-thirds of its aggregate Community-wide turnover within one and the same Member State.

3.   The thresholds laid down in paragraph 2 will be reviewed before the end of the fourth year following that of the adoption of this Regulation by the Council acting by a qualified majority on a proposal form from the Commission.

Article 2   Appraisal of concentrations

1.   Concentrations within the scope of this Regulation shall be appraised in accordance with the following provisions with a view to establishing whether or not they are compatible with the common market.

In making this appraisal, the Commission shall take into account:

(a)   the need to maintain and develop effective competition within the common market in view of, among other things, the structure of all the markets concerned and the actual or potential competition from undertakings located either within or outwith the Community;

(b)   the market position of the undertakings concerned and their economic and financial power, the alternatives available to suppliers and users, their access to supplies or markets, any legal or other barriers to entry, supply and demand trends for the relevant goods and services, the interests of the intermediate and ultimate consumers, and the development of technical and economic progress provided that it is to consumers' advantage and does not form an obstacle to competition.

2.   A concentration which does not create or strengthen a dominant position as a result of which effective competition would be significantly impeded in the common market or in a substantial part of it shall be declared compatible with the common market.

3.   A concentration which creates or strengthens a dominant position as a result of which effective competition would be significantly impeded in the common market or in a substantial part of it shall be declared incompatible with the common market.

Article 3   Definition of concentration

1.   A concentration shall be deemed to arise where:

(a)   two or more previously independent undertakings merge, or

(b)   —   one or more persons already controlling at least one undertaking, or
       —   one or more undertakings

acquire, whether by purchase of securities or assets, by contract or by any other means, direct or indirect control of the whole or parts of one or more other undertakings.

2.   An operation, including the creation of a joint venture, which has as its object or effect the coordination of the competitive behaviour of undertakings which remain independent shall not constitute a concentration within the meaning of paragraph 1(b).

The creation of a joint venture performing on a lasting basis all the functions of an autonomous economic entity, which does not give rise to coordination of the competitive behaviour of the parties amongst themselves or between them and the joint venture, shall constitute a concentration within the meaning of paragraph 1(b).

3.   For the purposes of this Regulation, control shall be constituted by rights, contracts or any other means which, either separately or in combination and having regard to the considerations of fact or law involved, confer the possibility of exercising decisive influence on an undertaking, in particular by:

(a)   ownership or the right to use all or part of the assets of an undertaking;

(b) rights or contracts which confer decisive influence on the composition, voting or decisions of the organs of an undertaking.

4. Control is acquired by persons or undertakings which:

(a) are holders of the rights or entitled to rights under the contracts concerned; or
(b) while not being holders of such rights or entitled to rights under such contracts, have the power to exercise the rights deriving therefrom.

5. A concentration shall not be deemed to arise where:

(a) credit institutions or other financial institutions or insurance companies, the normal activities of which include transactions and dealing in securities for their own account or for the account of others, hold on a temporary basis securities which they have acquired in an undertaking with a view to reselling them, provided that they do not exercise voting rights in respect of those securities with a view to determining the competitive behaviour of that undertaking or provided that they exercise such voting rights only with a view to preparing the disposal of all or part of that undertaking or of its assets or the disposal of those securities and that any such disposal takes place within one year of the date of acquisition; that period may be extended by the Commission on request where such institutions or companies can show that the disposal was not reasonably possible within the period set;
(b) control is acquired by an office-holder according to the law of a Member State relating to liquidation, winding up, insolvency, cessation of payments, compositions or analogous proceedings;
(c) the operations referred to in paragraph 1(b) are carried out by the financial holding companies referred to in Article 5(3) of the Fourth Council Directive 78/660/EEC of 25 July 1978 on the annual accounts of certain types of companies([4]), as last amended by Directive 84/569/EEC([5]), provided however that the voting rights in respect of the holding are exercised, in particular in relation to the appointment of members of the management and supervisory bodies of the undertakings in which they have holdings, only to maintain the full value of those investments and not to determine directly or indirectly the competitive conduct of those undertakings.

Article 4   Prior notification of concentrations

1. Concentrations with a Community dimension defined in this Regulation shall be notified to the Commission not more than one week after the conclusion of the agreement, or the announcement of the public bid, or the acquisition of a controlling interest. That week shall begin when the first of those events occurs.

2. A concentration which consists of a merger within the meaning of Article 3(1)(a) or in the acquisition of joint control within the meaning of Article 3(1)(b) shall be notified jointly by the parties to the merger or by those acquiring joint control as the case may be. In all other cases, the notification shall be effected by the person or undertaking acquiring control of the whole or parts of one or more undertakings.

3. Where the Commission finds that a notified concentration falls within the scope of this Regulation, it shall publish the fact of the notification, at the same time indicating

---

([4])   OJ No L 222, 14. 8. 1978, p. 11.
([5])   OJ No L 314, 4. 12. 1984, p. 28.

the names of the parties, the nature of the concentration and the economic sectors involved. The Commission shall take account of the legitimate interest of undertakings in the protection of their business secrets.

Article 5   Calculation of turnover

1.   Aggregate turnover within the meaning of Article 1(2) shall comprise the amounts derived by the undertakings concerned in the preceding financial year from the sale of products and the provision of services falling within the undertakings' ordinary activities after deduction of sales rebates and of value added tax and other taxes directly related to turnover. The aggregate turnover of an undertaking concerned shall not include the sale of products or the provision of services between any of the undertakings referred to in paragraph 4.

Turnover, in the Community or in a Member State, shall comprise products sold and services provided to undertakings or consumers, in the Community or in that Member State as the case may be.

2.   By way of derogation from paragraph 1, where the concentration consists in the acquisition of parts, whether or not constituted as legal entities, of one or more undertakings, only the turnover relating to the parts which are the subject of the transaction shall be taken into account with regard to the seller or sellers.

However, two or more transactions within the meaning of the first subparagraph which take place within a two-year period between the same persons or undertakings shall be treated as one and the same concentration arising on the date of the last transaction.

3.   In place of turnover the following shall be used:

   (a)   for credit institutions and other financial institutions, as regards Article 1(2)(a), one-tenth of their total assets.
         As regards Article 1(2)(b) and the final part of Article 1(2), total Community-wide turnover shall be replaced by one-tenth of total assets multiplied by the ratio between loans and advances to credit institutions and customers in transactions with Community residents and the total sum of those loans and advances.
         As regards the final part of Article 1(2), total turnover within one Member State shall be replaced by one-tenth of total assets multiplied by the ratio between loans and advances to credit institutions and customers in transactions with residents of that Member State and the total sum of those loans and advances;
   (b)   for insurance undertakings, the value of gross premiums written which shall comprise all amounts received and receivable in respect of insurance contracts issued by or on behalf of the insurance undertakings, including also outgoing reinsurance premiums, and after deduction of taxes and parafiscal contributions or levies charged by reference to the amounts of individual premiums or the total volume of premiums; as regards Article 1(2)(b) and the final part of Article 1(2), gross premiums received from Community residents and from residents of one Member State respectively shall be taken into account.

4.   Without prejudice to paragraph 2, the aggregate turnover of an undertaking concerned within the meaning of Article 1(2) shall be calculated by adding together the respective turnovers of the following:

   (a)   the undertaking concerned;
   (b)   those undertakings in which the undertaking concerned, directly or indirectly:
         —   owns more than half the capital or business assets, or

-   has the power to exercise more than half the voting rights, or
-   has the power to appoint more than half the members of the supervisory board, the administrative board or bodies legally representing the undertakings, or
-   has the right to manage the undertakings' affairs;

(c)   those undertakings which have in the undertaking concerned the rights or powers listed in (b);

(d)   those undertakings in which an undertaking as referred to in (c) has the rights or powers listed in (b);

(e)   those undertakings in which two or more undertakings as referred to in (a) to (d) jointly have the rights or powers listed in (b).

5.   Where undertakings concerned by the concentration jointly have the rights or powers listed in paragraph 4 (b), in calculating the aggregate turnover of the undertakings concerned for the purposes of Article 1(2):

(a)   no account shall be taken of the turnover resulting from the sale of products or the provision of services between the joint undertaking and each of the undertakings concerned or any other undertaking connected with any one of them, as set out in paragraph 4 (b) to (e);

(b)   account shall be taken of the turnover resulting from the sale of products and the provision of services between the joint undertaking and any third undertakings. This turnover shall be apportioned equally amongst the undertakings concerned.

Article 6   Examination of the notification and initiation of proceedings

1.   The Commission shall examine the notification as soon as it is received.

(a)   Where it concludes that the concentration notified does not fall within the scope of this Regulation, it shall record that finding by means of a decision.

(b)   Where it finds that the concentration notified, although falling within the scope of this Regulation, does not raise serious doubts as to its compatibility with the common market, it shall decide not to oppose it and shall declare that it is compatible with the common market.

(c)   If, on the other hand, it finds that the concentration notified falls within the scope of this Regulation and raises serious doubts as to its compatibility with the common market, it shall decide to initiate proceedings.

2.   The Commission shall notify its decision to the undertakings concerned and the competent authorities of the Member States without delay.

Article 7   Suspension of concentrations

1.   For the purposes of paragraph 2 a concentration as defined in Article 1 shall not be put into effect either before its notification or within the first three weeks following its notification.

2.   Where the Commission, following a preliminary examination of the notification within the period provided for in paragraph 1, finds it necessary in order to ensure the full effectiveness of any decision taken later pursuant to Article 8(3) and (4), it may decide on its own initiative to continue the suspension of a concentration in whole or in part until it takes a final decision, or to take other interim measures to that effect.

3. Paragraphs 1 and 2 shall not prevent the implementation of a public bid which has been notified to the Commission in accordance with Article 4(1), provided that the acquirer does not exercise the voting rights attached to the securities in question or does so only to maintain the full value of those investments and on the basis of a derogation granted by the Commission under paragraph 4.

4. The Commission may, on request, grant a derogation from the obligations imposed in paragraphs 1, 2 or 3 in order to prevent serious damage to one or more undertakings concerned by a concentration or to a third party. That derogation may be made subject to conditions and obligations in order to ensure conditions of effective competition. A derogation may be applied for and granted at any time, even before notification or after the transaction.

5. The validity of any transaction carried out in contravention of paragraph 1 or 2 shall be dependent on a decision pursuant to Article 6(1)(b) or Article 8(2) or (3) or on a presumption pursuant to Article 10(6).

This Article shall, however, have no effect on the validity of transactions in securities including those convertible into other securities admitted to trading on a market which is regulated and supervised by authorities recognized by public bodies, operates regularly and is accessible directly or indirectly to the public, unless the buyer and seller knew or ought to have known that the transaction was carried out in contravention of paragraph 1 or 2.

Article 8   Powers of decision of the Commission

1. Without prejudice to Article 9, all proceedings initiated pursuant to Article 6(1)(c) shall be closed by means of a decision as provided for in paragraphs 2 to 5.

2. Where the Commission finds that, following modification by the undertakings concerned if necessary, a notified concentration fulfils the criterion laid down in Article 2(2), it shall issue a decision declaring the concentration compatible with the common market.

It may attach to its decision conditions and obligations intended to ensure that the undertakings concerned comply with the commitments they have entered into *vis-à-vis* the Commission with a view to modifying the original concentration plan. The decision declaring the concentration compatible shall also cover restrictions directly related and necessary to the implementation of the concentration.

3. Where the Commission finds that a concentration fulfils the criterion laid down in Article 2(3), it shall issue a decision declaring that the concentration is incompatible with the common market.

4. Where a concentration has already been implemented, the Commission may, in a decision pursuant to paragraph 3 or by separate decision, require the undertakings or assets brought together to be separated or the cessation of joint control or any other action that may be appropriate in order to restore conditions of effective competition.

5. The Commission may revoke the decision it has taken pursuant to paragraph 2 where:

(a) the declaration of compatibility is based on incorrect information for which one of the undertakings is responsible or where it has been obtained by deceit; or
(b) the undertakings concerned commit a breach of an obligation attached to the decision.

6. In the cases referred to in paragraph 5, the Commission may take a decision under paragraph 3, without being bound by the deadline referred to in Article 10 (3).

Article 9   Referral to the competent authorities of the Member States

1. The Commission may, by means of a decision notified without delay to the undertakings concerned and the competent authorities of the other Member States, refer a notified concentration to the competent authorities of the Member State concerned in the following circumstances.

2. Within three weeks of the date of receipt of the copy of the notification a Member State may inform the Commission, which shall inform the undertakings concerned, that a concentration threatens to create or to strengthen a dominant position as a result of which effective competition would be significantly impeded on a market, within that Member State, which presents all the characteristics of a destinct market, be it a substantial part of the common market or not.

3. If the Commission considers that, having regard to the market for the products or services in question and the geographical reference market within the meaning of paragraph 7, there is such a distinct market and that such a threat exists, either:

(a)   it shall itself deal with the case in order to maintain or restore effective competition on the market concerned; or
(b)   it shall refer the case to the competent authorities of the Member State concerned with a view to the application of that State's national competition law.

If, however, the Commission considers that such a distinct market or threat does not exist it shall adopt a decision to that effect which it shall address to the Member State concerned.

4. A decision to refer or not to refer pursuant to paragraph 3 shall be taken:

(a)   as a general rule within the six-week period provided for in Article 10(1), second subparagraph, where the Commission, pursuant to Article 6(1)(b) has not initiated proceedings; or
(b)   within three months at most of the notification of the concentration concerned where the Commission has initiated proceedings under Article 6(1)(c), without taking the preparatory steps in order to adopt the necessary measures under Article 8(2), second subparagraph, (3) or (4) to maintain or restore effective competition on the market concerned.

5. If within the three months referred to in paragraph 4 (b) the Commission, despite a reminder from the Member State concerned, has not taken a decision on referral in accordance with paragraph 3 nor has taken the preparatory steps referred to in paragraph 4 (b), it shall be deemed to have taken a decision to refer the case to the Member State concerned in accordance with paragraph 3 (b).

6. The publication of any report or the announcement of the findings of the examination of the concentration by the competent authority of the Member State concerned shall be effected not more than four months after the Commission's referral.

7. The geographical reference market shall consist of the area in which the undertakings concerned are involved in the supply and demand of products or services, in

which the conditions of competition are sufficiently homogeneous and which can be distinguished from neighbouring areas because, in particular, conditions of competition are appreciably different in those areas. This assessment should take account in particular the nature and characteristics of the products or services concerned, of the existence of entry barriers of consumer preferences, of appreciable differences of the undertakings' market shares between the area concerned and neighbouring areas or of substantial price differences.

8. In applying the provisions of this Article, the Member State concerned may take only the measures strictly necessary to safeguard or restore effective competition on the market concerned.

9. In accordance with the relevant provisions of the Treaty, any Member State may appeal to the Court of Justice, and in particular request the application of Article 186, for the purpose of applying its national competition law.

10. This Article will be reviewed before the end of the fourth year following that of the adoption of this Regulation.

Article 10 Time limits for initiating proceedings and for decisions

1. The decisions referred to in Article 6(1) must be taken within one month at most. That period shall begin on the day following that of the receipt of a notification or, if the information to be supplied with the notification is incomplete, on the day following that of the receipt of the complete information.

That period shall be increased to six weeks if the Commission receives a request from a Member State in accordance with Article 9(2).

2. Decisions taken pursuant to Article 8(2) concerning notified concentrations must be taken as soon as it appears that the serious doubts referred to in Article 6(1)(c) have been removed, particularly as a result of modifications made by the undertakings concerned, and at the latest by the deadline laid down in paragraph 3.

3. Without prejudice to Article 8(6), decisions taken pursuant to Article 8(3) concerning notified concentrations must be taken within not more than four months of the date on which proceedings are initiated.

4. The period set by paragraph 3 shall exceptionally be suspended where, owing to circumstances for which one of the undertakings involved in the concentration is responsible, the Commission has had to request information by decision pursuant to Article 11 or to order an investigation by decision pursuant to Article 13.

5. Where the Court of Justice gives a Judgement which annuls the whole or part of a Commission decision taken under this Regulation, the periods laid down in this Regulation shall start again from the date of the Judgement.

6. Where the Commission has not taken a decision in accordance with Article 6(1)(b) or (c) or Article 8(2) or (3) within the deadlines set in paragraphs 1 and 3 respectively, the concentration shall be deemed to have been declared compatible with the common market, without prejudice to Article 9.

Article 11 Requests for information

1. In carrying out the duties assigned to it by this Regulation, the Commission may obtain all necessary information from the Governments and competent authorities of

the Member States, from the persons referred to in Article 3(1)(b), and from undertakings and associations of undertakings.

2.   When sending a request for information to a person, an undertaking or an association of undertakings, the Commission shall at the same time send a copy of the request to the competent authority of the Member State within the territory of which the residence of the person or the seat of the undertaking or association of undertakings is situated.

3.   In its request the Commission shall state the legal basis and the purpose of the request and also the penalties provided for in Article 14(1)(c) for supplying incorrect information.

4.   The information requested shall be provided, in the case of undertakings, by their owners or their representatives and, in the case of legal persons, companies or firms, or of associations having no legal personality, by the persons authorized to represent them by law or by their statutes.

5.   Where a person, an undertaking or an association of undertakings does not provide the information requested within the period fixed by the Commission or provides incomplete information, the Commission shall by decision require the information to be provided. The decision shall specify what information is required, fix an appropriate period within which it is to be supplied and state the penalties provided for in Articles 14(1)(c) and 15(1)(a) and the right to have the decision reviewed by the Court of Justice.

6.   The Commission shall at the same time send a copy of its decision to the competent authority of the Member State within the territory of which the residence of the person or the seat of the undertaking or association of undertakings is situated.

Article 12   Investigations by the authorities of the Member States

1.   At the request of the Commission, the competent authorities of the Member States shall undertake the investigations which the Commission considers to be necessary under Article 13(1), or which it has ordered by decision pursuant to Article 13(3). The officials of the competent authorities of the Member States responsible for conducting those investigations shall exercise their powers upon production of an authorization in writing issued by the competent authority of the Member State within the territory of which the investigation is to be carried out. Such authorization shall specify the subject matter and purpose of the investigation.

2.   If so requested by the Commission or by the competent authority of the Member State within the territory of which the investigation is to be carried out, officials of the Commission may assist the officials of that authority in carrying out their duties.

Article 13   Investigative powers of the Commission

1.   In carrying out the duties assigned to it by this Regulation, the Commission may undertake all necessary investigations into undertakings and associations of undertakings.

To that end the officials authorized by the Commission shall be empowered:

   (a)   to examine the books and other business records;

(b) to take or demand copies of or extracts from the books and business records;

(c) to ask for oral explanations on the spot;

(d) to enter any premises, land and means of transport of undertakings.

2. The officials of the Commission authorized to carry out the investigations shall exercise their powers on production of an authorization in writing specifying the subject matter and purpose of the investigation and the penalties provided for in Article 14 (1) (d) in cases where production of the required books or other business records is incomplete. In good time before the investigation, the Commission shall inform, in writing, the competent authority of the Member State within the territory of which the investigation is to be carried out and of the identities of the authorized officials.

3. Undertakings and associations of undertakings shall submit to investigations ordered by decision of the Commission. The decision shall specify the subject matter and purpose of the investigation, appoint the date on which it shall begin and state the penalties provided for in Articles 14(1)(d) and 15(1)(b) and the right to have the decision reviewed by the Court of Justice.

4. The Commission shall in good time and in writing inform the competent authority of the Member State within the territory of which the investigation is to be carried out of its intention of taking a decision pursuant to paragraph 3. It shall hear the competent authority before taking its decision.

5. Officials of the competent authority of the Member State within the territory of which the investigation is to be carried out may, at the request of that authority or of the Commission, assist the officials of the Commission in carrying out their duties.

6. Where an undertaking or association of undertakings opposes an investigation ordered pursuant to this Article, the Member State concerned shall afford the necessary assistance to the officials authorized by the Commission to enable them to carry out their investigation. To this end the Member States shall, after consulting the Commission, take the necessary measures within one year of the entry into force of this Regulation.

Article 14   Fines

1. The Commission may by decision impose on the persons referred to in Article 3(1)(b), undertakings or associations of undertakings fines of from ECU 1 000 to 50 000 where intentionally or negligently:

(a) they fail to notify a concentration in accordance with Article 4;

(b) they supply incorrect or misleading information in a notification pursuant to Article 4;

(c) they supply incorrect information in response to a request made pursuant to Article 11 or fail to supply information within the period fixed by a decision taken pursuant to Article 11;

(d) they produce the required books or other business records in incomplete form during investigations under Article 12 or 13, or refuse to submit to an investigation ordered by decision taken pursuant to Article 13.

2. The Commission may by decision impose fines not exceeding 10 % of the aggregate turnover of the undertakings concerned within the meaning of Article 5 on the persons or undertakings concerned where, either intentionally or negligently, they:

(a) fail to comply with an obligation imposed by decision pursuant to Article 7(4) or 8(2), second subparagraph;

(b) put into effect a concentration in breach of Article 7(1) or disregard a decision taken pursuant to Article 7(2);

(c) put into effect a concentration declared incompatible with the common market by decision pursuant to Article 8(3) or do not take the measures ordered by decision pursuant to Article 8(4).

3. In setting the amount of a fine, regard shall be had to the nature and gravity of the infringements.

4. Decisions taken pursuant to paragraphs 1 and 2 shall not be of criminal law nature.

Article 15   Periodic penalty payments

1. The Commission may by decision impose on the persons referred to in Article 3(1)(b), undertakings or associations of undertakings concerned periodic penalty payments of up to ECU 25 000 for each day of delay calculated from the date set in the decision, in order to compel them:

(a) to supply complete and correct information which it has requested by decision pursuant to Article 11;

(b) to submit to an investigation which it has ordered by decision pursuant to Article 13.

2. The Commission may by decision impose on the persons referred to in Article 3(1)(b) or on undertakings periodic penalty payments of up to ECU 100 000 for each day of delay calculated from the date set in the decision, in order to compel them:

(a) to comply with an obligation imposed by decision pursuant to Article 7(4) or Article 8(2), second sub-paragraph, or

(b) to apply the measures ordered by decision pursuant to Article 8(4).

3. Where the persons referred to in Article 3(1)(b), undertakings or associations of undertakings have satisfied the obligation which it was the purpose of the periodic penalty payment to enforce, the Commission may set the total amount of the periodic penalty payments at a lower figure than that which would arise under the original decision.

Article 16   Review by the Court of Justice

The Court of Justice shall have unlimited jurisdiction within the meaning of Article 172 of the Treaty to review decisions whereby the Commission has fixed a fine or periodic penalty payments; it may cancel, reduce or increase the fine or periodic penalty payments imposed.

Article 17   Professional secrecy

1. Information acquired as a result of the application of Article 11, 12, 13 and 18 shall be used only for the purposes of the relevant request, investigation or hearing.

2. Without prejudice to Articles 4(3), 18 and 20, the Commission and the competent authorities of the Member States, their officials and other servants shall not disclose

information they have acquired through the application of this Regulation of the kind covered by the obligation of professional secrecy.

3. Paragraphs 1 and 2 shall not prevent publication of general information or of surveys which do not contain information relating to particular undertakings or associations of undertakings.

Article 18   Hearing of the parties and of third persons

1. Before taking any decision provided for in Articles 7(2) and (4), Article 8(2), second subparagraph, and (3) to (5) and Articles 14 and 15, the Commission shall give the persons, undertakings and associations of undertakings concerned the opportunity, at every stage of the procedure up to the consultation of the Advisory Committee, of making known their views on the objections against them.

2. By way of derogation from paragraph 1, a decision to continue the suspension of a concentration or to grant a derogation from suspension as referred to in Article 7(2) or (4) may be taken provisionally, without the persons, undertakings or associations of undertakings concerned being given the opportunity to make known their views beforehand, provided that the Commission gives them that opportunity as soon as possible after having taken its decision.

3. The Commission shall base its decision only on objections on which the parties have been able to submit their observations. The rights of the defence shall be fully respected in the proceedings. Access to the file shall be open at least to the parties directly involved, subject to the legitimate interest of undertakings in the protection of their business secrets.

4. In so far as the Commission or the competent authorities of the Member States deem it necessary, they may also hear other natural or legal persons. Natural or legal persons showing a sufficient interest and especially members of the administrative or management bodies of the undertakings concerned or the recognized representatives of their employees shall be entitled, upon application, to be heard.

Article 19   Liaison with the authorities of the Member States

1. The Commission shall transmit to the competent authorities of the Member States copies of notifications within three working days and, as soon as possible, copies of the most important documents lodged with or issued by the Commission pursuant to this Regulation.

2. The Commission shall carry out the procedures set out in this Regulation in close and constant liaison with the competent authorities of the Member States, which may express their views upon those procedures. For the purposes of Article 9 it shall obtain information from the competent authority of the Member State as referred to in paragraph 2 of that Article and give it the opportunity to make known its views at every stage of the procedure up to the adoption of a decision pursuant to paragraph 3 of that Article; to that end it shall give it access to the file.

3. An Advisory Committee on concentrations shall be consulted before any decision is taken pursuant to Article 8(2) to (5), 14 or 15, or any provisions are adopted pursuant to Article 23.

4. The Advisory Committee shall consist of representatives of the authorities of the Member States. Each Member State shall appoint one or two representatives; if unable to

attend, they may be replaced by other representatives. At least one of the representatives of a Member State shall be competent in matters of restrictive practices and dominant positions.

5. Consultation shall take place at a joint meeting convened at the invitation of and chaired by the Commission. A summary of the case, together with an indication of the most important documents and a preliminary draft of the decision to be taken for each case considered, shall be sent with the invitation. The meeting shall take place not less than 14 days after the invitation has been sent. The Commission may in exceptional cases shorten that period as appropriate in order to avoid serious harm to one or more of the undertakings concerned by a concentration.

6. The Advisory Committee shall deliver an opinion on the Commission's draft decision, if necessary by taking a vote. The Advisory Committee may deliver an opinion even if some members are absent and unrepresented. The opinion shall be delivered in writing and appended to the draft decision. The Commission shall take the utmost account of the opinion delivered by the Committee. It shall inform the Committee of the manner in which its opinion has been taken into account.

7. The Advisory Committee may recommend publication of the opinion. The Commission may carry out such publication. The decision to publish shall take due account of the legitimate interest of undertakings in the protection of their business secrets and of the interest of the undertakings concerned in such publication's taking place.

Article 20   Publication of decisions

1. The Commission shall publish the decisions which it takes pursuant to Article 8(2) to (5) in the *Official Journal of the European Communities*.

2. The publication shall state the names of the parties and the main content of the decision; it shall have regard to the legitimate interest of undertakings in the protection of their business secrets.

Article 21   Jurisdiction

1. Subject to review by the Court of Justice, the Commission shall have sole jurisdiction to take the decisions provided for in this Regulation.

2. No Member State shall apply its national legislation on competition to any consideration that has a Community dimension.

The first subparagraph shall be without prejudice to any Member State's power to carry out any enquiries necessary for the application of Article 9(2) or after referral, pursuant to Article 9(3), first subparagraph, indent (b), or (5), to take the measures strictly necessary for the application of Article 9(8).

3. Notwithstanding paragraphs 1 and 2, Member States may take appropriate measures to protect legitimate interests other than those taken into consideration by this Regulation and compatible with the general principles and other provisions of Community law.

Public security, plurality of the media and prudential rules shall be regarded as legitimate interests within the meaning of the first subparagraph.

Any other public interest must be communicated to the Commission by the Member State concerned and shall be recognized by the Commission after an assessment of its compatibility with the general principles and other provisions of Community law before the measures referred to above may be taken. The Commission shall inform the Member State concerned of its decision within one month of that communication.

Article 22   Application of the Regulation

1.   This Regulation alone shall apply to concentrations as defined in Article 3.

2.   Regulations No 17([6]), (EEC) No 1017/68 ([7]), (EEC) No 4056/86 ([8]) and (EEC) No 3975/87 ([9]) shall not apply to concentrations as defined in Article 3.

3.   If the Commission finds, at the request of a Member State, that a concentration as defined in Article 3 that has no Community dimension within the meaning of Article 1 creates or strengthens a dominant position as a result of which effective competition would be significantly impeded within the territory of the Member State concerned it may, in so far as the concentration affects trade between Member States, adopt the decisions provided for in Article 8(2), second subparagraph, (3) and (4).

4.   Articles 2(1)(a) and (b), 5, 6, 8 and 10 to 20 shall apply. The period within which proceedings may be initiated pursuant to Article 10(1) shall begin on the date of the receipt of the request from the Member State. The request must be made within one month at most of the date on which the concentration was made known to the Member State or effected. This period shall begin on the date of the first of those events.

5.   Pursuant to paragraph 3 the Commission shall take only the measures strictly necessary to maintain or store effective competition within the territory of the Member State at the request of which it intervenes.

6.   Paragraphs 3 to 5 shall continue to apply until the thresholds referred to in Article 1(2) have been reviewed.

Article 23   Implementing provisions

The Commission shall have the power to adopt implementing provisions concerning the form, content and other details of notifications pursuant to Article 4, time limits pursuant to Article 10, and hearings pursuant to Article 18.

Article 24   Relations with non-member countries

1.   The Member States shall inform the Commission of any general difficulties encountered by their undertakings with concentrations as defined in Article 3 in a non-member country.

([6])   OJ No 13, 21. 2. 1962, p. 204/62.
([7])   OJ No L 175, 23. 7. 1968, p. 1.
([8])   OJ No L 378, 31. 12. 1986, p. 4.
([9])   OJ No L 374, 31. 12. 1987, p. 1.

2.   Initially not more than one year after the entry into force of this Regulation and thereafter periodically the Commission shall draw up a report examining the treatment accorded to Community undertakings, in the terms referred to in paragraphs 3 and 4, as regards concentrations in non-member countries. The Commission shall submit those reports to the Council, together with any recommendations.

3.   Whenever it appears to the Commission, either on the basis of the reports referred to in paragraph 2 or on the basis of other information, that a non-member country does not grant Community undertakings treatment comparable to that granted by the Community to undertakings from that non-member country, the Commission may submit proposals to the Council for an appropriate mandate for negotiation with a view to obtaining comparable treatment for Community undertakings.

4.   Measures taken under this Article shall comply with the obligations of the Community or of the Member States, without prejudice to Article 234 of the Treaty, under international agreements, whether bilateral or multilateral.

Article 25   Entry into force

1.   This Regulation shall enter into force on 21 September 1990.

2.   This Regulation shall not apply to any concentration which was the subject of an agreement or announcement or where control was acquired within the meaning of Article 4(1) before the date of this Regulation's entry into force and it shall not in any circumstances apply to any concentration in respect of which proceedings were initiated before that date by a Member State's authority with responsibility for competition.

This Regulation shall be binding in its entirety and directly applicable in all Member States.

Done at Brussels, 21 December 1989.

For the Council
The President
E. CRESSON

Annex 1B

COUNCIL REGULATION (EC) NO 1310/97 OF 30 JUNE 1997 AMENDING REGULATION (EEC) NO 4064/89 ON THE CONTROL OF CONCENTRATIONS BETWEEN UNDERTAKINGS

THE COUNCIL OF THE EUROPEAN UNION,

Having regard to the Treaty establishing the European Community, and in particular Articles 87 and 235 thereof,

Having regard to the proposal from the Commission ([1]),

Having regard to the opinion of the European Parliament ([2]),

Having regard to the opinion of the Economic and Social Committee ([3]),

(1) Whereas concentrations with a significant impact in several Member States that fall below the thresholds referred to in Council Regulation (EEC) No 4064/89 of 21 December 1989 on the control of concentrations between undertakings ([4]) may qualify for examination under a number of national merger control systems; whereas multiple notification of the same transaction increases legal uncertainty, effort and cost for companies and may lead to conflicting assessments;

(2) Whereas extending the scope of Community merger control to concentrations with a significant impact in several Member States will ensure that a 'one-stop shop' system applies and will allow, in compliance with the subsidiarity principle, for an appreciation of the competition impact of such concentrations in the Community as a whole;

(3) Whereas additional criteria should be established for the application of Community merger control in order to meet the abovementioned objectives; whereas those criteria should consist of new thresholds established in terms of the total turnover of the undertakings concerned achieved world-wide, at Community level and in at least three Member States;

([1]) OJ No C 350, 21. 11. 1996, pp. 8 and 10.

([2]) OJ No C 362, 2. 12. 1996, p. 130.

([3]) OJ No C 56, 24. 2. 1997, p. 71.

([4]) OJ No L 395, 30. 12. 1989, p. 1. Regulation rectified by OJ No L 257, 21. 9. 1990, p. 13 and amended by the 1994 Act of Accession.

(4) Whereas at the end of the initial phase of application of this Regulation the Commission should report to the Council on the implementation of all applicable thresholds and criteria, so that the Council is in a position, acting in accordance with Article 145 of the Treaty, to change the criteria or adjust the thresholds laid down in this Regulation;

(5) Whereas it is appropriate to define the concept of concentration in such a manner as to cover operations bringing about a lasting change in the structure of the undertakings concerned; whereas in the specific case of joint ventures it is appropriate to include within the scope and procedure of Regulation (EEC) No 4064/89 all full-function joint ventures; whereas, in addition to the dominance test set out in Article 2 of that Regulation, it should be provided that the Commission apply the criteria of Article 85(1) and (3) of the Treaty to such joint ventures, to the extent that their creation has as its direct consequence an appreciable restriction of competition between undertakings that remain independent; whereas, if the effects of such joint ventures on the market are primarily structural, Article 85(1) does not as a general rule apply; whereas Article 85(1) may apply if two or more parent companies remain active in the market of the joint venture, or, possibly, if the creation of the joint venture has as its object or effect the prevention, restriction or distortion of competition between the parent companies in upstream, downstream or neighbouring markets; whereas, in this context, the appraisal of all competition aspects of the creation of the joint venture must be made within the same procedure;

(6) Whereas, for the purposes of calculating the turnover of credit and financial institutions, banking income is a better criterion than a proportion of assets, because it reflects more accurately the economic reality of the whole banking sector;

(7) Whereas it should be expressly provided that decisions taken at the end of the first phase of the procedure cover restrictions directly related and necessary for the implementation of a concentration;

(8) Whereas the Commission may declare a concentration compatible with the common market in the second phase of the procedure, following commitments by the parties that are proportional to and would entirely eliminate the competition problem; whereas it is also appropriate to accept commitments in the first phase of the procedure where the competition problem is readily identifiable and can easily be remedied; whereas it should be expressly provided that in these cases the Commission may attach to its decision conditions and obligations; whereas transparency and effective consultation of Member States and interested third parties should be ensured in both phases of the procedure;

(9) Whereas, to ensure effective control, concentrations should be suspended until a final decision has been taken; whereas, on the other hand, it should be possible to waive a suspension, where appropriate; whereas, in deciding whether or not to grant a waiver, the Commission should take account of all pertinent factors, such as the nature and gravity of damage to the undertakings concerned by a concentration or to third parties, and the threat to competition posed by the concentration;

(10) Whereas the rules governing the referral of concentrations between the Commission and Member States should be reviewed at the same time as the additional criteria for implementation of Community merger control are established; whereas these rules protect the competition interests of the Member States in an adequate manner and take due account of legal security and the 'one-stop shop' principle; whereas, however, certain aspects of the referral procedures should be improved or clarified;

(11) Whereas, in particular, the Commission can declare a concentration incompatible with the common market only if it impedes effective competition in a substantial part thereof; whereas the application of national competition law is,

therefore, particularly appropriate where a concentration affects competition on a distinct market within a Member State that does not constitute a substantial part of the common market: whereas in this case it should not be necessary to demonstrate, in the request for referral, that the concentration threatens to create or to strengthen a dominant position on this distinct market;

(12) Whereas it should be possible to suspend exceptionally the period within which the Commission must take a decision within the first phase of the procedure;

(13) Whereas it should be expressly provided that two or more Member States may make a joint request pursuant to Article 22 of Regulation (EEC) No 4064/89; whereas to ensure effective control, provision should be made for the suspension of concentrations referred to the Commission by one or more Member States;

(14) Whereas the Commission should be given the power to adopt implementing provisions where necessary,

HAS ADOPTED THIS REGULATION:

Article 1   Regulation (EEC) No 4064/89 is hereby amended as follows:

1. in Article 1:

    (a) paragraph 1 shall be replaced by the following:
        '1.   Without prejudice to Article 22, this Regulation shall apply to all concentrations with a Community dimension as defined in paragraphs 2 and 3.';

    (b) paragraph 3 shall be replaced by the following:
        '3.   For the purposes of this Regulation, a concentration that does not meet the thresholds laid down in paragraph 2 has a Community dimension where:
        (a)   the combined aggregate worldwide turnover of all the undertakings concerned is more than ECU 2 500 million;
        (b)   in each of at least three Member States, the combined aggregate turnover of all the undertakings concerned is more than ECU 100 million;
        (c)   in each of at least three Member States included for the purpose of point (b), the aggregate turnover of each of at least two of the undertakings concerned is more than ECU 25 million; and
        (d)   the aggregate Community-wide turnover of each of at least two of the undertakings concerned is more than ECU 100 million;
        unless each of the undertakings concerned achieves more than two-thirds of its aggregate Community-wide turnover within one and the same Member State.';

    (c) the following paragraphs shall be added:
        '4.   Before 1 July 2000 the Commission shall report to the Council on the operation of the thresholds and criteria set out in paragraphs 2 and 3.
        5.   Following the report referred to in paragraph 4 and on a proposal from the Commission, the Council, acting by a qualified majority, may revise the thresholds and criteria mentioned in paragraph 3.';

2. in Article 2, the following paragraph shall be added:
    '4.   To the extent that the creation of a joint venture constituting a concentration pursuant to Article 3 has as its object or effect the coordination of the competitive behaviour of undertakings that remain independent, such coordination shall be appraised in accordance with the criteria of Article 85(1) and (3) of the Treaty,

with a view to establishing whether or not the operation is compatible with the common market.

In making this appraisal, the Commission shall take into account in particular:

— whether two or more parent companies retain to a significant extent activities in the same market as the joint venture or in a market which is downstream or upstream from that of the joint venture or in a neighbouring market closely related to this market,

— whether the coordination which is the direct consequence of the creation of the joint venture affords the undertakings concerned the possibility of eliminating competition in respect of a substantial part of the products or services in question.';

3. in Article 3, paragraph 2 shall be amended as follows:

(a) the first subparagraph shall be deleted;

(b) in the second subparagraph the phrase 'which does not give rise to the coordination of the competitive behaviour of the parties amongst themselves or between them and the joint venture' shall be deleted.

4. in Article 5:

— paragraph 3 shall be replaced by the following:

'3. In place of turnover the following shall be used:

(a) for credit institutions and other financial institutions, as regards Article 1(2) and (3), the sum of the following income items as defined in Council Directive 86/635/EEC of 8 December 1986 on the annual accounts and consolidated accounts of banks and other financial institutions (*), after deduction of value added tax and other taxes directly related to those items, where appropriate:

(i) interest income and similar income;

(ii) income from securities:

— income from shares and other variable yield securities,

— income from participating interests,

— income from shares in affiliated undertakings;

(iii) commissions receivable;

(iv) net profit on financial operations;

(v) other operating income.

The turnover of a credit or financial institution in the Community or in a Member State shall comprise the income items, as defined above, which are received by the branch or division of that institution established in the Community or in the Member State in question, as the case may be;

(b) for insurance undertakings, the value of gross premiums written which shall comprise all amounts received and receivable in respect of insurance contracts issued by or on behalf of the insurance undertakings, including also outgoing reinsurance premiums, and after deduction of taxes and parafiscal contributions or levies charged by reference to the amounts of individual premiums or the total volume of premiums; as regards Article 1(2)(b) and (3)(b), (c) and (d) and the final part of Article 1(2) and (3), gross premiums received from Community residents and from residents of one Member State respectively shall be taken into account.'

— in paragraph 4, the introductory sentence shall be replaced by the following:

'4. Without prejudice to paragraph 2, the aggregate turnover of an undertaking concerned within the meaning of Article 1(2) and (3)

(*) OJ No L 372, 31. 12. 1986, p.1.

100

shall be calculated by adding together the respective turnovers of the following:';
— in paragraph 5, the introductory sentence shall be replaced by the following:
'5. Where undertakings concerned by the concentration jointly have the rights or powers listed in paragraph 4 (b), in calculating the aggregate turnover of the undertakings concerned for the purposes of Article 1(2) and (3):';

5. in Article 6:

(a) in paragraph 1:
    — in point (b) the following subparagraph shall be added:
    'The decision declaring the concentration compatible shall also cover restrictions directly related and necessary to the implementation of the concentration.';
    — point (c) shall be replaced by the following:
    '(c) Without prejudice to paragraph 1 (a), where the Commission finds that the concentration notified falls within the scope of this Regulation and raises serious doubts as to its compatibility with the common market, it shall decide to initiate proceedings.';
(b) the following paragraphs shall be inserted:
    '1a. Where the Commission finds that, following modification by the undertakings concerned, a notified concentration no longer raises serious doubts within the meaning of paragraph 1 (c), it may decide to declare the concentration compatible with the common market pursuant to paragraph 1 (b).
    The Commission may attach to its decision under paragraph 1 (b) conditions and obligations intended to ensure that the undertakings concerned comply with the commitments they have entered into vis-à-vis the Commission with a view to rendering the concentration compatible with the common market.
    1b. The Commission may revoke the decision it has taken pursuant to paragraph 1 (a) or (b) where:
    (a) the decision is based on incorrect information for which one of the undertakings is responsible or where it has been obtained by deceit, or
    (b) the undertakings concerned commit a breach of an obligation attached to the decision.
    1c. In the cases referred to in paragraph 1 (b), the Commission may take a decision under paragraph 1, without being bound by the deadlines referred to in Article 10(1).';

6. in Article 7:

(a) paragraph 1 shall be replaced by the following:
    '1. A concentration as defined in Article 1 shall not be put into effect either before its notification or until it as been declared compatible with the common market pursuant to a decision under Article 6(1)(b) or Article 8(2) or on the basis of a presumption according to Article 10(6).';
(b) paragraph 2 shall be deleted;
(c) paragraph 3 shall be amended as follows:
    the words 'paragraphs 1 and 2' at the beginning of the paragraph shall be replaced by the words paragraph 1';
(d) paragraph 4 shall be replaced by the following:
    '4. The Commission may, on request, grant a derogation from the obligations imposed in paragraphs 1 or 3. The request to grant a derogation must

be reasoned. In deciding on the request, the Commission shall take into account inter alia the effects of the suspension on one or more undertakings concerned by a concentration or on a third party and the threat to competition posed by the concentration. That derogation may be made subject to conditions and obligations in order to ensure conditions of effective competition. A derogation may be applied for and granted at any time, even before notification or after the transaction.';

(e) paragraph 5 shall be replaced by the following:

'5. The validity of any transaction carried out in contravention of paragraph 1 shall be dependent on a decision pursuant to Article 6(1)(b) or Article 8(2) or (3) or on a presumption pursuant to Article 10(6).

This Article shall, however, have no effect on the validity of transactions in securities including those convertible into other securities admitted to trading on a market which is regulated and supervised by authorities recognized by public bodies, operates regularly and is accessible directly or indirectly to the public, unless the buyer and seller knew or ought to have known that the transaction was carried out in contravention of paragraph 1.';

7. in Article 8:

(a) paragraph 2 shall be replaced by the following:

'2. Where the Commission finds that, following modification by the undertakings concerned if necessary, a notified concentration fulfils the criterion laid down in Article 2(2) and, in the cases referred to in Article 2(4), the criteria laid down in Article 85(3) of the Treaty, it shall issue a decision declaring the concentration compatible with the common market.

It may attach to its decision conditions and obligations intended to ensure that the undertakings concerned comply with the commitments they have entered into *vis-à-vis* the Commission with a view to rendering the concentration compatible with the common market. The decision declaring the concentration compatible with the common market shall also cover restrictions directly related and necessary to the implementation of the concentration.';

(b) paragraph 3 shall be replaced by the following:

'3. Where the Commission finds that a concentration fulfils the criterion defined in. Article 2(3) or, in the cases referred to in Article 2(4), does not fulfil the criteria laid down in Article 85(3) of the Treaty, it shall issue a decision declaring that the concentration is incompatible with the common market.';

8. in Article 9:

(a) paragraph 2 shall be replaced by the following:

'2. Within three weeks of the date of receipt of the copy of the notification a Member State may inform the Commission, which shall inform the undertakings concerned, that:

(a) a concentration threatens to create or to strengthen a dominant position as a result of which effective competition will be significantly impeded on a market within that Member State, which presents all the characteristics of a distinct market, or

(b) a concentration affects competition on a market within that Member State, which presents all the characteristics of a distinct market and which does not constitute a substantial part of the common market.';

(b) in paragraph 3:

— point (b) shall be replaced by the following:

'(b) it shall refer the whole or part of the case to the competent authorities of the Member State concerned with a view to the application of that State's national competition law.',

— the following subparagraph shall be added:
'In cases where a Member State informs the Commission that a concentration affects competition in a distinct market within its territory that does not form a substantial part of the common market, the Commission shall refer the whole or part of the case relating to the distinct market concerned, if it considers that such a distinct market is affected.';

(c) paragraph 10 shall be replaced by the following:
'10. This Article may be re-examined at the same time as the thresholds referred to in Article 1.';

9. in Article 10:

(a) in paragraph 1, the following text shall be added at the end of the second subparagraph:
'or where, after notification of a concentration, the undertakings concerned submit commitments pursuant to Article 6(1a), which are intended by the parties to form the basis for a decision pursuant to Article 6(1)(b).';

(b) at the beginning of paragraph 4 the phrase 'The period set by paragraph 3' shall be replaced by the phrase 'The periods set by paragraphs 1 and 3';

10. in Article 18:

(a) in paragraph 1 the words: 'Article 7(2) and (4)' shall be replaced by the words 'Article 7(4)';

(b) paragraph 2 shall be replaced by the following:
'2. By way of derogation from paragraph 1, a decision to grant a derogation from suspension as referred to in Article 7(4) may be taken provisionally, without the persons, undertakings or associations of undertakings concerned being given the opportunity to make known their views beforehand, provided that the Commission gives them that opportunity as soon as possible after having taken its decision.';

11. in Article 19, the following text shall be added at the end of paragraph 1:
'Such documents shall include commitments which are intended by the parties to form the basis for a decision pursuant to Articles 6(1)(b) or 8(2).';

12. in Article 22:

(a) paragraphs 1 and 2 shall be replaced by the following:
'1. This Regulation alone shall apply to concentrations as defined in Article 3, and Regulations No 17(^{1}), (EEC) No 1017/68 (^{2}), (EEC) No 4056/86 (^{3}) and (EEC) No 3975/87 (^{4}) shall not apply, except in relation to joint ventures that do not have a Community dimension and which have their object or effect the coordination of the competitive behaviour of undertakings that remain independent.';

(b) paragraph 3 shall be amended as follows:
'3. If the Commission finds, at the request of a Member State or at the joint request of two or more Member States, that a concentration as defined in Article 3 that has no Community dimension within the meaning of Article 1 creates or strengthens a dominant position as a result of which effective competition would be significantly impeded within the territory of the Member State or States making the joint request, it may, insofar as that concentration affects trade between Member States, adopt the decisions provided for in Article 8(2), second subparagraph, (3) and (4).';

(c) paragraph 4 shall be replaced by the following:

'4.   Articles 2(1)(a) and (b), 5, 6, 8 and 10 to 20 shall apply to a request made pursuant to paragraph 3. Article 7 shall apply to the extent that the concentration has not been put into effect on the date on which the Commission informs the parties that a request has been made.

The period within which proceedings may be initiated pursuant to Article 10(1) shall begin on the day following that of the receipt of the request from the Member State or States concerned. The request must be made within one month at most of the date on which the concentration was made known to the Member State or to all Member States making a joint request or effected. This period shall begin on the date of the first of those events.';

(d)   in paragraph 5 the phrase 'or States' shall be inserted after the phrase 'within the territory of the Member State';

(e)   paragraph 6 shall be deleted;

13.   in Article 23:

(a)   these phrase 'time limits pursuant to Article 10' shall be replaced by the phrase 'time limits pursuant to Articles 7, 9, 10 and 22';

(b)   the following subparagraph shall be added:
'The Commission shall have the power to lay down the procedure and time limits for the submission of commitments pursuant to Articles 6(1a) and 8(2).'

Article 2

This Regulation shall not apply to any concentration which was the subject of an agreement or announcement or where control was acquired within the meaning of Article 4(1) of Regulation (EEC) No 4064/89, before 1 March 1998 and it shall not in any circumstances apply to any concentration in respect of which proceedings were initiated before 1 March 1998 by a Member State's authority with responsibility for competition.

Article 3

This Regulation shall enter into force on 1 March 1998.

This Regulation shall be binding in its entirety and directly applicable in all Member States.

Done at Luxembourg, 30 June 1997.

For the Council
The President
A. NUIS

Annex 1C

This is a working document prepared for the facility of the reader. Only texts published in the Official Journal of the European Communities are authentic.

CONSOLIDATED TEXT OF COUNCIL REGULATION (EEC) NO 4064/89 OF 21 DECEMBER 1989 ON THE CONTROL OF CONCENTRATIONS BETWEEN UNDERTAKINGS (PUBLISHED IN THE OFFICIAL JOURNAL. ONLY THE PUBLISHED TEXT IS AUTHENTIC: OJ L395, 30 DECEMBER 1989, OJ L257, 21 SEPTEMBER 1990) WITH AMENDMENTS INTRODUCED BY COUNCIL REGULATION (EC) NO. 1310/97 OF 30 JUNE 1997, OJ L180, p. 1, 09 JULY 1997

THE COUNCIL OF THE EUROPEAN COMMUNITIES,

. . .

Recitals

. . .

HAS ADOPTED THIS REGULATION:

Article 1   Scope

1.   Without prejudice to Article 22, this Regulation shall apply to all concentrations with a Community dimension as defined in *paragraphs 2 and 3*.

2.   For the purposes of this Regulation, a concentration has a Community dimension where:

(a)   the combined aggregate worldwide turnover of all the undertakings concerned is more than ECU 5 000 million; and

(b)   the aggregate Community-wide turnover of each of at least two of the undertakings concerned is more than ECU 250 million, unless each of the undertakings concerned achieves more than two-thirds of its aggregate Community-wide turnover within one and the same Member State.

3. ~~The thresholds laid down in paragraph 2 will be reviewed before the end of the fourth year following that of the adoption of this Regulation by the Council acting by a qualified majority on a proposal from the Commission.~~

3. *For the purposes of this Regulation, a concentration that does not meet the thresholds laid down in paragraph 2 has a Community dimension where:*

    (a) *the combined aggregate worldwide turnover of all the undertakings concerned is more than ECU 2 500 million;*
    (b) *in each of at least three Member States, the combined aggregate turnover of all the undertakings concerned is more than ECU 100 million;*
    (c) *in each of at least three Member States included for the purpose of point (b), the aggregate turnover of each of at least two of the undertakings concerned is more than ECU 25 million; and*
    (d) *the aggregate Community-wide turnover of each of at least two of the undertakings concerned is more than ECU 100 million;*
    unless each of the undertakings concerned achieves more than two-thirds of its aggregate Community-wide turnover within one and the same Member State.

4. Before 1 July 2000 the Commission shall report to the Council on the operation of the thresholds and criteria set out in paragraphs 2 and 3.

5. Following the report referred to in paragraph 4 and on a proposal from the Commission, the Council, acting by a qualified majority, may revise the thresholds and criteria mentioned in paragraph 3.

Article 2   Appraisal of concentrations

1. Concentrations within the scope of this Regulation shall be appraised in accordance with the following provisions with a view to establishing whether or not they are compatible with the common market. In making this appraisal, the Commission shall take into account:

    (a) the need to maintain and develop effective competition within the common market in view of, among other things, the structure of all the markets concerned and the actual or potential competition from undertakings located either within or outwith the Community;
    (b) the market position of the undertakings concerned and their economic and financial power, the alternatives available to suppliers and users, their access to supplies or markets, any legal or other barriers to entry, supply and demand trends for the relevant goods and services, the interests of the intermediate and ultimate consumers, and the development of technical and economic progress provided that it is to consumers' advantage and does not form an obstacle to competition.

2. A concentration which does not create or strengthen a dominant position as a result of which effective competition would be significantly impeded in the common market or in a substantial part of it shall be declared compatible with the common market.

3. A concentration which creates or strengthens a dominant position as a result of which effective competition would be significantly impeded in the common market or in a substantial part of it shall be declared incompatible with the common market.

4. *To the extent that the creation of a joint venture constituting a concentration pursuant to Article 3 has as its object or effect the coordination of the competitive behaviour of*

106

undertakings that remain independent, such coordination shall be appraised in accordance with the criteria of Article 85(1) and (3) of the Treaty, with a view to establishing whether or not the operation is compatible with the common market.

In making this appraisal, the Commission shall take into account in particular:

— *whether two or more parent companies retain to a significant extent activities in the same market as the joint venture or in a market which is downstream or upstream from that of the joint venture or in a neighbouring market closely related to this market;*
— *whether the coordination which is the direct consequence of the creation of the joint venture affords the undertakings concerned the possibility of eliminating competition in respect of a substantial part of the products or services in question.*

Article 3   Definition of concentration

1.   A concentration shall be deemed to arise where:

(a)   two or more previously independent undertakings merge, or
(b)   — one or more persons already controlling at least one undertaking, or
     — one or more undertakings

acquire, whether by purchase of securities or assets, by contract or by any other means, direct or indirect control of the whole or parts of one or more other undertakings.

2.   ~~An operation, including the creation of a joint venture, which has as its object or effect the coordination of the competitive behaviour of undertakings which remain independent shall not constitute a concentration within the meaning of paragraph 1 (b).~~

The creation of a joint venture performing on a lasting basis all the functions of an autonomous economic entity, ~~which does not give rise to coordination of the competitive behaviour of the parties amongst themselves or between them and the joint venture~~, shall constitute a concentration within the meaning of paragraph 1 (b).

3.   For the purposes of this Regulation, control shall be constituted by rights, contracts or any other means which, either separately or in combination and having regard to the considerations of fact or law involved, confer the possibility of exercising decisive influence on an undertaking, in particular by:

(a)   ownership or the right to use all or part of the assets of an undertaking;
(b)   rights or contracts which confer decisive influence on the composition, voting or decisions of the organs of an undertaking.

4.   Control is acquired by persons or undertakings which:
(a)   are holders of the rights or entitled to rights under the contracts concerned, or
(b)   while not being holders of such rights or entitled to rights under such contracts, have the power to exercise the rights deriving therefrom.

5.   A concentration shall not be deemed to arise where:

(a)   credit institutions or other financial institutions or insurance companies, the normal activities of which include transactions and dealing in securities for their own account or for the account of others, hold on a temporary basis securities which they have acquired in an undertaking with a view to reselling them, provided that they do not exercise voting rights in respect of those securities with a view to determining the competitive behaviour of that undertaking or provided that they exercise such voting rights only with a view to preparing the disposal of all or part of that undertaking or of its assets or the disposal of those securities and that any such disposal takes place within one year of the date of acquisition; that period may be extended by the Commission on request where such institutions or companies can show that the disposal was not reasonably possible within the period set;

(b) control is acquired by an office-holder according to the law of a Member State relating to liquidation, winding up, insolvency, cessation of payments, compositions or analogous proceedings;

(c) the operations referred to in paragraph 1(b) are carried out by the financial holding companies referred to in Article 5(3) of the Fourth Council Directive 78/660/EEC of 25 July 1978 on the annual accounts of certain types of companies[1], as last amended by Directive 84/569/EEC[2], provided however that the voting rights in respect of the holding are exercised, in particular in relation to the appointment of members of the management and supervisory bodies of the undertakings in which they have holdings, only to maintain the full value of those investments and not to determine directly or indirectly the competitive conduct of those undertakings.

Article 4   Prior notification of concentrations

1. Concentrations with a Community dimension defined in this Regulation shall be notified to the Commission not more than one week after the conclusion of the agreement, or the announcement of the public bid, or the acquisition of a controlling interest. That week shall begin when the first of those events occurs.

2. A concentration which consists of a merger within the meaning of Article 3 (1) (a) or in the acquisition of joint control within the meaning of Article 3 (1) (b) shall be notified jointly by the parties to the merger or by those acquiring joint control as the case may be. In all other cases, the notification shall be effected by the person or undertaking acquiring control of the whole or parts of one or more undertakings.

3. Where the Commission finds that a notified concentration falls within the scope of this Regulation, it shall publish the fact of the notification, at the same time indicating the names of the parties, the nature of the concentration and the economic sectors involved. The Commission shall take account of the legitimate interest of undertakings in the protection of their business secrets.

Article 5   Calculation of turnover

1. Aggregate turnover within the meaning of Article 1(2) shall comprise the amounts derived by the undertakings concerned in the preceding financial year from the sale of products and the provision of services falling within the undertakings' ordinary activities after deduction of sales rebates and of value added tax and other taxes directly related to turnover. The aggregate turnover of an undertaking concerned shall not include the sale of products or the provision of services between any of the undertakings referred to in paragraph 4.

---

[1]   OJ No L 222 14.8.1978, p. 11.
[2]   OJ No L 314, 4.12.1984, p.28.

Turnover, in the Community or in a Member State, shall comprise products sold and services provided to undertakings or consumers, in the Community or in that Member State as the case may be.

2.   By way of derogation from paragraph 1, where the concentration consists in the acquisition of parts, whether or not constituted as legal entities, of one or more undertakings, only the turnover relating to the parts which are the subject of the transaction shall be taken into account with regard to the seller or sellers.

However, two or more transactions within the meaning of the first subparagraph which take place within a two-year period between the same persons or undertakings shall be treated as one and the same concentration arising on the date of the last transaction.

3.   In place of turnover the following shall be used:

(a)   ~~for credit institutions and other financial institutions, as regards Article 1 (2) (a), one tenth of their total assets. As regards Article 1 (2) (b) and the final part of Article 1 (2), total Community wide turnover shall be replaced by one tenth of total assets multiplied by the ratio between loans and advances to credit institutions and customers in transactions with Community residents and the total sum of those loans and advances.~~

   ~~As regards the final part of Article 1 (2), total turnover within one Member State shall be replaced by one tenth of total assets multiplied by the ratio between loans and advances to credit institutions and customers in transactions with residents of that Member State and the total sum of those loans and advances;~~

(a)   *for credit institutions and other financial institutions, as regards Article 1(2) and (3), the sum of the following income items as defined in Council Directive 86/635/EEC of 8 December 1986 on the annual accounts and consolidated accounts of banks and other financial institutions[3], after deduction of value added tax and other taxes directly related to those items, where appropriate:*
   (i)   *interest income and similar income;*
   (ii)   *income from securities:*
       —   *income from shares and other variable yield securities,*
       —   *income from participating interests,*
       —   *income from shares in affiliated undertakings;*
   (iii)   *commissions receivable;*
   (iv)   *net profit on financial operations;*
   (v)   *other operating income.*

The turnover of a credit or financial institution in the Community or in a Member State shall comprise the income items, as defined above, which are received by the branch or division of that institution established in the Community or in the Member State in question, as the case may be.

(b)   for insurance undertakings, the value of gross premiums written which shall comprise all amounts received and receivable in respect of insurance contracts issued by or on behalf of the insurance undertakings, including also outgoing reinsurance premiums, and after deduction of taxes and parafiscal contributions or levies charged by reference to the amounts of individual premiums or the total volume of premiums; as regards Article 1(2)(b) *and (3)(b), (c) and (d)* and the final part of Article 1(2) *and (3)*, gross premiums received from

---

[3]   OJ No L 372, 31. 12. 1986, p.1.

Community residents and from residents of one Member State respectively shall be taken into account.

4.   Without prejudice to paragraph 2, the aggregate turnover of an undertaking concerned within the meaning of Article 1(2) *and 3* shall be calculated by adding together the respective turnovers of the following:

(a)   the undertaking concerned;
(b)   those undertakings in which the undertaking concerned, directly or indirectly;
— owns more than half the capital or business assets, or
— has the power to exercise more than half the voting rights, or
— has the power to appoint more than half the members of the supervisory board, the administrative board or bodies legally representing the undertakings, or
— has the right to manage the undertakings' affairs;
(c)   those undertakings which have in an undertaking concerned the rights or powers listed in (b);
(d)   those undertakings in which an undertaking as referred to in (c) has the rights or powers listed in (b);
(e)   those undertakings in which two or more undertakings as referred to in (a) to (d) jointly have the rights or powers listed in (b).

5.   Where undertakings concerned by the concentration jointly have the rights or powers listed in paragraph 4 (b), in calculating the aggregate turnover of the undertakings concerned for the purposes of Article 1(2) *and (3)*:

(a)   no account shall be taken of the turnover resulting from the sale of products or the provision of services between the joint undertaking and each of the undertakings concerned or any other undertaking connected with any one of them, as set out in paragraph 4 (b) to (e);
(b)   account shall be taken of the turnover resulting from the sale of products and the provision of services between the joint undertaking and any third undertakings. This turnover shall be apportioned equally amongst the undertakings concerned.

Article 6   Examination of the notification and initiation of proceedings

1.   The Commission shall examine the notification as soon as it is received.

(a)   Where it concludes that the concentration notified does not fall within the scope of this Regulation, it shall record that finding by means of a decision.
(b)   Where it finds that the concentration notified, although falling within the scope of this Regulation, does not raise serious doubts as to its compatibility with the common market, it shall decide not to oppose it and shall declare that it is compatible with the common market.
The decision declaring the concentration compatible shall also cover restrictions directly related and necessary to the implementation of the concentration.
(c)   ~~If, on the other hand, it~~ *Without prejudice to paragraph 2, where the Commission* finds that the concentration notified falls within the scope of this Regulation and raises serious doubts as to its compatibility with the common market, it shall decide to initiate proceedings.

2.   Where the Commission finds that, following modification by the undertakings concerned, a notified concentration no longer raises serious doubts within the meaning of paragraph 1(c), it may decide to declare the concentration compatible with the common market pursuant to paragraph 1(b).

The Commission may attach to its decision under paragraph 1(b) conditions and obligations intended to ensure that the undertakings concerned comply with the commitments they have entered into vis-à-vis the Commission with a view to rendering the concentration compatible with the common market.

3.   *The Commission may revoke the decision it has taken pursuant to paragraph 1(a) or (b) where:*

   (a)   *the decision is based on incorrect information for which one of the undertakings is responsible or where it has been obtained by deceit, or*
   (b)   *the undertakings concerned commit a breach of an obligation attached to the decision.*

4.   In the cases referred to in paragraph 3, the Commission may take a decision under paragraph 1, without being bound by the deadlines referred to in Article 10(1).

~~2.~~ 5.   The Commission shall notify its decision to the undertakings concerned and the competent authorities of the Member States without delay.

Article 7   Suspension of concentrations

1.   ~~For the purposes of paragraph 2 a~~ A concentration as defined in Article 1 shall not be put into effect either before its notification or ~~within the first three weeks following its notification~~ *until it has been declared compatible with the common market pursuant to a decision under Article 6(1)(b) or Article 8(2) or on the basis of a presumption according to Article 10(6).*

~~2.   Where the Commission, following a preliminary examination of the notification within the period provided for in paragraph 1, finds it necessary in order to ensure the full effectiveness of any decision taken later pursuant to Article 8 (3) and (4), it may decide on its own initiative to continue the suspension of a concentration in whole or in part until it takes a final decision, or to take other interim measures to that effect.~~

3.   Paragraph~~s~~ 1 ~~and 2~~ shall not prevent the implementation of a public bid which has been notified to the Commission in accordance with Article 4(1), provided that the acquirer does not exercise the voting rights attached to the securities in question or does so only to maintain the full value of those investments and on the basis of a derogation granted by the Commission under paragraph 4.

4.   The Commission may, on request, grant a derogation from the obligations imposed in paragraphs 1 ~~2 or 3~~ *or 3.* ~~in order to prevent serious damage to one or more undertakings concerned by a concentration or to a third party.~~ *The request to grant a derogation must be reasoned. In deciding on the request, the Commission shall take into account inter alia the effects of the suspension on one or more undertakings concerned by a concentration or on a third party and the threat to competition posed by the concentration.* That derogation may be made subject to conditions and obligations in order to ensure conditions of effective competition. A derogation may be applied for and granted at any time, even before notification or after the transaction.

5.   The validity of any transaction carried out in contravention of paragraph 1 ~~or 2~~ shall be dependent on a decision pursuant to Article 6(1)(b) or 8(2) or (3) or on a presumption pursuant to Article 10(6).

This Article shall, however, have no effect on the validity of transactions in securities including those convertible into other securities admitted to trading on a market which is regulated and supervised by authorities recognized by public bodies, operates regularly and is accessible directly or indirectly to the public, unless the buyer and seller knew or ought to have known that the transaction was carried out in contravention of paragraph 1 ~~or 2~~.

Article 8   Powers of decision of the Commission

1.   Without prejudice to Article 9, all proceedings initiated pursuant to Article 6(1)(c) shall be closed by means of a decision as provided for in paragraphs 2 to 5.

2.   Where the Commission finds that, following modification by the undertakings concerned if necessary, a notified concentration fulfils the criterion laid down in Article 2(2) *and, in the cases referred to in Article 2(4), the criteria laid down in Article 85(3) of the Treaty*, it shall issue a decision declaring the concentration compatible with the common market.

It may attach to its decision conditions and obligations intended to ensure that the undertakings concerned comply with the commitments they have entered into *vis-à-vis* the Commission with a view to ~~modifying the original concentration plan~~ *rendering the concentration compatible with the common market*. The decision declaring the concentration compatible *with the common market* shall also cover restrictions directly related and necessary to the implementation of the concentration.

3.   Where the Commission finds that a concentration fulfils the criterion ~~laid down~~ *defined* in Article 2(3) *or, in the cases referred to in Article 2(4), does not fulfil the criteria laid down in Article 85(3) of the Treaty*, it shall issue a decision declaring that the concentration is incompatible with the common market.

4.   Where a concentration has already been implemented, the Commission may, in a decision pursuant to paragraph 3 or by separate decision, require the undertakings or assets brought together to be separated or the cessation of joint control or any other action that may be appropriate in order to restore conditions of effective competition.

5.   The Commission may revoke the decision it has taken pursuant to paragraph 2 where:

    (a)   the declaration of compatibility is based on incorrect information for which one of the undertakings is responsible or where it has been obtained by deceit, or

    (b)   the undertakings concerned commit a breach of an obligation attached to the decision.

6.   In the cases referred to in paragraph 5, the Commission may take a decision pursuant to paragraph 3, without being bound by the deadline referred to in Article 10(3).

Article 9   Referral to the competent authorities of the Member States

1.   The Commission may, by means of a decision notified without delay to the undertakings concerned and the competent authorities of the other Member States, refer a notified concentration to the competent authorities of the Member State concerned in the following circumstances.

2. Within three weeks of the date of receipt of the copy of the notification a Member State may inform the Commission, which shall inform the undertakings concerned, that:

(a) a concentration threatens to create or to strengthen a dominant position as a result of which effective competition ~~would~~ will be significantly impeded on a market within that Member State, which presents all the characteristics of a distinct market, ~~be it a substantial part of the common market~~ or

(b) *a concentration affects competition on a market within that Member State, which presents all the characteristics of a distinct market and which does not constitute a substantial part of the common market.*

~~not.~~

3. If the Commission considers that, having regard to the market for the products or services in question and the geographical reference market within the meaning of paragraph 7, there is such a distinct market and that such a threat exists, either:

(a) it shall itself deal with the case in order to maintain or restore effective competition on the market concerned, or

(b) it shall refer *the whole or part of* the case to the competent authorities of the Member State concerned with a view to the application of that State's national competition law.

If, however, the Commission considers that such a distinct market or threat does not exist it shall adopt a decision to that effect which it shall address to the Member State concerned.

In cases where a Member State informs the Commission that a concentration affects competition in a distinct market within its territory that does not form a substantial part of the common market, the Commission shall refer the whole or part of the case relating to the distinct market concerned, if it considers that such a distinct market is affected.

4. A decision to refer or not to refer pursuant to paragraph 3 shall be taken where:

(a) as a general rule within the six-week period provided for in Article 10(1), second subparagraph, where the Commission, pursuant to Article 6(1)(b), has not initiated proceedings, or

(b) within three months at most of the notification of the concentration concerned where the Commission has initiated proceedings under Article 6(1)(c), without taking the preparatory steps in order to adopt the necessary measures under Article 8(2), second subparagraph, (3) or (4) to maintain or restore effective competition on the market concerned.

5. If within the three months referred to in paragraph 4 (b) the Commission, despite a reminder from the Member State concerned, has not taken a decision on referral in accordance with paragraph 3 nor has taken the preparatory steps referred to in paragraph 4 (b), it shall be deemed to have taken a decision to refer the case to the Member State concerned in accordance with paragraph 3 (b).

6. The publication of any report or the announcement of the findings of the examination of the concentration by the competent authority of the Member State concerned shall be effected not more than four months after the Commission's referral.

7. The geographical reference market shall consist of the area in which the undertakings concerned are involved in the supply and demand of products or services, in which the conditions of competition are sufficiently homogeneous and which can be

distinguished from neighbouring areas because, in particular, conditions of competition are appreciably different in those areas. This assessment should take account in particular of the nature and characteristics of the products or services concerned, of the existence of entry barriers or of consumer preferences, of appreciable differences of the undertakings' market shares between the area concerned and neighbouring areas or of substantial price differences.

8.   In applying the provisions of this Article, the Member State concerned may take only the measures strictly necessary to safeguard or restore effective competition on the market concerned.

9.   In accordance with the relevant provisions of the Treaty, any Member State may appeal to the Court of Justice, and in particular request the application of Article 186, for the purpose of applying its national competition law.

10.   ~~This Article will be reviewed before the end of the fourth year following that of the adoption of this Regulation.~~ *This Article may be re-examined at the same time as the thresholds referred to in Article 1.*

Article 10   Time limits for initiating proceedings and for decisions

1.   The decisions referred to in Article 6(1) must be taken within one month at most. That period shall begin on the day following that of the receipt of a notification or, if the information to be supplied with the notification is incomplete, on the day following that of the receipt of the complete information.

That period shall be increased to six weeks if the Commission receives a request from a Member State in accordance with Article 9(2), *or where, after notification of a concentration, the undertakings concerned submit commitments pursuant to Article 6(2), which are intended by the parties to form the basis for a decision pursuant to Article 6(1)(b).*

2.   Decisions taken pursuant to Article 8(2) concerning notified concentrations must be taken as soon as it appears that the serious doubts referred to in Article 6(1)(c) have been removed, particularly as a result of modifications made by the undertakings concerned, and at the latest by the deadline laid down in paragraph 3.

3.   Without prejudice to Article 8(6), decisions taken pursuant to Article 8 (3) concerning notified concentrations must be taken within not more than four months of the date on which proceedings are initiated.

4.   The periods set by paragraphs *1 and* 3 shall exceptionally be suspended where, owing to circumstances for which one of the undertakings involved in the concentration is responsible, the Commission has had to request information by decision pursuant to Article 11 or to order an investigation by decision pursuant to Article 13.

5.   Where the Court of Justice gives a Judgement which annuls the whole or part of a Commission decision taken under this Regulation, the periods laid down in this Regulation shall start again from the date of the Judgement.

6.   Where the Commission has not taken a decision in accordance with Article 6(1)(b) or (c) or Article 8(2) or (3) within the deadlines set in paragraphs 1 and 3 respectively, the concentration shall be deemed to have been declared compatible with the common market, without prejudice to Article 9.

Article 11   Requests for information

1.   In carrying out the duties assigned to it by this Regulation, the Commission may obtain all necessary information from the Governments and competent authorities of the Member States, from the persons referred to in Article 3(1)(b), and from undertakings and associations of undertakings.

2.   When sending a request for information to a person, an undertaking or an association of undertakings, the Commission shall at the same time send a copy of the request to the competent authority of the Member State within the territory of which the residence of the person or the seat of the undertaking or association of undertakings is situated.

3.   In its request the Commission shall state the legal basis and the purpose of the request and also the penalties provided for in Article 14(1)(c) for supplying incorrect information.

4.   The information requested shall be provided, in the case of undertakings, by their owners or their representatives and, in the case of legal persons, companies or firms, or of associations having no legal personality, by the persons authorized to represent them by law or by their statutes.

5.   Where a person, an undertaking or an association of undertakings does not provide the information requested within the period fixed by the Commission or provides incomplete information, the Commission shall by decision require the information to be provided. The decision shall specify what information is required, fix an appropriate period within which it is to be supplied and state the penalties provided for in Articles 14(1)(c) and 15(1)(a) and the right to have the decision reviewed by the Court of Justice.

6.   The Commission shall at the same time send a copy of its decision to the competent authority of the Member State within the territory of which the residence of the person or the seat of the undertaking or association of undertakings is situated.

Article 12   Investigations by the authorities of the Member States

1.   At the request of the Commission, the competent authorities of the Member States shall undertake the investigations which the Commission considers to be necessary under Article 13(1), or which it has ordered by decision pursuant to Article 13(3). The officials of the competent authorities of the Member States responsible for conducting those investigations shall exercise their powers upon production of an authorization in writing issued by the competent authority of the Member State within the territory of which the investigation is to be carried out. Such authorization shall specify the subject matter and purpose of the investigation.

2.   If so requested by the Commission or by the competent authority of the Member State within the territory of which the investigation is to be carried out, officials of the Commission may assist the officials of that authority in carrying out their duties.

Article 13   Investigative powers of the Commission

1.   In carrying out the duties assigned to it by this Regulation, the Commission may undertake all necessary investigations into undertakings and associations of undertakings. To that end the officials authorized by the Commission shall be empowered:

(a) to examine the books and other business records;
(b) to take or demand copies of or extracts from the books and business records;
(c) to ask for oral explanations on the spot;
(d) to enter any premises, land and means of transport of undertakings.

2.   The officials of the Commission authorized to carry out the investigations shall exercise their powers on production of an authorization in writing specifying the subject matter and purpose of the investigation and the penalties provided for in Article 14(1)(d) in cases where production of the required books or other business records is incomplete. In good time before the investigation, the Commission shall inform, in writing, the competent authority of the Member State within the territory of which the investigation is to be carried out of the investigation and of the identities of the authorized officials.

3.   Undertakings and associations of undertakings shall submit to investigations ordered by decision of the Commission. The decision shall specify the subject matter and purpose of the investigation, appoint the date on which it shall begin and state the penalties provided for in Articles 14(1)(d) and 15(1)(b) and the right to have the decision reviewed by the Court of Justice.

4.   The Commission shall in good time and in writing inform the competent authority of the Member State within the territory of which the investigation is to be carried out of its intention of taking a decision pursuant to paragraph 3. It shall hear the competent authority before taking its decision.

5.   Officials of the competent authority of the Member State within the territory of which the investigation is to be carried out may, at the request of that authority or of the Commission, assist the officials of the Commission in carrying out their duties.

6.   Where an undertaking or association of undertakings opposes an investigation ordered pursuant to this Article, the Member State concerned shall afford the necessary assistance to the officials authorized by the Commission to enable them to carry out their investigation. To this end the Member States shall, after consulting the Commission, take the necessary measures within one year of the entry into force of this Regulation.

Article 14   Fines

1.   The Commission may by decision impose on the persons referred to in Article 3 (1) (b), undertakings or associations of undertakings fines of from ECU 1 000 to 50 000 where intentionally or negligently:

(a) they fail to notify a concentration in accordance with Article 4;
(b) they supply incorrect or misleading information in a notification pursuant to Article 4;
(c) they supply incorrect information in response to a request made pursuant to Article 11 or fail to supply information within the period fixed by a decision taken pursuant to Article 11;
(d) they produce the required books or other business records in incomplete form during investigations under Article 12 or 13, or refuse to submit to an investigation ordered by decision taken pursuant to Article 13.

2.   The Commission may by decision impose fines not exceeding 10% of the aggregate turnover of the undertakings concerned within the meaning of Article 5 on the persons or undertakings concerned where, either intentionally or negligently, they;

(a) fail to comply with an obligation imposed by decision pursuant to Article 7(4) or 8(2), second subparagraph;

(b) put into effect a concentration in breach of Article 7(1) or disregard a decision taken pursuant to Article 7(2);

(c) put into effect a concentration declared incompatible with the common market by decision pursuant to Article 8(3) or do not take the measures ordered by decision pursuant to Article 8(4).

3.   In setting the amount of a fine, regard shall be had to the nature and gravity of the infringement.

4.   Decisions taken pursuant to paragraphs 1 and 2 shall not be of criminal law nature.

Article 15   Periodic penalty payments

1.   The Commission may by decision impose on the persons referred to in Article 3(1)(b), undertakings or associations of undertakings concerned periodic penalty payments of up to ECU 25 000 for each day of delay calculated from the date set in the decision, in order to compel them:

(a) to supply complete and correct information which it has requested by decision pursuant to Article 11;

(b) to submit to an investigation which it has ordered by decision pursuant to Article 13.

2.   The Commission may by decision impose on the persons referred to in Article 3(1)(b) or on undertakings periodic penalty payments of up to ECU 100 000 for each day of delay calculated from the date set in the decision, in order to compel them:

(a) to comply with an obligation imposed by decision pursuant to Article 7(4) or Article 8(2), second subparagraph, or

(b) to apply the measures ordered by decision pursuant to Article 8(4).

3.   Where the persons referred to in Article 3(1)(b), undertakings or associations of undertakings have satisfied the obligation which it was the purpose of the periodic penalty payment to enforce, the Commission may set the total amount of the periodic penalty payments at a lower figure than that which would arise under the original decision.

Article 16   Review by the Court of Justice

The Court of Justice shall have unlimited jurisdiction within the meaning of Article 172 of the Treaty to review decisions whereby the Commission has fixed a fine or periodic penalty payments; it may cancel, reduce or increase the fine or periodic penalty payments imposed.

Article 17   Professional secrecy

1.   Information acquired as a result of the application of Articles 11, 12, 13 and 18 shall be used only for the purposes of the relevant request, investigation or hearing.

2.   Without prejudice to Articles 4 (3), 18 and 20, the Commission and the competent authorities of the Member States, their officials and other servants shall not disclose information they have acquired through the application of this Regulation of the kind covered by the obligation of professional secrecy.

3.   Paragraphs 1 and 2 shall not prevent publication of general information or of surveys which do not contain information relating to particular undertakings or associations of undertakings.

Article 18   Hearing of the parties and of third persons

1.   Before taking any decision provided for in Article 7 (2) and (4), Article 8 (2), second subparagraph, and (3) to (5), and Articles 14 and 15, the Commission shall give the persons, undertakings and associations of undertakings concerned the opportunity, at every stage of the procedure up to the consultation of the Advisory Committee, of making known their views on the objections against them.

2.   By way of derogation from paragraph 1, a decision to continue the suspension of a concentration or to grant a derogation from suspension as referred to in Article 7 (2) or (4) may be taken provisionally, without the persons, undertakings or associations of undertakings concerned being given the opportunity to make known their views beforehand, provided that the Commission gives them that opportunity as soon as possible after having taken its decision.

3.   The Commission shall base its decision only on objections on which the parties have been able to submit their observations. The rights of the defence shall be fully respected in the proceedings. Access to the file shall be open at least to the parties directly involved, subject to the legitimate interest of undertakings in the protection of their business secrets.

4.   Insofar as the Commission or the competent authorities of the Member States deem it necessary, they may also hear other natural or legal persons. Natural or legal persons showing a sufficient interest and especially members of the administrative or management bodies of the undertakings concerned or the recognized representatives of their employees shall be entitled, upon application, to be heard.

Article 19   Liaison with the authorities of the Member States

1.   The Commission shall transmit to the competent authorities of the Member States copies of notifications within three working days and, as soon as possible, copies of the most important documents lodged with or issued by the Commission pursuant to this Regulation. *Such documents shall include commitments which are intended by the parties to form the basis for a decision pursuant to Articles 6(1)(b) or 8(2).*

2.   The Commission shall carry out the procedures set out in this Regulation in close and constant liaison with the competent authorities of the Member States, which may express their views upon those procedures. For the purposes of Article 9 it shall obtain information from the competent authority of the Member State as referred to in paragraph 2 of that Article and give it the opportunity to make known its views at every stage of the procedure up to the adoption of a decision pursuant to paragraph 3 of that Article; to that end it shall give it access to the file.

3.   An Advisory Committee on concentrations shall be consulted before any decision is taken pursuant to Articles 8(2) to (5), 14 or 15, or any provisions are adopted pursuant to Article 23.

4.   The Advisory Committee shall consist of representatives of the authorities of the Member States. Each Member State shall appoint one or two representatives; if unable to attend, they may be replaced by other representatives. At least one of the representatives of a Member State shall be competent in matters of restrictive practices and dominant positions.

5.   Consultation shall take place at a joint meeting convened at the invitation of and chaired by the Commission. A summary of the case, together with an indication of the most important documents and a preliminary draft of the decision to be taken for each case considered, shall be sent with the invitation. The meeting shall take place not less than 14 days after the invitation has been sent. The Commission may in exceptional cases shorten that period as appropriate in order to avoid serious harm to one or more of the undertakings concerned by a concentration.

6.   The Advisory Committee shall deliver an opinion on the Commission's draft decision, if necessary by taking a vote. The Advisory Committee may deliver an opinion even if some members are absent and unrepresented. The opinion shall be delivered in writing and appended to the draft decision. The Commission shall take the utmost account of the opinion delivered by the Committee. It shall inform the Committee of the manner in which its opinion has been taken into account.

7.   The Advisory Committee may recommend publication of the opinion. The Commission may carry out such publication. The decision to publish shall take due account of the legitimate interest of undertakings in the protection of their business secrets and of the interest of the undertakings concerned in such publication's taking place.

Article 20   Publication of decisions

1.   The Commission shall publish the decisions which it takes pursuant to Article 8(2) to (5) in the *Official Journal of the European Communities.*

2.   The publication shall state the names of the parties and the main content of the decision; it shall have regard to the legitimate interest of undertakings in the protection of their business secrets.

Article 21   Jurisdiction

1.   Subject to review by the Court of Justice, the Commission shall have sole jurisdiction to take the decisions provided for in this Regulation.

2.   No Member State shall apply its national legislation on competition to any concentration that has a Community dimension.

The first subparagraph shall be without prejudice to any Member State's power to carry out any enquiries necessary for the application of Article 9 (2) or after referral, pursuant to Article 9 (3), first subparagraph, indent (b), or (5), to take the measures strictly necessary for the application of Article 9 (8).

3.   Notwithstanding paragraphs 1 and 2, Member States may take appropriate measures to protect legitimate interests other than those taken into consideration by this Regulation and compatible with the general principles and other provisions of Community law.

Public security, plurality of the media and prudential rules shall be regarded as legitimate interests within the meaning of the first subparagraph.

119

Any other public interest must be communicated to the Commission by the Member State concerned and shall be recognized by the Commission after an assessment of its compatibility with the general principles and other provisions of Community law before the measures referred to above may be taken. The Commission shall inform the Member State concerned of its decision within one month of that communication.

Article 22   Application of the Regulation

1.   This Regulation alone shall apply to concentrations as defined in Article 3, *and* Regulations No 17,[4] (EEC) No 1017/68,[5] (EEC) No 4056/86[6] and (EEC) No 3975/87[7] shall not apply ~~to concentrations as defined in Article 3~~, *except in relation to joint ventures that do not have a Community dimension and which have as their object or effect the coordination of the competitive behaviour of undertakings that remain independent.*

3.   If the Commission finds, at the request of a Member State *or at the joint request of two or more Member States*, that a concentration as defined in Article 3 that has no Community dimension within the meaning of Article 1 creates or strengthens a dominant position as a result of which effective competition would be significantly impeded within the territory of the Member State ~~concerned~~ *or States making the joint request*, it may, ~~in so far~~ *insofar* as ~~the~~ *that* concentration affects trade between Member States, adopt the decisions provided for in Article 8(2), second subparagraph, (3) and (4).

4.   Articles 2(1)(a) and (b), 5, 6, 8 and 10 to 20 shall apply *to a request made pursuant to paragraph 3. Article 7 shall apply to the extent that the concentration has not been put into effect on the date on which the Commission informs the parties that a request has been made.*

The period within which proceedings may be initiated pursuant to Article 10 (1) shall begin on the ~~date~~ *day following that* of the receipt of the request from the Member State *or States concerned.* The request must be made within one month at most of the date on which the concentration was made known to the Member State *or to all Member States making a joint request* or effected. This period shall begin on the date of the first of those events.

5.   Pursuant to paragraph 3 the Commission shall take only the measures strictly necessary to maintain or restore effective competition within the territory of the Member State *or States* at the request of which it intervenes.

~~6.   Paragraphs 3 to 5 shall continue to apply until the thresholds referred to in Article 1 (2) have been reviewed.~~

Article 23   Implementing provisions

The Commission shall have the power to adopt implementing provisions concerning the form, content and other details of notifications pursuant to Article 4, time limits pursuant to Articles *7, 9,* 10 *and* 22 and hearings pursuant to Article 18.

---

[4]   OJ No 13, 21. 2. 1962, p. 204/62.
[5]   OJ No L 175, 23. 7. 1968, p. 1.
[6]   OJ No L 378, 31. 12. 1986, p. 4.
[7]   OJ No L 374, 31. 12. 1987, p. 1.

The Commission shall have the power to lay down the procedure and time limits for the submission of commitments pursuant to Articles 6(2) and 8(2).

Article 24   Relations with non-member countries

1.   The Member States shall inform the Commission of any general difficulties encountered by their undertakings with concentrations as defined in Article 3 in a non-member country.

2.   Initially not more than one year after the entry into force of this Regulation and thereafter periodically the Commission shall draw up a report examining the treatment accorded to Community undertakings, in the terms referred to in paragraphs 3 and 4, as regards concentrations in non-member countries. The Commission shall submit those reports to the Council, together with any recommendations.

3.   Whenever it appears to the Commission, either on the basis of the reports referred to in paragraph 2 or on the basis of other information, that a non-member country does not grant Community undertakings treatment comparable to that granted by the Community to undertakings from that non-member country, the Commission may submit proposals to the Council for an appropriate mandate for negotiation with a view to obtaining comparable treatment for Community undertakings.

4.   Measures taken under this Article shall comply with the obligations of the Community or of the Member States, without prejudice to Article 234 of the Treaty, under international agreements, whether bilateral or multilateral.

Article 25   Entry into force

1.   This Regulation shall enter into force on 21 September 1990.

2.   This Regulation shall not apply to any concentration which was the subject of an agreement or announcement or where control was acquired within the meaning of Article 4(1) before the date of this Regulation's entry into force and it shall not in any circumstances apply to any concentration in respect of which proceedings were initiated before that date by a Member State's authority with responsibility for competition.

3.   As regards concentrations to which this Regulation applies by virtue of accession, the date of accession shall be substituted for the date of entry into force of this Regulation. The provision of paragraph 2, second alternative, applies in the same way to proceedings initiated by a competition authority of the new Member States or by the EFTA Surveillance Authority.[8]

This Regulation shall be binding in its entirety and directly applicable
in all Member States.

---

[8]   Introduced by the Act concerning the conditions of accession of the Kingdom of Norway, the Republic of Austria, the Republic of Finland and the Kingdom of Sweden and the adjustments to the Treaties on which the European Union is founded, ANNEX I — List referred to in Article 29 of the Act of Accession — III. COMPETITION B. PROCEDURAL REGULATIONS; OJ No. C 241, 29/08/94 P. 0057.

ANNEX 2

COMMISSION REGULATION (EC) NO 447/98 OF 1 MARCH 1998 ON THE NOTIFICATIONS, TIME LIMITS AND HEARINGS PROVIDED FOR IN COUNCIL REGULATION (EEC) NO 4064/89 ON THE CONTROL OF CONCENTRATIONS BETWEEN UNDERTAKINGS

(Text with EEA relevance)

THE COMMISSION OF THE EUROPEAN COMMUNITIES,

Having regard to the Treaty establishing the European Community,

Having regard to the Agreement on the European Economic Area,

Having regard to Council Regulation (EEC) No 4064/89 of 21 December 1989 on the control of concentrations between undertakings ([1]), as last amended by Regulation (EC) No 1310/97 ([2]), and in particular Article 23 thereof,

Having regard to Council Regulation No 17 of 6 February 1962, First Regulation implementing Articles 85 and 86 of the Treaty ([3]), as last amended by the Act of Accession of Austria, Finland and Sweden, and in particular Article 24 thereof,

Having regard to Council Regulation (EEC) No 1017/68 of 19 July 1968 applying rules of competition to transport by rail, road and inland waterway ([4]), as last amended by the Act of Accession of Austria, Finland and Sweden, and in particular Article 29 thereof,

Having regard to Council Regulation (EEC) No 4056/86 of 22 December 1986 laying down detailed rules for the application of Articles 85 and 86 of the Treaty to maritime transport ([5]), as amended by the Act of Accession of Austria, Finland and Sweden, and in particular Article 26 thereof,

Having regard to Council Regulation (EEC) No 3975/87 of 14 December 1987 laying down the procedure for the application of the rules on competition to undertakings in

---

([1]) OJ L 395, 30.12.1989, p. 1; corrected version, OJ L 257,21.9.1990, p. 13.
([2]) OJ L 180, 9.7.1997, p. 1.
([3]) OJ 13, 21.2.1962, p. 204/62.
([4]) OJ L 175, 23.7.1968, p. 1.
([5]) OJ L 378, 31.12.1986, p. 4.

the air transport sector (⁶), as last amended by Regulation (EEC) No 2410/92 (⁷), and in particular Article 19 thereof,

Having consulted the Advisory Committee on Concentrations,

(1) Whereas Regulation (EEC) No 40641/89 and in particular Article 23 thereof has been amended by Regulation (EC) No 1310/97;

(2) Whereas Commission Regulation (EC) No 3384/94 (⁸), implementing Regulation (EEC) No 4064/89, must be modified in order to take account of those amendments; whereas experience in the application of Regulation (EC) No 3384/94 has revealed the need to improve certain procedural aspects thereof; whereas for the sake of clarity it should therefore be replaced by a new regulation;

(3) Whereas the Commission has adopted Decision 94/810/ECSC, EC of 12 December 1994 on the terms of reference of hearing officers in competition procedures before the Commission (⁹);

(4) Whereas Regulation (EEC) No 4064/89 is based on the principle of compulsory notification of concentrations before they are put into effect; whereas, on the one hand, a notification has important legal consequences which are favourable to the parties to the concentration plan, while, on the other hand, failure to comply with the obligation to notify renders the parties liable to a fine and may also entail civil law disadvantages for them; whereas it is therefore necessary in the interests of legal certainty to define precisely the subject matter and content of the information to be provided in the notification;

(5) Whereas it is for the notifying parties to make full and honest disclosure to the Commission of the facts and circumstances which are relevant for taking a decision on the notified concentration;

(6) Whereas in order to simplify and expedite examination of the notification, it is desirable to prescribe that a form be used;

(7) Whereas since notification sets in motion legal time limits pursuant to Regulation (EEC) No 4064/89, the conditions governing such time-limits and the time when they become effective must also be determined;

(8) Whereas rules must be laid down in the interests of legal certainty for calculating the time limits provided for in Regulation (EEC) No 4064/89; whereas in particular, the beginning and end of the period and the circumstances suspending the running of the period must be determined, with due regard to the requirements resulting from the exceptionally short legal time-limits referred to above; whereas in the absence of specific provisions the determination of rules applicable to periods, dates and time-limits should be based on the principles of Council Regulation (EEC, Euratom) No 1182/71(¹⁰);

(9) Whereas the provisions relating to the Commission's procedure must be framed in such a way as to safeguard fully the right to be heard and the rights of defence; whereas for these purposes the Commission should distinguish between the parties who notify the concentration, other parties involved in the concentration plan, third parties and parties regarding whom the Commission intends to take a decision imposing a fine or periodic penalty payments;

(10) Whereas the Commission should give the notifying parties and other parties involved, if they so request, an opportunity before notification to discuss the intended concentration informally and in strict confidence; whereas in addition it should, after notification, maintain close contact with those parties to the

---

(⁶)   OJ L 374, 31.12.1987, p. 1.
(⁷)   OJ L 240, 24.8.1992, p. 18.
(⁸)   OJ L 377, 31.12.1994, p. 1.
(⁹)   OJ L 330, 21.12.1994, p. 67.
(¹⁰) OJ L 124, 8.6.1971, p. 1.

extent necessary to discuss with them any practical or legal problems which it discovers on a first examination of the case and if possible to remove such problems by mutual agreement;

(11) Whereas in accordance with the principle of the rights of defence, the notifying parties must be given the opportunity to submit their comments on all the objections which the Commission proposes to take into account in its decisions; whereas the other parties involved should also be informed of the Commission's objections and granted the opportunity to express their views;

(12) Whereas third parties having sufficient interest must also be given the opportunity of expressing their views where they make a written application;

(13) Whereas the various persons entitled to submit comments should do so in writing, both in their own interest and in the interest of good administration, without prejudice to their right to request a formal oral hearing where appropriate to supplement the written procedure; whereas in urgent cases, however, the Commission must be able to proceed immediately to formal oral hearings of the notifying parties, other parties involved or third parties;

(14) Whereas it is necessary to define the rights of persons who are to be heard, to what extent they should be granted access to the Commission's file and on what conditions they may be represented or assisted;

(15) Whereas the Commission must respect the legitimate interest of undertakings in the protection of their business secrets and other confidential information;

(16) Whereas, in order to enable the Commission to carry out a proper assessment of commitments that have the purpose of rendering the concentration compatible with the common market, and to ensure due consultation with other parties involved, third patties and the authorities of the Member States as provided for in Regulation (EEC) No 4064/89, in particular Article 18(1) and (4) thereof, the procedure and time-limits for submitting such commitments as provided for in Article 6(2) and Article 8(2) of Regulation (EEC) No 4064/89 must be laid down;

(17) Whereas it is also necessary to define the rules for fixing and calculating the time limits for reply fixed by the Commission;

(18) Whereas the Advisory Committee on Concentrations must deliver its opinion on the basis of a preliminary draft decision; whereas it must therefore be consulted on a case after the inquiry into that case has been completed; whereas such consultation does not, however, prevent the Commission from reopening an inquiry if need be,

HAS ADOPTED THIS REGULATION:

CHAPTER I   NOTIFICATIONS

Article 1   Persons entitled to submit notifications

1.   Notifications shall be submitted by the persons or undertakings referred to in Article 4(2) of Regulation (EEC) No 4064/89.

2.   Where notifications are signed by representatives of persons or of undertakings, such representatives shall produce written proof that they are authorised to act.

3.   Joint notifications should be submitted by a joint representative who is authorised to transmit and to receive documents on behalf of all notifying parties.

Article 2   Submission of notifications

1.   Notifications shall be submitted in the manner prescribed by form CO as shown in the Annex. Joint notifications shall be submitted on a single form.

2.   One original and 23 copies of the form CO and the supporting documents shall be submitted to the Commission at the address indicated in form CO.

3.   The supporting documents shall be either originals or copies of the originals; in the latter case the notifying parties shall confirm that they are true and complete.

4.   Notifications shall be in one of the official languages of the Community. This language shall also be the language of the proceeding for the notifying parties. Supporting documents shall be submitted in their original language. Where the original language is not one of the official languages of the Community, a translation into the language of the proceeding shall be attached.

5.   Where notifications are made pursuant to Article 57 of the EEA Agreement, they may also be in one of the official languages of the EFTA States or the working language of the EFTA Surveillance Authority. If the language chosen for the notifications is not an official language of the Community, the notifying parties shall simultaneously supplement all documentation with a translation into an official language of the Community. The language which is chosen for the translation shall determine the language used by the Commission as the language of the proceedings for the notifying parties.

Article 3   Information and documents to be provided

1.   Notifications shall contain the information, including documents, requested by form CO. The information must be correct and complete.

2.   The Commission may dispense with the obligation to provide any particular information, including documents, requested by form CO where the Commission considers that such information is not necessary for the examination of the case.

3.   The Commission shall without delay acknowledge in writing to the notifying parties or their representatives receipt of the notification and of any reply to a letter sent by the Commission pursuant to Article 4(2) and (4).

Article 4   Effective date of notification

1.   Subject to paragraphs 2, 3 and 4, notifications shall become effective on the date on which they are received by the Commission.

2.   Where the information, including documents, contained in the notification is incomplete in a material respect, the Commission shall inform the notifying parties or their representatives in writing without delay and shall set an appropriate time-limit for the completion of the information. In such cases, the notification shall become effective on the date on which the complete information is received by the Commission.

3.   Material changes in the facts contained in the notification which the notifying parties know or ought to have known must be communicated to the Commission without delay. In such cases, when these material changes could have a significant

125

effect on the appraisal of the concentration, the notification may be considered by the Commission as becoming effective on the date on which the information on the material changes is received by the Commission; the Commission shall inform the notifying parties or their representatives of this in writing and without delay.

4.   Incorrect or misleading information shall be considered to be incomplete information.

5.   When the Commission publishes the fact of the notification pursuant to Article 4(3) of Regulation (EEC) No 4064/89, it shall specify the date upon which the notification has been received. Where, further to the application of paragraphs 2, 3 and 4, the effective date of notification is later than the date specified in this publication, the Commission shall issue a further publication in which it will state the later date.

Article 5   Conversion of notifications

1.   Where the Commission finds that the operation notified does not constitute a concentration within the meaning of Article 3 of Regulation (EEC) No 4064/89, it shall inform the notifying parties or their representatives in writing. In such a case, the Commission shall, if requested by the notifying parties, as appropriate and subject to paragraph 2 of this Article, treat the notification as an application within the meaning of Article 2 or a notification within the meaning of Article 4 of Regulation No 17, as an application within the meaning of Article 12 or a notification within the meaning of Article 14 of Regulation (EEC) No 1017/68, as an application within the meaning of Article 12 of Regulation (EEC) No 4056/86 or as an application within the meaning of Article 3(2) or of Article 5 of Regulation (EEC) No 3975/87.

2.   In cases referred to in paragraph 1, second sentence, the Commission may require that the information given in the notification be supplemented within an appropriate time-limit fixed by it in so far as this is necessary for assessing the operation on the basis of the Regulations referred to in that sentence. The application or notification shall be deemed to fulfil the requirements of such Regulations from the date of the original notification where the additional information is received by the Commission within the time-limit fixed.

CHAPTER II   TIME-LIMITS

Article 6   Beginning of periods

1.   The period referred to in Article 9(2) of Regulation (EEC) No 4064/89 shall start at the beginning of the working day following the date of the receipt of the copy of the notification by the Member State.

2.   The period referred to in Article 9(4)(b) of Regulation (EEC) No 4064/89 shall start at the beginning of the working day following the effective date of the notification, within the meaning of Article 4 of this Regulation.

3.   The period referred to in Article 9(6) of Regulation (EEC) No 4064/89 shall start at the beginning of the working day following the date of the Commission's referral.

4.   The periods referred to in Article 10(1) of Regulation (EEC) No 4064/89 shall start at the beginning of the working day following the effective date of the notification, within the meaning of Article 4 of this Regulation.

5. The period referred to in Article 10(3) of Regulation (EEC) No 4064/89 shall start at the beginning of the working day following the day on which proceedings were initiated.

6. The period referred to in Article 22(4), second subparagraph, second sentence, of Regulation (EEC) No 4064/89 shall start at the beginning of the working day following the date of the first of the events referred to.

Article 7   End of periods

1. The period referred to in Article 9(2) of Regulation (EEC) No 4064/89 shall end with the expiry of the day which in the third week following that in which the period began is the same day of the week as the day from which the period runs.

2. The period referred to in Article 9(4)(b) of Regulation (EEC) No 4064/89 shall end with the expiry of the day which in the third month following that in which the period began falls on the same date as the day from which the period runs. Where such a day does not occur in that month, the period shall end with the expiry of the last day of that month.

3. The period referred to in Article 9(6) of Regulation (EEC) No 4064/89 shall end with the expiry of the day which in the fourth month following that in which the period began falls on the same date as the day from which the period runs. Where such a day does not occur in that month, the period shall end with the expiry of the last day of that month.

4. The period referred to in Article 10(1), first subparagraph, of Regulation (EEC) No 4064/89 shall end with the expiry of the day which in the month following that in which the period began falls on the same date as the day from which the period runs. Where such a day does not occur in that month, the period shall end with the expiry of the last day of that month.

5. The period referred to in Article 10(1), second subparagraph, of Regulation (EEC) No 4064/89 shall end with the expiry of the day which in the sixth week following that in which the period began is the same day of the week as the day from which the period runs.

6. The period referred to in Article 10(3) of Regulation (EEC) No 4064/89 shall end with the expiry of the day which in the fourth month following that in which the period began falls on the same date as the day from which the period runs. Where such a day does not occur in that month, the period shall end with the expiry of the last day of that month.

7. The period referred to in Article 22(4), second subparagraph, second sentence, of Regulation (EEC) No 4064/89 shall end with the expiry of the day which in the month following that in which the period began falls on the same date as the day from which the period runs. Where such a day does not occur in that month, the period shall end with the expiry of the last day of that month.

8. Where the last day of the period is not a working day, the period shall end with the expiry of the following working day.

Article 8   Recovery of holidays

Once the end of the period has been determined in accordance with Article 7, if public holidays or other holidays of the Commission referred to in Article 23 fall within the periods referred to in Articles 9, 10 and 22 of Regulation (EEC) No 4064/89, a corresponding number of working days shall be added to those periods.

Article 9 Suspension of time limit

1.   The periods referred to in Article 10(1) and (3) of Regulation (EEC) No 4064/89 shall be suspended where the Commission, pursuant to Article 11(5) and Article 13(3) of that Regulation, has to take a decision because:

(a)   information which the Commission has requested pursuant to Article 11(1) of Regulation (EEC) No 4064/89 from one of the notifying parties or another involved party, as defined in Article 11 of this Regulation, is not provided or not provided in full within the time limit fixed by the Commission;

(b)   information which the Commission has requested pursuant to Article 11(1) of Regulation (EEC) No 4064/89 from a third party, as defined in Article 11 of this Regulation, is not provided or not provided in full within the time limit fixed by the Commission owing to circumstances for which one of the notifying parties or another involved party, as defined in Article 11 of this Regulation, is responsible;

(c)   one of the notifying parties or another involved party, as defined in Article 11 of this Regulation, has refused to submit to an investigation deemed necessary by the Commission on the basis of Article 13(1) of Regulation (EEC) No 4064/89 or to cooperate in the carrying out of such an investigation in accordance with that provision;

(d)   the notifying parties have failed to inform the Commission of material changes in the facts contained in the notification.

2.   The periods referred to in Article 10(1) and (3) of Regulation (EEC) No 4064/89 shall be suspended:

(a)   in the cases referred to in paragraph 1(a) and (b), for the period between the end of the time limit fixed in the request for information and the receipt of the complete and correct information required by decision;

(b)   in the cases referred to in paragraph 1(c), for the period between the unsuccessful attempt to carry out the investigation and the completion of the investigation ordered by decision;

(c)   in the cases referred to in paragraph 1(d), for the period between the occurrence of the change in the facts referred to therein and the receipt of the complete and correct information requested by decision or the completion of the investigation ordered by decision.

3.   The suspension of the time limit shall begin on the day following that on which the event causing the suspension occurred. It shall end with the expiry of the day on which the reason for suspension is removed. Where such a day is not a working day, the suspension of the time-limit shall end with the expiry of the following working day.

Article 10 Compliance with the time-limits

1.   The time limits referred to in Article 9(4) and (5), and Article 10(1) and (3) of Regulation (EEC) No 4064/89 shall be met where the Commission has taken the relevant decision before the end of the period.

2.   The time limit referred to in Article 9(2) of Regulation (EEC) No 4064/89 shall be met where a Member State informs the Commission before the end of the period in writing.

128

3.   The time limit referred to in Article 9(6) of Regulation (EEC) No 4064/89 shall be met where the competent authority of the Member State concerned publishes any report or announces the findings of the examination of the concentration before the end of the period.

4.   The time limit referred to in Article 22(4), second subparagraph, second sentence, of Regulation (EEC) No 4064/89 shall be met where the request made by the Member State or the Member States is received by the Commission before the end of the period.

CHAPTER III   HEARING OF THE PARTIES AND OF THIRD PARTIES

Article 11   Parties to be heard

For the purposes of the rights to be heard pursuant to Article 18 of Regulation (EEC) No 4064/89, the following parties are distinguished:

(a)   notifying parties, that is, persons or undertakings submitting a notification pursuant to Article 4(2) of Regulation (EEC) No 4064/89;

(b)   other involved parties, that is, parties to the concentration plan other than the notifying parties, such as the seller and the undertaking which is the target of the concentration;

(c)   third parties, that is, natural or legal persons showing a sufficient interest, including customers, suppliers and competitors, and especially members of the administration or management organs of the undertakings concerned or recognised workers' representatives of those undertakings;

(d)   parties regarding whom the Commission intends to take a decision pursuant to Article 14 or 15 of Regulation (EEC) No 4064/89.

Article 12   Decisions on the suspension of concentrations

1.   Where the Commission intends to take a decision pursuant to Article 7(4) of Regulation (EEC) No 4064/89 which adversely affects one or more of the parties, it shall, pursuant to Article 18(1) of that Regulation, inform the notifying parties and other involved parties in writing of its objections and shall fix a time limit within which they may make known their views.

2.   Where the Commission, pursuant to Article 18(2) of Regulation (EEC) No 4064/89, has taken a decision referred to in paragraph 1 of this Article provisionally without having given the notifying parties and other involved parties the opportunity to make known their views, it shall without delay send them the text of the provisional decision and shall fix a time limit within which they may make known their views.

Once the notifying parties and other involved parties have made known their views, the Commission shall take a final decision annulling, amending or confirming the provisional decision. Where they have not made known their views within the time limit fixed, the Commission's provisional decision shall become final with the expiry of that period.

3.   The notifying parties and other involved parties shall make known their views in writing or orally within the time limit fixed. They may confirm their oral statements in writing.

Article 13   Decisions on the substance of the case

1.   Where the Commission intends to take a decision pursuant to Article 8(2), second subparagraph, or Article 8(3), (4) or (5) of Regulation (EEC) No 4064/89, it shall, before consulting the Advisory Committee on Concentrations, hear the parties pursuant to Article 18(1) and (3) of that Regulation.

2.   The Commission shall address its objections in writing to the notifying parties.

The Commission shall, when giving notice of objections, set a time limit within which the notifying parties may inform the Commission of their views in writing.

The Commission shall inform other involved parties in writing of these objections.

The Commission shall also set a time limit within which those other involved parties may inform the Commission of their views in writing.

3.   After having addressed its objections to the notifying parties, the Commission shall, upon request, give them access to the file for the purpose of enabling them to exercise their rights of defence.

The Commission shall, upon request, also give the other involved parties who have been informed of the objections access to the file in so far as this is necessary for the purposes of preparing their observations.

4.   The parties to whom the Commission's objections have been addressed or who have been informed of those objections shall, within the time limit fixed, make known in writing their views on the objections. In their written comments, they may set out all matters relevant to the case and may attach any relevant documents in proof of the facts set out. They may also propose that the Commission hear persons who may corroborate those facts. They shall submit one original and 29 copies of their response to the Commission at the address indicated in form CO.

5.   Where the Commission intends to take a decision pursuant to Article 14 or 15 of Regulation (EEC) No 4064/89 it shall, before consulting the Advisory Committee on Concentrations, hear pursuant to Article 18(1) and (3) of that Regulation the parties regarding whom the Commission intends to take such a decision.

The procedure provided for in paragraph 2, first and second subparagraphs, paragraph 3, first subparagraph, and paragraph 4 is applicable, *mutatis mutandis.*

Article 14   Oral hearings

1.   The Commission shall afford the notifying parties who have so requested in their written comments the opportunity to put forward their arguments orally in a formal hearing if such parties show a sufficient interest. It may also in other cases afford such parties the opportunity of expressing their views orally.

2.   The Commission shall afford other involved parties who have so requested in their written comments the opportunity to express their views orally in a formal hearing if they show a sufficient interest. It may also in other cases afford such parties the opportunity of expressing their views orally.

3.   The Commission shall afford parties on whom it proposes to impose a fine or periodic penalty payment who have so requested in their written comments the

130

opportunity to put forward their arguments orally in a formal hearing. It may also in other cases afford such parties the opportunity of expressing their views orally.

4. The Commission shall invite the persons to be heard to attend on such date as it shall appoint.

5. The Commission shall invite the competent authorities of the Member States, to take part in the hearing.

Article 15   Conduct of formal oral hearings

1. Hearings shall be conducted by the Hearing Officer.

2. Persons invited to attend shall either appear in person or be represented by legal representatives or representatives authorised by their constitution appropriate. Undertakings and associations of undertakings may be represented by a duly authorised agent appointed from among their permanent staff.

3. Persons heard by the Commission may be assisted by their legal adviser or other qualified persons admitted by the Hearing Officer.

4. Hearings shall not be public. Each person shall be heard separately or in the presence of other persons invited to attend. In the latter case, regard shall be had to the legitimate interest of the undertakings in the protection of their business secrets and other confidential information.

5. The statements made by each person heard shall be recorded.

Article 16   Hearing of third parties

1. If third parties apply in writing to be heard pursuant to Article 18(4), second sentence, of Regulation (EEC) No 4064/89, the Commission shall inform them in writing of the nature and subject matter of the procedure and shall fix a time limit within which they may make known their views.

2. The third parties referred to in paragraph 1 shall make known their views in writing within the time limit fixed. The Commission may, where appropriate, afford the parties who have so requested in their written comments the opportunity to participate in a formal hearing. It may also in other cases afford such parties the opportunity of expressing their views orally.

3. The Commission may likewise afford to any other third parties the opportunity of expressing their views.

Article 17   Confidential information

1. Information, including documents, shall not be communicated or made accessible in so far as it contains business secrets of any person or undertaking, including the notifying parties, other involved parties or of third parties, or other confidential information the disclosure of which is not considered necessary by the Commission for the purpose of the procedure, or where internal documents of the authorities are concerned.

2. Any party which makes known its views under the provisions of this Chapter shall clearly identify any material which it considers to be confidential, giving reasons, and provide a separate non-confidential version within the time limit fixed by the Commission.

CHAPER IV COMMITMENTS RENDERING THE CONCENTRATION COMPATIBLE

Article 18 Time limits for commitments

1. Commitments proposed to the Commission by the undertakings concerned pursuant to Article 6(2) of Regulation (EEC) No 4064/89 which are intended by the parties to form the basis for a decision pursuant to Article 6(1)(b) of that Regulation shall be submitted to the Commission within not more than three weeks from the date of receipt of the notification.

2. Commitments proposed to the Commission by the undertakings concerned pursuant to Article 8(2) of Regulation (EEC) No 4064/89 which are intended by the parties to form the basis for a decision pursuant to that Article shall be submitted to the Commission within not more than three months from the date on which proceedings were initiated. The Commission may in exceptional circumstances extend this period.

3. Articles 6 to 9 shall apply *mutatis mutandis* to paragraphs 1 and 2 of this Article.

Article 19 Procedure for commitments

1. One original and 29 copies of commitments proposed to the Commission by the undertakings concerned pursuant to Article 6(2) or Article 8(2) of Regulation (EEC) No 4064/89 shall be submitted to the Commission at the address indicated in form CO.

2. Any party proposing commitments to the Commission pursuant to Articles 6(2) or Article 8(2) of Regulation (EEC) No 4064/89 shall clearly identify any material which it considers to be confidential, giving reasons, and provide a separate non-confidential version within the time limit fixed by the Commission.

CHAPTER V MISCELLANEOUS PROVISIONS

Article 20 Transmission of documents

1. Transmission of documents and invitations from the Commission to the addressees may be effected in any of the following ways:

    (a) delivery by hand against receipt;
    (b) registered letter with acknowledgement of receipt;
    (c) fax with a request for acknowledgement of receipt;
    (d) telex;
    (e) electronic mail with a request for acknowledgement of receipt.

2.   Unless otherwise provided in this Regulation, paragraph 1 also applies to the transmission of documents from the notifying parties, from other involved parties or from third parties to the Commission.

3.   Where a document is sent by telex, by fax or by electronic mail, it shall be presumed that it has been received by the addressee on the day on which it was sent.

Article 21   Setting of time limits

In fixing the time limits provided for pursuant to Article 4(2), Article 5(2), Article 12(1) and (2), Article 13(2) and Article 16(1), the Commission shall have regard to the time required for preparation of statements and to the urgency of the case. It shall also take account of working days as well as public holidays in the country of receipt of the Commission's communication.

These time limits shall be set in terms of a precise calendar date.

Article 22   Receipt of documents by the Commission

1.   In accordance with the provisions of Article 4(1) of this Regulation, notifications must be delivered to the Commission at the address indicated in form CO or have been dispatched by registered letter to the address indicated in form CO before the expiry of the period referred to in Article 4(1) of Regulation (EEC) No 4064/89.

Additional information requested to complete notifications pursuant to Article 4(2) and (4) or to supplement notifications pursuant to Article 5(2) must reach the Commission at the aforesaid address or have been dispatched by registered letter before the expiry of the time limit fixed in each case.

Written comments on Commission communications pursuant to Article 12(1) and (2), Article 13(2) and Article 16(1) must have reached the Commission at the aforesaid address before the expiry of the time limit fixed in each case.

2.   Time limits referred to in subparagraphs two and three of paragraph 1 shall be determined in accordance with Article 21.

3.   Should the last day of a time limit fall on a day which is not a working day or which is a public holiday in the country of dispatch, the time limit shall expire on the following working day.

Article 23   Definition of working days

The expression 'working days' in this Regulation means all days other than Saturdays, Sundays, public holidays and other holidays as determined by the Commission and published in the *Official Journal of the European Communities* before the beginning of each year.

Article 24   Repeal

Regulation (EEC) No 3384/94 is repealed.

Article 25   Entry into force

This Regulation shall enter into force on 21 March 1998.

This Regulation shall be binding in its entirety and directly applicable in all Member States.

Done at Brussels, 1 March 1998.

For the Commission
Karel VAN MIERT
Member of the Commission

ANNEX: FORM CO RELATING TO THE NOTIFICATION OF A CONCENTRATION PURSUANT TO REGULATION (EEC) NO 4064/89

Introduction

A.   The purpose of this form

This form specifies the information that must be provided by an undertaking or undertakings when notifying the Commission of a concentration with a Community dimension. A 'concentration' is defined in Article 3 of Regulation (EEC) No 4064/89 (hereinafter referred to as 'the Merger Regulation') and 'Community dimension' in Article 1 thereof.

Your attention is drawn to the Merger Regulation and to Regulation (EC) No 447/98 (hereinafter referred to as 'the Implementing Regulation') and to the corresponding provisions of the Agreement on the European Economic Area ([11]).

Experience has shown that prenotification meetings are extremely valuable to both the notifying parties and the Commission in determining the precise amount of information required in a notification and, in the large majority of cases, will result in a significant reduction of the information required. Accordingly, notifying parties are encouraged to consult the Commission regarding the possibility of dispensing with the obligation to provide certain information (see Section B(g) on the possibility of dispensation).

B.   The need for a correct and complete notification

All information required by this form must be correct and complete. The information required must be supplied in the appropriate section of this form. Annexes to this form shall only be used to supplement the information supplied in the form itself.

([11])   Hereinafter referred to as 'the EEA Agreement'; see in particular Article 57 of the EEA Agreement (point 1 of Annex XIV to the EEA Agreement and Protocol 4 to the Agreement between the EFTA States on the establishment of a Surveillance Authority and a Court of Justice), as well as Protocols 21 and 24 to the EEA Agreement and Article 1, and the Agreed Minutes of the Protocol adjusting the EEA Agreement. In particular, any reference to EFTA States shall be understood to mean those EFTA States which are Contracting Parties to the EEA Agreement.

In particular you should note that:

(a) In accordance with Article 10(1) of the Merger Regulation and Article 4(2) and (4) of the Implementing Regulation, the time limits of the Merger Regulation linked to the notification will not begin to run until all the information that has to be supplied with the notification has been received by the Commission. This requirement is to ensure that the Commission is able to assess the notified concentration within the strict time-limits provided by the Merger Regulation.

(b) The notifying parties should check carefully, in the course of preparing their notification, that contact names and numbers, and in particular fax numbers, provided to the Commission are accurate, relevant and up-to-date.

(c) Incorrect or misleading information in the notification will be considered to be incomplete information (Article 4(4) of the Implementing Regulation).

(d) If a notification is incomplete, the Commission will inform the notifying parties or their representatives of this in writing and without delay. The notification will only become effective on the date on which the complete and accurate information is received by the Commission (Article 10(1) of the Merger Regulation, Article 4(2) and (4) of the Implementing Regulation).

(e) Article 14(1)(b) of the Merger Regulation provides that incorrect or misleading information, where supplied intentionally or negligently, can make the notifying party or parties liable to fines of up to ECU 50 000. In addition, pursuant to Article 6(3)(a) and Article 8(5)(a) of the Merger Regulation the Commission may also revoke its decision on the compatibility of a notified concentration where it is based on incorrect information for which one of the undertakings is responsible.

(f) You may request that the Commission accept that the notification is complete notwithstanding the failure to provide information required by this form, if such information is not reasonably available to you in part or in whole (for example, because of the unavailability of information on a target company during a contested bid).

The Commission will consider such a request, provided that you give reasons for the unavailability of that information, and provide your best estimates for missing data together with the sources for the estimates. Where possible, indications as to where any of the requested information that is unavailable to you could be obtained by the Commission should also be provided.

(g) You may request that the Commission accept that the notification is complete notwithstanding the failure to provide information required by this form, if you consider that any particular information requested by this form, in the full or short form version, may not be necessary for the Commission's examination of the case.

The Commission will consider such a request, provided that you give reasons why that information is not relevant and necessary to its inquiry into the notified operation. You may explain this during your pre-notification contacts with the Commission and/or in your notification and ask the Commission to dispense with the obligation to provide that information, pursuant to Article 3(2) of the Implementing Regulation.

C. Notification in short form

(a) In cases where a joint venture has no, or *de minimis*, actual or foreseen activities within the EEA territory, the Commission intends to allow notification of the operation by means of short form. Such cases occur where joint control is acquired by two or more undertakings, and where:

    (i)   the turnover (^{12}) of the joint venture and/or the turnover of the contributed activities (^{13}), is less than ECU 100 million in the EEA territory; and

    (ii)   the total value of assets (^{14}) transferred to the joint venture is less than ECU 100 million in the EEA territory (^{15}).

(b)   If you consider that the operation to be notified meets these qualifications, you may explain this in your notification and ask the Commission to dispense with the obligation to provide the full-form notification, pursuant to Article 3(2) of the Implementing Regulation, and to allow you to notify by means of short form.

(c)   Short-form notification allows the notifying parties to limit the information provided in the notification to the following sections and questions:

- Section 1,
- Section 2, except questions 2.1 (a, b and d), 2.3.4, and 2.3.5,
- Section 3, only questions 3.1 and 3.2 (a),
- Section 5, only questions 5.1 and 5.3,
- Section 6,
- Section 10,
- Section 11 (optional for the convenience of the parties), and
- Section 12,
- the five largest independent customers, the five largest independent suppliers, and the five largest competitors in the markets in which the joint venture will be active. Provide the name, address, telephone number, fax number and appropriate contact person of each such customer, supplier and competitor.

(d)   In addition, with respect to the affected markets of the joint venture as defined in Section 6, indicate for the EEA territory, for the Community as a whole, for each Member State and EFTA State, and where different, in the opinion of the notifying parties, for the relevant geographic market, the sales in value and volume, as well as the market shares, for the year preceding the operation.

(e)   The Commission may require full, or where appropriate partial, notification under the form CO where:

- the notified operation does not meet the short-form thresholds, or
- this appears to be necessary for an adequate investigation with respect to possible competition problems.

In such cases, the notification may be considered incomplete in a material respect pursuant to Article 4(2) of the Implementing Regulation. The Commis-

---

(^{12})   The turnover of the joint venture should be determined according to the most recent audited accounts of the parent companies, or the joint venture itself, depending upon the availability of separate accounts for the resources combined in the joint venture.

(^{13})   The expression 'and-or' refers to the variety of situations covered by the short form; for example:
- in the case of the joint acquisition of a target company, the turnover to be taken into account is the turnover of this target (the joint venture),
- in the case of the creation of a joint venture to which the parent companies contribute their activities, the turnover to be taken into account is that of the contributed activities,
- in the case of entry of a new controlling party into an existing joint venture, the turnover of the joint venture and the turnover of the activities contributed by the new parent company (if any) must be taken into account.

(^{14})   The total value of assets of the joint venture should be determined according to the last regularly prepared and approved balance sheet of each parent company. The term 'assets' includes: (1) all tangible and intangible assets that will be transferred to the joint venture (examples of tangible assets include production plants, wholesale or retail outlets, and inventory of goods), and (2) any amount of credit or any obligations of the joint venture which any parent company of the joint venture has agreed to extend or guarantee.

(^{15})   Where the assets transferred generate turnover, then neither the value of the assets nor that of the turnover may exceed ECU 100 million.

sion will inform the notifying parties or their representatives of this in writing and without delay and will fix a deadline for the submission of a full or, where appropriate, partial notification. The notification will only become effective on the dare on which all information required is received.

D. Who must notify

In the case of a merger within the meaning of Article 3(1)(a) of the Merger Regulation or the acquisition of joint control in an undertaking within the meaning of Article 3(1)(b) of the Merger Regulation, the notification shall be completed jointly by the parties to the merger or by those acquiring joint control as the case may be.

In case of the acquisition of a controlling interest in one undertaking by another, the acquirer must complete the notification.

In the case of a public bid to acquire an undertaking, the bidder must complete the notification.

Each party completing the notification is responsible for the accuracy of the information which it provides.

E. How to notify

The notification must be completed in one of the official languages of the European Community. This language will thereafter be the language of the proceedings for all notifying parties. Where notifications are made in accordance with Article 12 of Protocol 24 to the EEA Agreement in an official language of an EFTA State which is not an official language of the Community, the notification must simultaneously be supplemented with a translation into an official language of the Community.

The information requested by this form is to be set out using the sections and paragraph numbers of the form, signing a declaration as provided in Section 12, and annexing supporting documentation.

Supporting documents are to be submitted in their original language; where this is not an official language of the Community, they must be translated into the language of the proceeding (Article 2(4) of the Implementing Regulation).

Supporting documents may be originals or copies of the originals. In the latter case, the notifying party must confirm that they are true and complete.

One original and 23 copies of the form CO and all supporting documents must be provided.

The notification must be delivered to the Commission on working days as defined by Article 23 of the Implementing Regulation. In order to enable it to be registered on the same day, it must be delivered before 17.00 on Mondays to Thursdays and before 16.00 on Fridays, at the following address:
Commission of the European Communities
Directorate-General for Competition (DG IV)
Merger Task Force
150 avenue de Cortenberg/Kortenberglaan 150
B-1049 Brussels.

137

F. Confidentiality

Article 214 of the Treaty and Article 17(2) of the Merger Regulation as well as the corresponding provisions of the EEA Agreement ([16]) require the Commission, the Member States, the EFTA Surveillance Authority and the EFTA States, their officials and other servants not to disclose information they have acquired through the application of the Regulation of the kind covered by the obligation of professional secrecy. The same principle must also apply to protect confidentiality between notifying parties.

If you believe that your interests would be harmed if any of the information you are asked to supply were to be published or otherwise divulged to other parties, submit this information separately with each page clearly marked 'Business Secrets'. You should also give reasons why this information should not be divulged or published.

In the case of mergers or joint acquisitions, or in other cases where the notification is completed by more than one of the parties, business secrets may be submitted under separate cover, and referred to in the notification as an annex. All such annexes must be included in the submission in order for a notification to be considered complete.

G. Definitions and instructions for purposes of this form

Notifying party or parties: in cases where a notification is submitted by only one of the undertakings party to an operation, 'notifying parties' is used to refer only to the undertaking actually submitting the notification.
Party(parties) to the concentration: these terms relate to both the acquiring and acquired parties, or to the merging parties, including all undertakings in which a controlling interest is being acquired or which is the subject of a public bid.

Except where otherwise specified, the terms 'notifying party(parties)' and 'party(parties) to the concentration' include all the undertakings which belong to the same groups as those 'parties'.
Affected markets: Section 6 of this form requires the notifying parties to define the relevant product markets, and further to identify which of those relevant markets are likely to be affected by the notified operation. This definition of affected market is used as the basis for requiring information for a number of other questions contained in this form. The definitions thus submitted by the notifying parties are referred to in this form as the affected market(s). This term can refer to a relevant market made up either of products or of services.
Year: all references to the word 'year' in this form should be read as meaning calendar year, unless otherwise stated. All information requested in this form must, unless otherwise specified, relate to the year preceding that of the notification.

The financial data requested in Sections 2.3 to 2.5 must be provided in ecus at the average conversion rates prevailing for the years or other periods in question.

All references contained in this form are to the relevant Articles and paragraphs of Council Regulation (EEC) No 4064/89, unless otherwise stated.

([16]) See, in particular, Article 122 of the EEA Agreement, Article 9 of Protocol 24 to the EEA Agreement and Article 17(2) of Chapter XIII of Protocol 4 to the Agreement between the EFTA States on the establishment of a Surveillance Authority and a Court of Justice (ESA Agreement).

Section 1

Background information

1.1.   *Information on notifying party (or parties)*
       Give details of:
1.1.1. name and address of undertaking;
1.1.2. nature of the undertaking's business;
1.1.3. name, address, telephone number, fax number and/or telex of, and position held by, the appropriate contact person.
1.2.   *Information on other parties ([17]) to the concentration*
       For each party to the concentration (except the notifying party or parties) give details of:
1.2.1. name and address of undertaking;
1.2.2. nature of undertaking's business;
1.2.3. name, address, telephone number, fax number and/or telex of, and position held by the appropriate contact person.
1.3.   *Address for service*
       Give an address (in Brussels if available) to which all communications may be made and documents delivered.
1.4.   *Appointment of representatives*
       Where notifications are signed by representatives of undertakings, such representatives must produce written proof that they are authorised to act.
       If a joint notification is being submitted, has a joint representative been appointed?
       If yes, please give the details requested in Sections 1.4.1 to 1.4.4.
       If no, please give details of information of any representatives who have been authorised to act for each of the parties to the concentration, indicating whom they represent:
1.4.1. name of representative;
1.4.2. address of representative;
1.4.3. name of person to be contacted (and address, if different from 1.4.2);
1.4.4. telephone number, fax number and/or telex.

Section 2

Details of the concentration

2.1.   *Describe the nature of the concentration being notified. In doing so state:*
       (a) whether the proposed concentration is a full legal merger, an acquisition of sole or joint control, a full-function joint venture within the meaning of Article 3(2) of the Merger Regulation or a contract or other means of conferring direct or indirect control within the meaning of Article 3(3) of the Merger Regulation;
       (b) whether the whole or parts of parties are subject to the concentration;
       (c) a brief explanation of the economic and financial structure of the concentration;
       (d) whether any public offer for the securities of one party by another party

---

([17])   This includes the target company in the case of a contested bid, in which case the details should be completed as far as is possible.

has the support of the former's supervisory boards of management or other bodies legally representing that party;

(e) the proposed or expected date of any major events designed to bring about the completion of the concentration;

(f) the proposed structure of ownership and control after the completion of the concentration;

(g) any financial or other support received from whatever source (including public authorities) by any of the parties and the nature and amount of this support.

2.2. *List the economic sectors involved in the concentration*

2.3. *For each of the undertakings concerned by the concentration ([18]) provide the following data ([19]) for the last financial year:*

2.3.1. worldwide turnover;

2.3.2. Community-wide turnover;

2.3.3. EFTA-wide turnover;

2.3.4. turnover in each Member State;

2.3.5. turnover in each EFTA State;

2.3.6. the Member State, if any, in which more than two thirds of Community-wide turnover is achieved ([20]);

2.3.7. the EFTA State, if any, in which more than two thirds of EFTA-wide turnover is achieved.

2.4. *For the purposes of Article 1(3) of the Merger Regulation, if the operation does not meet the thresholds set out in Article 1(2), provide the following data for the last financial year:*

2.4.1. the Member States, if any, in which the combined aggregate turnover of all the undertakings concerned is more than ECU 100 million;

2.4.2. the Member States, if any, in which the aggregate turnover of each of at least two of the undertakings concerned is more than ECU 25 million.

2.5. *Provide the following information with respect to the last financial year:*

2.5.1. does the combined turnover of the undertakings concerned in the territory of the EFTA States equal 25% or more of their total turnover in the EEA territory?

2.5.2. does each of at least two undertakings concerned have a turnover exceeding ECU 250 million in the territory of the EFTA States?

Section 3

Ownership and control ([21])

For each of the parties to the concentration provide a list of all undertakings belonging to the same group.

This list must include:

([18]) See Commission notice on the concept of undertakings concerned.

([19]) See, generally, the Commission notice on calculation of turnover. Turnover of the acquiring party or parties to the concentration should include the aggregated turnover of all undertakings within the meaning of Article 5(4). Turnover of the acquired party or parties should include the turnover relating to the parts subject to the transaction within the meaning of Article 5(2). Special provisions are contained in Articles 5(3), (4) and 5(5) for credit, insurance, other financial institutions and joint undertakings.

([20]) Sea Guidance Note III for the calculation of turnover in one Member State with respect to Community-wide turnover.

([21]) See Article 3(3), (4) and (5) and Article 5(4).

3.1.   all undertakings or persons controlling these parties, directly or indirectly;
3.2.   all undertakings active on any affected market (^{22}) that are controlled, directly or indirectly:
        (a) by these parties;
        (b) by any other undertaking identified in 3.1.
For each entry listed above, the nature and means of control should be specified.

The information sought in this section may be illustrated by the use of organisation charts or diagrams to show the structure of ownership and control of the undertakings.

Section 4

Personal and financial links and previous acquisitions

With respect to the parties to the concentration and each undertaking or person identified in response to Section 3, provide:
4.1.   a list of all other undertakings which are active on affected markets (affected markets are defined in Section 6 in which the undertakings, or persons, of the group hold individually or collectively 10% or more of the voting rights, issued share capital or other securities;
        in each case identify the holder and state the percentage held;
4.2.   a list for each undertaking of the members of their boards of management who are also members of the boards of management or of the supervisory boards of any other undertaking which is active on affected markets; and (where applicable) for each undertaking a list of the members of their supervisory boards who are also members of the boards of management of any other undertaking which is active on affected markets;
        in each case identify the name of the other undertaking and the positions held;
4.3.   details of acquisitions made during the last three years by the groups identified above (Section 3) of undertakings active in affected markets as defined in Section 6.
        Information provided here may be illustrated by the use of organisation charts or diagrams to give a better understanding.

Section 5

Supporting documentation

Notifying parties must provide the following:
5.1.   copies of the final or most recent versions of all documents bringing about the concentration, whether by agreement between the parties to the concentration, acquisition of a controlling interest or a public bid;
5.2.   in a public bid, a copy of the offer document; if it is unavailable at the time of notification, it should be submitted as soon as possible and not later than when it is posted to shareholders;
5.3.   copies of the most recent annual reports and accounts of all the parties to the concentration;

(^{22}) See Section 6 for the definition of affected markets.

5.4. where at least one affected market is identified:
copies of analyses, reports, studies and surveys submitted to or prepared for any member(s) of the board of directors, the supervisory board, or the shareholders' meeting, for the purpose of assessing or analysing the concentration with respect to competitive conditions, competitors (actual and potential), and market conditions.

Section 6

Market definitions

The relevant product and geographic markets determine the scope within which the market power of the new entity resulting from the concentration must be assessed ([23]).

The notifying party or parties must provide the data requested having regard to the following definitions:

I. *Relevant product markets*
A relevant product market comprises all those products and/or services which are regarded as interchangeable or substitutable by the consumer, by reason of the products' characteristics, their prices and their intended use. A relevant product market may in some cases be composed of a number of individual products and/ or services which present largely identical physical or technical characteristics and are interchangeable.

Factors relevant to the assessment of the relevant product market include the analysis of why the products or services in these markets are included and why others are excluded by using the above definition, and having regard to, for example, substitutability, conditions of competition, prices, cross-price elasticity of demand or other factors relevant for the definition of the product markets.

II. *Relevant geographic markets*
The relevant geographic market comprises the area in which the undertakings concerned are involved in the supply and demand of relevant products or services, in which the conditions of competition are sufficiently homogeneous and which can be distinguished from neighbouring geographic areas because, in particular, conditions of competition are appreciably different in those areas.
Factors relevant to the assessment of the relevant geographic market include the nature and characteristics of the products or services concerned, the existence of entry barriers, consumer preferences, appreciable differences in the undertakings' market shares between neighbouring geographic areas or substantial price differences.

III. *Affected markets*
For purposes of information required in this form, affected markets consist of relevant product markets where, in the EEA territory, in the Community, in the territory of the EFTA States, in any Member State or in any EFTA State:
(a) two or more of the parties to the concentration are engaged in business activities in the same product market and where the concentration will lead

---

([23]) See Commission notice on the definition of the relevant market for the purposes of Community competition law.

to a combined market share of 15% or more. These are horizontal relationships;

(b) one or more of the parties to the concentration are engaged in business activities in a product market, which is upstream or downstream of a product market in which any other party to the concentration is engaged, and any of their individual or combined market shares is 25% or more, regardless of whether there is or is not any existing supplier/customer relationship between the parties to the concentration. These are vertical relationships.

On the basis of the above definitions and market share thresholds, provide the following information:

6.1. Identify each affected market within the meaning of Section III, at:

(a) the EEA, Community or EFTA level;

(b) the individual Member States or EFTA States level.

IV. *Markets related to affected markets within the meaning of Section III*

6.2. Describe the relevant product and geographic markets concerned by the notified operation, which are closely related to the affected market(s) (in upstream, downstream and horizontal neighbouring markets), where any of the parties to the concentration are active and which are not themselves affected markets within the meaning of Section Ill.

V. *Non-affected markets*

6.3. In case there are no affected markets in the meaning of Section 6.1, describe the product and geographic scope of the markets on which the notified operation would have an impact.

Section 7

Information on affected markets

For each affected relevant product market, for each of the last three financial years ([24]):

(a) for the EEA territory,

(b) for the Community as a whole,

(c) for the territory of the EFTA States as a whole,

(d) individually for each Member State and EFTA State where the parties to the concentration do business,

(e) and, where in the opinion of the notifying parties, the relevant geographic market is different,

provide the following:

7.1. an estimate of the total size of the market in terms of sales value (in ecus) and volume (units) ([25]). Indicate the basis and sources for the calculations and provide documents where available to confirm these calculations;

7.2. the sales in value and volume, as well as an estimate of the market shares, of each of the parties to the concentration;

7.3. an estimate of the market share in value (and where appropriate volume) of all competitors (including importers) having at least 10% of the geographic market

---

([24]) Without prejudice to Article 3(2) of the Implementing Regulation, the information required under 7.1 and 7.2 below must be provided with regard to all the territories under (a), (b), (c), (d) and (e).

([25]) The value and volume of a market should reflect output less exports plus imports for the geographic areas under consideration.

under consideration. Provide documents where available to confirm the calculation of these market shares and provide the name, address, telephone number, fax number and appropriate contact person, of these competitors;

7.4. an estimate of the total value and volume and source of imports from outside the EEA territory and identify:
   (a) the proportion of such imports that are derived from the groups to which the parties to the concentration belong,
   (b) an estimate of the extent to which any quotas, tariffs or non-tariff barriers to trade, affect these imports, and
   (c) an estimate of the extent to which transportation and other costs affect these imports,

7.5. the extent to which trade among States within the EEA territory is affected by:
   (a) transportation and other costs, and
   (b) other non-tariff barriers to trade;

7.6. the manner in which the parties to the concentration produce and sell the products and/or services; for example, whether they manufacture locally, or sell through local distribution facilities;

7.7. a comparison of price levels in each Member State and EFTA State by each party to the concentration and a similar comparison of price levels between the Community, the EFTA States and other areas where these products are produced (e.g. eastern Europe, the United States of America, Japan, or other relevant areas);

7.8. the nature and extent of vertical integration of each of the parties to the concentration compared with their largest competitors.

Section 8

General conditions in affected markets

8.1. Identify the five largest independent ([26]) suppliers to the parties and their individual shares of purchases from each of these suppliers (of raw materials or goods used for purposes of producing the relevant products). Provide the name, address, telephone number, fax number and appropriate contact person, of these suppliers.

Structure of supply in affected markets

8.2. Explain the distribution channels and service networks that exist on the affected markets. In so doing, take account of the following where appropriate:
   (a) the distribution systems prevailing on the market and their importance. To what extent is distribution performed by third parties and/or undertakings belonging to the same group as the parties identified in Section 3?
   (b) the service networks (for example, maintenance and repair) prevailing and their importance in these markets. To what extent are such services performed by third parties and/or undertakings belonging to the same group as the parties identified in Section 3?

([26]) That is suppliers which are not subsidiaries, agents or undertakings forming part of the group of the party in question. In addition to those five independent suppliers the notifying parties can, if they consider it necessary for a proper assessment of the case, identify the intra-group suppliers. The same will apply in 8.5 in relation to customers.

8.3. Where appropriate, provide an estimate of the total Community-wide and EFTA-wide capacity for the last three years. Over this period what proportion of this capacity is accounted for by each of the parties to the concentration, and what have been their respective rates of capacity utilisation.

8.4. If you consider any other supply-side considerations to be relevant, they should be specified.

Structure of demand in affected markets

8.5. Identify the five largest independent customers of the parties in each affected market and their individual share of total sales for such products accounted for by each of those customers. Provide the name, address, telephone number, fax number and appropriate contact person, of each of these customers.

8.6. Explain the structure of demand in terms of:
   (a) the phases of the markets in terms of, for example, take-off, expansion, maturity and decline, and a forecast of the growth rate of demand;
   (b) the importance of customer preferences, in terms of brand loyalty, product differentiation and the provision of a full range of products;
   (c) the degree of concentration or dispersion of customers;
   (d) segmentation of customers into different groups with a description of the 'typical customer' of each group;
   (e) the importance of exclusive distribution contracts and other types of long-term contracts;
   (f) the extent to which public authorities, government agencies, State enterprises or similar bodies are important participants as a source of demand.

Market entry

8.7. Over the last five years, has there been any significant entry into any affected markets? If the answer is 'yes', where possible provide their name, address, telephone number, fax number and appropriate contact person, and an estimate of their current market shares.

8.8. In the opinion of the notifying parties are there undertakings (including those at present operating only in extra-Community or extra-EEA markets) that are likely to enter the market? If the answer is 'yes', please explain why and identify such entrants by name, address, telephone number, fax number and appropriate contact person, and an estimate of the time within which such entry is likely to occur.

8.9. Describe the various factors influencing entry into affected markets that exist in the present case, examining entry from both a geographical and product viewpoint. In so doing, take account of the following where appropriate:
   (a) the total costs of entry (R & D, establishing distribution systems, promotion, advertising, servicing, etc.) on a scale equivalent to a significant viable competitor, indicating the market share of such a competitor;
   (b) any legal or regulatory barriers to entry, such as government authorisation or standard setting in any form;
   (c) any restrictions created by the existence of patents, know-how and other intellectual property rights in these markets and any restrictions created by licensing such rights;
   (d) the extent to which each of the parties to the concentration are licensees or licensors of patents, know-how and other rights in the relevant markets;
   (e) the importance of economies of scale for the production of products in the affected markets;
   (f) access to sources of supply, such as availability of raw materials.

Research and development

8.10.   Give an account of the importance of research and development in the ability of a firm operating on the relevant market(s) to compete in the long term. Explain the nature of the research and development in affected markets carried out by the parties to the concentration.

In so doing, take account of the following, where appropriate:
(a)   trends and intensities of research and development ([27]) in these markets and for the parties to the concentration;
(b)   the course of technological development for these markets over an appropriate time period (including developments in products and/or services, production processes, distribution systems, etc.);
(c)   the major innovations that have been made in these markets and the undertakings responsible for these innovations;
(d)   the cycle of innovation in these markets and where the parties are in this cycle of innovation.

Cooperative agreements

8.11.   To what extent do cooperative agreements (horizontal or vertical) exist in the affected markets?
8.12.   Give details of the most important cooperative agreements engaged in by the parties to the concentration in the affected markets, such as research and development, licensing, joint production, specialisation, distribution, long term supply and exchange of information agreements.

Trade associations

8.13.   With respect to the trade associations in the affected markets:
(a)   identify those in which the parties to the concentration are members;
(b)   identify the most important trade associations to which the customers and suppliers of the parties to the concentration belong.
Provide the name, address, telephone number, fax number and appropriate contact person of all trade associations listed above.

Section 9

General market information

Market data on conglomerate aspects
Where any of the parties to the concentration hold individually a market share of 25% or more for any product market in which there is no horizontal or vertical relationship as described above, provide the following information:
9.1.   a description of each product market and explain why the products and/or services in these markets are included (and why others are excluded) by reason of their characteristics, prices and their intended use;

([27])   Research and development intensity is defined as research development expenditure as a proportion of turnover.

146

9.2. an estimate of the value of the market and the market shares of each of the groups to which the parties belong for each product market identified in 9.1 for the last financial year:
    (a) for the EEA territory as a whole;
    (b) for the Community as a whole;
    (c) for the territory of the EFTA States as a whole;
    (d) individually for each Member State and EFTA State where the groups to which the parties belong do business;
    (e) and, where different, for the relevant geographic market.

Overview of the markets

9.3. Describe the worldwide context of the proposed concentration, indicating the position of each of the parties to the concentration outside of the EEA territory in terms of size and competitive strength.

9.4. Describe how the proposed concentration is likely to affect the interests of intermediate and ultimate consumers and the development of technical and economic progress.

Section 10

Cooperative effects of a joint venture

10. For the purpose of Article 2(4) of the Merger Regulation please answer the following questions:
    (a) Do two or more parents retain to a significant extent activities in the same market as the joint venture or in a market which is downstream or upstream from that of the joint venture or in a neighbouring market closely related to this market ([28])?
        If the answer is affirmative, please indicate for each of the markets referred to here:
        — the turnover of each parent company in the preceding financial year,
        — the economic significance of the activities of the joint venture in relation to this turnover,
        — the market share of each parent.
        If the answer is negative, please justify your answer.
    (b) If the answer to (a) is affirmative and in your view the creation of the joint venture does not lead to coordination between independent undertakings that restricts competition within the meaning of Article 85(1) of the EC Treaty, give your reasons.
    (c) Without prejudice to the answers to (a) and (b) and in order to ensure that a complete assessment of the case can be made by the Commission, please explain how the criteria of Article 85(3) apply.
        Under Article 85(3), the provisions of Article 85(1) may be declared inapplicable if the operation:
        (i) contributes to improving the production or distribution of goods, or to promoting technical or economic progress;
        (ii) allows consumers a fair share of the resulting benefit;
        (iii) does not impose on the undertakings concerned restrictions which are not indispensable to the attainment of these objectives; and
        (iv) does not afford such undertakings the possibility of eliminating competition in respect of a substantial part of the products in question.

([28]) For market definitions refer to Section 6.

For guidance, please refer to form A/B, and in particular Sections 16 and 17 thereof, annexed to Commission Regulation (EC) No 3385/94 ([29]).

Section 11

General matters

Ancillary restraints

11.1.   If the parties to the concentration, and/or other involved parties (including the seller and minority shareholders), enter into ancillary restrictions directly related and necessary to the implementation of the concentration, these restrictions may be assessed in conjunction with the concentration itself (see Article 6(1)(b) and Article 8(2) of the Merger Regulation, recital 25 to the Merger Regulation, recital 7 to Regulation (EC) No 1310/97 and the Commission notice on restrictions ancillary to concentrations) ([30]).

    (a)   Identify each ancillary restriction in the agreements provided with the notification for which you request an assessment in conjunction with the concentration; and

    (b)   explain why these are directly related and necessary to the implementation of the concentration.

Conversion of notification

11.2.   In the event that the Commission finds that the operation notified does not constitute a concentration within the meaning of Article 3 of the Merger Regulation, do you request that it be treated as an application for negative clearance from, or a notification to obtain an exemption from Article 85 of the EC Treaty?

Section 12

Declaration

Article 1(2) of the Implementing Regulation states that where notifications are signed by representatives of undertakings, such representatives must produce written proof that they are authorised to act. Such written authorisation must accompany the notification.

The notification must conclude with the following declaration which is to be signed by or on behalf of all the notifying parties:

The undersigned declare that, to the best of their knowledge and belief, the information given in this notification is true, correct, and complete, that complete copies of documents required by form CO, have been supplied, and that all estimates are identified as such and are their best estimates of the underlying facts and that all the opinions expressed are sincere.

They are aware of the provisions of Article 14(1)(b) of the Merger Regulation.

Place and date:

([29])   OJ L 377, 31.12.1994, p. 28.
([30])   OJ L 180, 9.7.1997, p. 1.

Signatures:

Name/s:

On behalf of:

Guidance note I

Calculation of turnover for insurance undertakings (Article 5(3)(a))

For the calculation of turnover for insurance undertakings, we give the following example (proposed concentration between insurance A and B):

I.   *Consolidated profit and loss account*

(million ECU)

Income	Insurance A	Insurance B
Gross premiums written	5 000	300
— gross premiums received from Community residents	(4 500)	(300)
— gross premiums received from residents of one (and the same) Member State X	(3 600)	(270)
Other income	500	50
Total income	5 500	350

II. *Calculation of turnover*
1. Aggregate worldwide turnover is replaced by the value of gross premiums written worldwide, the sum of which is ECU 5 300 million.
2. Community-wide turnover is replaced, for each insurance undertakings, by the value of gross premiums written with Community residents. For each of the insurance undertakings, this amount is more than ECU 250 million.
3. Turnover within one (and the same) Member State X is replaced, for insurance undertakings, by the value of gross premiums written with residents of one (and the same) Member State X. For insurance A, it achieves 80% of its gross premiums written with Community residents within Member State X, whereas for insurance B, it achieves 90% of its gross premiums written with Community residents in that Member State X.
III. *Conclusion*
Since
(a) the aggregate worldwide turnover of insurances A and B, as replaced by the value of gross premiums written worldwide, is more than ECU 5 000 million;
(b) for each of the insurance undertakings, the value of gross premiums written with Community residents is more than ECU 250 million; but
(c) each of the insurance undertakings achieves more than two thirds of its gross premiums written with Community residents in one (and the same) Member State X,
the proposed concentration would not fall under the scope of the Regulation.

149

Guidance note II

Calculation of turnover for joint undertakings

A.   Creation of a joint undertaking (Article 3(2))
In a case where two (or more) undertakings create a joint undertaking that constitutes a concentration, turnover is calculated for the undertakings concerned.

B.   Existence of a joint undertaking (Article 5(5))
For the calculation of turnover in case of the existence of a joint undertaking C between two undertakings A and B concerned in a concentration, we give the following example:

I.   *Profit and loss accounts*

(million ECU)

Turnover	Undertaking A	Undertaking B
Sales revenues worldwide	10 000	2 000
— Community	(8 000)	(1 500)
— Member State Y	(4 000)	(900)

(million ECU)

Turnover	Joint undertaking C
Sales revenue worldwide	100
— with undertaking A	(20)
— with undertaking B	(10)
Turnover with third undertakings	70
— Community-wide	(60)
— in Member State Y (50)	(50)

II.   *Consideration of the joint undertaking*
(a)   The undertaking C is jointly controlled (in the meaning of Article 3(3) and (4)) by the undertakings A and B concerned by the concentration, irrespective of any third undertaking participating in that undertaking C.
(b)   The undertaking C is not consolidated A and B in their profit and loss accounts.
(c)   The turnover of C resulting from operations with A and B shall not be taken into account.
(d)   The turnover of C resulting from operations with any third undertaking shall be apportioned equally amongst the undertakings A and B, irrespective of their individual shareholdings in C.

III.   *Calculation of turnover*
(a)   Undertaking A's aggregate worldwide turnover shall be calculated as follows: ECU 10 000 million and 50% of C's worldwide turnover with third undertakings (i.e. ECU 35 million), the sum of which is ECU 10 035 million.
         Undertaking B's aggregate worldwide turnover shall be calculated as follows: ECU 2 000 million and 50% of C's worldwide turnover with third undertakings (i.e. ECU 35 million), the sum of which is ECU 2 035 million.
(b)   The aggregate worldwide turnover of the undertakings concerned is ECU 12 070 million.
(c)   Undertaking A achieves ECU 4 025 million within Member State Y (50% of C's turnover in this Member State taken into account), and a Community-wide turnover of ECU 8 030 million (including 50% of C's Community-wide turnover).

Undertaking B achieves ECU 925 million within Member State Y (50% of C's turnover in this Member State taken into account), and a Community-wide turnover of ECU 1 530 million (including 50% of C's Community-wide turnover).

IV.   *Conclusion*
Since
(a)   the aggregate worldwide turnover of undertakings A and B is more than ECU 5 000 million;
(b)   each of the undertakings concerned by the concentration achieves more than ECU 250 million within the Community;
(c)   each of the undertakings concerned (undertaking A 50,1 % and undertaking B 60,5 %) achieves less than two thirds of its Community-wide turnover in one (and the same) Member State Y;
the proposed concentration would fall under the scope of the Regulation.

Guidance note III

Application of the two-thirds rule (Article 1)

For the application of the two thirds rule for undertakings, we give the following examples (proposed concentration between undertakings A and B):

I.   *Consolidated profit and loss accounts*
Example 1   *(million ECU)*

Turnover	Undertaking A	Undertaking B
Sales revenues worldwide	10 000	500
— within the Community	(8 000)	(400)
— in Member State X	(6 000)	(200)

Example 2(a)   *(million ECU)*

Turnover	Undertaking A	Undertaking B
Sale revenues worldwide	4 800	500
— within the Community	(2 400)	(400)
— in Member State X	(2 100)	(300)

Example 2(b)
Same figures as in example 2(a) but undertaking B achieves ECU 300 million in Member State Y.

II.   *Application of the two-thirds rule*

Example 1
1.   Community-wide turnover is, for undertaking A, ECU 8 000 million and for undertaking B ECU 400 million.
2.   Turnover in one (and the same) Member State X is, for undertaking A (ECU 6 000 million), 75% of its Community-wide turnover and is, for undertaking B (ECU 200 million), 50% of its Community-wide-turnover.
3.   Conclusion: In this case, although undertaking A achieves more than two thirds of its Community-wide turnover in Member State X, the proposed concentration would fall under the scope of the Regulation due to the fact that undertaking B achieves less than two thirds of its Community-wide turnover in Member State X.

Example 2(a)
1. Community-wide turnover of undertaking A is ECU 2 400 million and of undertaking B, ECU 400 million.
2. Turnover in one (and the same) Member State X is, for undertaking A, ECU 2 100 million (i.e. 87.5% of its Community-wide turnover); and, for undertaking B, ECU 300 million (i.e. 75% of its Community-wide turnover).
3. Conclusion: In this case, each of the undertakings concerned achieves more than two thirds of its Community-wide turnover in one (and the same) Member State X; the proposed concentration would not fall under the scope of the Regulation.

Example 2(b)
Conclusion: In this case, the two thirds rule would not apply due to the fact that undertakings A and B achieve more than two thirds of their Community-wide turnover in different Member States X and Y. Therefore, the proposed concentration would fall under the scope of the Regulation.

Annex 3

COMMISSION NOTICE ON THE CONCEPT OF FULL-FUNCTION JOINT VENTURES UNDER COUNCIL REGULATION (EEC) NO 4064/89 ON THE CONTROL OF CONCENTRATIONS BETWEEN UNDERTAKINGS (98/C 66/01)

(Text with EEA relevance)

I. Introduction

1. The purpose of this notice is to provide guidance as to how the Commission interprets Article 3 of Council Regulation (EEC) No 4064/89 (¹) as last amended by Regulation (EC) No 1310/97 (²) (hereinafter referred to as the Merger Regulation) in relation to joint ventures (³).

2. This Notice replaces the Notice on the distinction between concentrative and cooperative joint ventures. Changes made in this Notice reflect the amendments made to the Merger Regulation as well as the experience gained by the Commission in applying the Merger Regulation since its entry into force on 21 September 1990. The principles set out in this Notice will be followed and further developed by the Commission's practice in individual cases.

3. Under the Community competition rules, joint ventures are undertakings which are jointly controlled by two or more other undertakings (⁴). In practice joint ventures

---

(¹) OJ L 395, 30.12.1989, p. 1, corrected version No L 257, 21.9.1990, p. 13.

(²) OJ L 180, 9.7.1997, p. 1.

(³) The Commission intends, in due course, to provide guidance on the application of Article 2(4) of the Merger Regulation. Pending the adoption of such guidance, interested parties are referred to the principles set out in paragraphs 17 to 20 of Commission Notice on the distinction between concentrative and cooperative joint ventures, OJ C 385, 31.12.1994, p. 1.

(⁴) The concept of joint control is set out in the Notice on the concept of concentration.

encompass a broad range of operations, from merger-like operations to cooperation for particular functions such as R & D, production or distribution.

4. Joint ventures fall within the scope of the Merger Regulation if they meet the requirements of a concentration set out in Article 3 thereof.

5. According to recital 23 to Council Regulation (EEC) No 4064/89 it is appropriate to define the concept of concentration in such a manner as to cover only operations bringing about a lasting change in the structure of the undertakings concerned.

6. The structural changes brought about by concentrations frequently reflect a dynamic process of restructuring in the markets concerned. They are permitted under the Merger Regulation unless they result in serious damage to the structure of competition by creating or strengthening a dominant position.

7. The Merger Regulation deals with the concept of full-function joint ventures in Article 3(2) as follows:
'The creation of a joint venture performing on a lasting basis all the functions of an autonomous economic entity shall constitute a concentration within the meaning of paragraph 1(b).'

II. Joint ventures under article 3 of the merger regulation

8. In order to be a concentration within the meaning of Article 3 of the Merger Regulation, an operation must fulfil the following requirements:

1. Joint control

9. A joint venture may fall within the scope of the Merger Regulation where there is an acquisition of joint control by two or more undertakings, that is, its parent companies (Article 3(1)(b)). The concept of control is set out in Article 3(3). This provides that control is based on the possibility of exercising decisive influence over an undertaking, which is determined by both legal and factual considerations.

10. The principles for determining joint control are set out in detail in the Commission's Notice on the concept of concentration ([5]).

2. Structural change of the undertakings

11. Article 3(2) provides that the joint venture must perform, on a lasting basis, all the functions of an autonomous economic entity. Joint ventures which satisfy this requirement bring about a lasting change in the structure of the undertakings concerned. They are referred to in this Notice as 'full-function' joint ventures.

12. Essentially this means that a joint venture must operate on a market, performing the functions normally carried out by undertakings operating on the same market. In

---

([5]) Paragraphs 18 to 39.

order to do so the joint venture must have a management dedicated to its day-to-day operations and access to sufficient resources including finance, staff, and assets (tangible and intangible) in order to conduct on a lasting basis its business activities within the area provided for in the joint-venture agreement ([6]).

13. A joint venture is not full-function if it only takes over one specific function within the parent companies' business activities without access to the market. This is the case, for example, for joint ventures limited to R & D or production. Such joint ventures are auxiliary to their parent companies' business activities. This is also the case where a joint venture is essentially limited to the distribution or sales of its parent companies' products and, therefore, acts principally as a sales agency. However, the fact that a joint venture makes use of the distribution network or outlet of one or more of its parent companies normally will not disqualify it as 'full-function' as long as the parent companies are acting only as agents of the joint venture ([7]).

14. The strong presence of the parent companies in upstream or downstream markets is a factor to be taken into consideration in assessing the full-function character of a joint venture where this presence leads to substantial sales or purchases between the parent companies and the joint venture. The fact that the joint venture relies almost entirely on sales to its parent companies or purchases from them only for an initial start-up period does not normally affect the full-function character of the joint venture. Such a start-up period may be necessary in order to establish the joint venture on a market. It will normally not exceed a period of three years, depending on the specific conditions of the marker in question ([8]).

Where sales from the joint venture to the parent companies are intended to be made on a lasting basis, the essential question is whether, regardless of these sales, the joint venture is geared to play an active role on the market. In this respect the relative proportion of these sales compared with the total production of the joint venture is an important factor. Another factor is whether sales to the parent companies are made on the basis of normal commercial conditions ([9]).

In relation to purchases made by the joint venture from its parent companies, the full-function character of the joint venture is questionable in particular where little value is added to the products or services concerned at the level of the joint venture itself. In

---

([6]) Case IV/M.527 — Thomson CSF/Deutsche Aerospace, of 2 December 1994 (paragraph 10) — intellectual rights, Case IV/M.560 EDS/Lufthansa of 11 May 1995 (paragraph 11) — outsourcing, Case IV/M.585 — Voest Alpine Industrieanlagenbau GmbH/Davy International Ltd, of 7 September 1995 (paragraph 8) — joint venture's right to demand additional expertise and staff from its parent companies, Case IV/M.686 — Nokia/Autoliv, of 5 February 1996 (paragraph 7), joint venture able to terminate 'service agreements' with parent company and to move from site retained by parent company, Case IV/M.791 — British Gas Trading Ltd/Group 4 Utility Services Ltd, of 7 October 1996, (paragraph 9) joint venture's intended assets will be transferred to leasing company and leased by joint venture.

([7]) Case IV/M.102 — TNT/Canada Post etc. of 2 December 1991 (paragraph 14).

([8]) Case IV/M.560 — EDS/Lufthansa of 11 May 1995 (paragraph 11); Case IV/M.686 Nokia/Autoliv of 5 February 1996 (paragraph 6); to be contrasted with Case IV/M.904 — RSB/Tenex/Fuel Logistics of 2 April 1997 (paragraph 15–17) and Case IV/M.979 — Preussag/Voest-Alpine of 1 October 1997 (paragraph 9–12). A special case exists where sales by the joint venture to its parent are caused by a legal monopoly downstream of the joint venture (Case IV/M.468 — Siemens/Italtel of 17 February 1995 (paragraph 12), or where the sales to a parent company consist of by-products, which are of minor importance to the joint venture (Case IV/M.550 — Union Carbide/Enichem of 13 March 1995 (paragraph 14)).

([9]) Case lV/M.556 — Zeneca/Vanderhave of 9 April 1996 (paragraph 8); Case IV/M.751 — Bayer/Hüls of 3 July 1996 (paragraph 10).

155

such a situation, the joint venture may be closer to a joint sales agency. However, in contrast to this situation where a joint venture is active in a trade market and performs the normal functions of a trading company in such a market, it normally will not be an auxiliary sales agency but a full-function joint venture. A trade market is characterised by the existence of companies which specialise in the selling and distribution of products without being vertically integrated in addition to those which are integrated, and where different sources of supply are available for the products in question. In addition, many trade markets may require operators to invest in specific facilities such as outlets, stockholding, warehouses, depots, transport fleets and sales personnel. In order to constitute a full-function joint venture in a trade market, an undertaking must have the necessary facilities and be likely to obtain a substantial proportion of its supplies not only from its parent companies but also from other competing sources ([10]).

15.   Furthermore, the joint venture must be intended to operate on a lasting basis. The fact that the parent companies commit to the joint venture the resources described above normally demonstrates that this is the case. In addition, agreements setting up a joint venture often provide for certain contingencies, for example, the failure of the joint venture or fundamental disagreement as between the parent companies ([11]) This may be achieved by the incorporation of provisions for the eventual dissolution of the joint venture itself or the possibility for one or more parent companies to withdraw from the joint venture. This kind of provision does not prevent the joint venture from being considered as operating on a lasting basis. The same is normally true where the agreement specifies a period for the duration of the joint venture where this period is sufficiently long in order to bring about a lasting change in the structure of the undertakings concerned ([12]), or where the agreement provides for the possible continuation of the joint venture beyond this period. By contrast, the joint venture will not be considered to operate on a lasting basis where it is established for a short finite duration. This would be the case, for example, where a joint venture is established in order to construct a specific project such as a power plant, but it will not be involved in the operation of the plant once its construction has been completed.

III.   Final

16.   The creation of a full-function joint venture constitutes a concentration within the meaning of Article 3 of the Merger Regulation. Restrictions accepted by the parent companies of the joint venture that are directly related and necessary for the implementation of the concentration ('ancillary restrictions'), will be assessed together with the concentration itself ([13]).

Further, the creation of a full-function joint venture may as a direct consequence lead to the coordination of the competitive behaviour of undertakings that remain independent. In such cases Article 2(4) of the Merger Regulation provides that those cooperative effects will be assessed within the same procedure as the concentration. This assessment will be made in accordance with the criteria of Article 85(1) and (3) of the Treaty

---

([10])   Case IV/M.788 — AgrEVO/Marubeni of 3 September 1996 (paragraphs 9 and 10).

([11])   Case IV/M.891 — Deutsche Bank/Commerzbank/J.M. Voith of 23 April 1997 (paragraph 7).

([12])   Case IV/M.791 — British Gas Trading Ltd/Group 4 Utility Services Ltd of 7 October 1996, (paragraph 10); to be contrasted with Case IV/M.722 — Teneo/Merill Lynch/Bankers Trust of 15 April 1996 (paragraph 15).

([13])   See Commission Notice regarding restrictions ancillary to concentrations, OJ No C 203, 14.8.1990, p. 5.

with a view to establishing whether or not the operation is compatible with the common market.

The applicability of Article 85 of the Treaty to other restrictions of competition, that are neither ancillary to the concentration, nor a direct consequence of the creation of the joint venture, will normally have to be examined by means of Regulation No 17.

17.   The Commission's interpretation of Article 3 of the Merger Regulation with respect to joint ventures is without prejudice to the interpretation which may be given by the Court of Justice or the Court of First Instance of the European Communities.

ANNEX 4

COMMISSION NOTICE ON THE CONCEPT OF CONCENTRATION UNDER COUNCIL REGULATION (EEC) NO 4064/89 ON THE CONTROL OF CONCENTRATIONS BETWEEN UNDERTAKINGS (98/C 66/02)

(Text with EEA relevance)

I. Introduction

1. The purpose of this Notice is to provide guidance as to how the Commission interprets the term 'concentration' used in Article 3 of Council Regulation (EEC) No 4064/89 [1] as last amended by Regulation (EC) No 1310/97 [2] (hereinafter referred to as 'the Merger Regulation'). This formal guidance on the interpretation of Article 3 should enable firms to establish more quickly, in advance of any contact with the Commission, whether and to what extent their operations may be covered by Community merger control.

This Notice replaces the Notice on the notion of a concentration [3]. This Notice deals with paragraphs (1), (3), (4) and (5) of Article 3. The interpretation of Article 3 in

---

[1] OJ L 395, 30.12.1989, p. 1, corrected version OJ L 257, 21.9.1990, p. 13.
[2] OJ L 180, 9.7.1997, p. 1.
[3] OJ C 385, 31.12.1994, p. 5.

relation to joint ventures, dealt with in particular under Article 3(2), is set out in the Commission's Notice on the concept of full-function joint ventures.

2.   The guidance set out in this Notice reflects the Commission's experience in applying the Merger Regulation since it entered into force on 21 December 1990. The principles contained here will be applied and further developed by the Commission in individual cases.

3.   According to recital 23 to Regulation (EEC) No 4064/89, the concept of concentration is defined as covering only operations which bring about a lasting change in the structure of the undertakings concerned. Article 3(1) provides that such a structural change is brought about either by a merger between two previously independent undertakings or by the acquisition of control over the whole or part of another undertaking.

4.   The determination of the existence of a concentration under the Merger Regulation is based upon qualitative rather than quantitative criteria, focusing on the concept of control. These criteria include considerations of both law and fact. It follows, therefore, that a concentration may occur on a legal or a *de facto* basis.

5.   Article 3(1) of the Merger Regulation defines two categories of concentration:

— those arising from a merger between previously independent undertakings (point (a));
— those arising from an acquisition of control (point (b)).

These are treated respectively in Sections II and III below.

II.   *Mergers between previously independent undertakings*

6.   A merger within the meaning of Article 3(1)(a) of the Merger Regulation occurs when two or more independent undertakings amalgamate into a new undertaking and cease to exist as separate legal entities. A merger may also occur when an undertaking is absorbed by another, the latter retaining its legal identity while the former ceases to exist as a legal entity.

7.   A merger within the meaning of Article 3(1)(a) may also occur where, in the absence of a legal merger, the combining of the activities of previously independent undertakings results in the creation of a single economic unit ([4]). This may arise in particular where two or more undertakings, while retaining their individual legal personalities, establish contractually a common economic management ([5]). If this leads to a *de facto* amalgamation of the undertakings concerned into a genuine common economic unit, the operation is considered to be a merger. A prerequisite for the determination of a common economic unit is the existence of a permanent, single economic management. Other relevant factors may include internal profit and loss compensation as between the various undertakings within the group, and their joint

---

([4])   In determining the previous independence of undertakings, the issue of control may be relevant. Control is considered generally in paragraphs 12 *et seq.* below. For this specific issue, minority shareholders are deemed to have control if they have previously obtained a majority of votes on major decisions at shareholders meetings. The reference period in this context is normally three years.

([5])   This could apply for example, in the case of a 'Gleichordnungskonzern' in German law, certain 'Groupements d'Intérêt Economique' in French law, and certain partnerships.

liability externally. The *de facto* amalgamation may be reinforced by cross-shareholdings between the undertakings forming the economic unit.

III. *Acquisition of control*

8.   Article 3(1)(b) provides that a concentration occurs in the case of an acquisition of control. Such control may be acquired by one undertaking acting alone or by two or more undertakings acting jointly.

Control may also be acquired by a person in circumstances where that person already controls (whether solely or jointly) at least one other undertaking or, alternatively, by a combination of persons (which controls another undertaking) and/or undertakings. The term 'person' in this context extends to public bodies ([6]) and private entities, as well as individuals.

As defined, a concentration within the meaning of the Merger Regulation is limited to changes in control. Internal restructuring within a group of companies, therefore, cannot constitute a concentration.

An exceptional situation exists where both the acquiring and acquired undertakings are public companies owned by the same State (or by the same public body). In this case, whether the operation is to be regarded as an internal restructuring depends in turn on the question whether both undertakings were formerly part of the same economic unit within the meaning of recital 12 to Regulation (EEC) No 4064/89. Where the undertakings were formerly part of different economic units having an independent power of decision, the operation will be deemed to constitute a concentration and not an internal restructuring ([7]). Such independent power of decision does not normally exist, however, where the undertakings are within the same holding company ([8]).

9.   Whether an operation gives rise to an acquisition of control depends on a number of legal and/or factual elements. The acquisition of property rights and shareholders' agreements are important, but are not the only elements involved: purely economic relationships may also play a decisive role. Therefore, in exceptional circumstances, a situation of economic dependence may lead to control on a *de facto* basis where, for example, very important long-term supply agreements or credits provided by suppliers or customers, coupled with structural links, confer decisive influence ([9]).

There may also be acquisition of control even if it is not the declared intention of the parties ([10]). Moreover, the Merger Regulation clearly defines control as having 'the possibility of exercising decisive influence' rather than the actual exercise of such influence.

10.   Control is nevertheless normally acquired by persons or undertakings which are the holders of the rights or are entitled to rights conferring control (Article 3(4)(a)).

([6])   Including the State itself, e. g. Case IW/M.157 — Air France/Sabena, of 5 October 1992 in relation to the Belgian State, or other public bodies such as the Treuhand in Case IV/M.308 — Kali und Salz/MDK/Treuhand, of 14 December 1993.

([7])   Case IV/M.097 — Péchiney/Usinor, of 24 June 1991; Case IV/M.216 — CEA Industrie/France Telecom/SGS-Thomson, of 22 February 1993.

([8])   See paragraph 55 of the Notice on the concept of undertakings concerned.

([9])   For example, in the Usinor/Bamesa decision adopted by the Commission under the ECSC Treaty. See also Case IV/M.258 — CCIE/GTE, of 25 September 1992, and Case IV/M.697 — Lockheed Martin Corporation/Loral Corporation, of 27 March 1996.

([10])   Case IV/M.157 — Air France/Sabena, of 5 October 1992.

There may be exceptional situations where the formal holder of a controlling interest differs from the person or undertaking having in fact the real power to exercise the rights resulting from this interest. This may be the case, for example, where an undertaking uses another person or undertaking for the acquisition of a controlling interest and exercises the rights through this person or undertaking, even though the latter is formally the holder of the rights. In such a situation, control is acquired by the undertaking which in reality is behind the operation and in fact enjoys the power to control the target undertaking (Article 3(4)(b)). The evidence needed to establish this type of indirect control may include factors such as the source of financing or family links.

11.   The object of control can be one or more undertakings which constitute legal entities, or the assets of such entities, or only some of these assets (^{11}). The assets in question, which could be brands or licences, must constitute a business to which a market turnover can be clearly attributed.

12.   The acquisition of control may be in the form of sole or joint control. In both cases, control is defined as the possibility of exercising decisive influence on an undertaking on the basis of rights, contracts or any other means (Article 3(3)).

1. Sole control

13.   Sole control is normally acquired on a legal basis where an undertaking acquires a majority of the voting rights of a company. It is not in itself significant that the acquired shareholding is 50% of the share capital plus one share (^{12}) or that it is 100% of the share capital (^{13}). In the absence of other elements, an acquisition which does not include a majority of the voting rights does not normally confer control even if it involves the acquisition of a majority of the share capital.

14.   Sole control may also be acquired in the case of a 'qualified minority'. This can be established on a legal and/or *de facto* basis.

On a legal basis it can occur where specific rights are attached to the minority shareholding. These may be preferential shares leading to a majority of the voting rights or other rights enabling the minority shareholder to determine the strategic commercial behaviour of the target company, such as the power to appoint more than half of the members of the supervisory board or the administrative board.

A minority shareholder may also be deemed to have sole control on a *de facto* basis. This is the case, for example, where the shareholder is highly likely to achieve a majority at the shareholders meeting, given that the remaining shares are widely dispersed (^{14}). In such a situation it is unlikely that all the smaller shareholders will be present or represented at the shareholders' meeting. The determination of whether or not sole control exists in a particular case is based on the evidence resulting from the presence of shareholders in previous years. Where, on the basis of the number of shareholders attending the shareholders' meeting, a minority shareholder has a stable majority of the votes at this meeting, then the large minority shareholder is taken to have sole control (^{15}).

(^{11})   Case IV/M.286 — Zürich/MMI, of 2 April 1993.
(^{12})   Case IV/M.296 — Crédit Lyonnais/BFG Bank, of 11 January 1993.
(^{13})   Case IV/M.299 — Sara Lee/BP Food Division, of 8 February 1993.
(^{14})   Case IV/M.025 — Arjomari/Wiggins Teape, of 10 February 1990.
(^{15})   Case IV/M.343 — Société Générale de Belgique/Générale de Banque, of 3 August 1993.

Sole control can also be exercised by a minority shareholder who has the right to manage the activities of the company and to determine its business policy.

15. An option to purchase or convert shares cannot in itself confer sole control unless the option will be exercised in the near future according to legally binding agreements ([16]). However, the likely exercise of such an option can be taken into account as an additional element which, together with other elements, may lead to the conclusion that there is sole control.

16. A change from joint to sole control of an undertaking is deemed to be a concentration within the meaning of the Merger Regulation because decisive influence exercised alone is substantially different from decisive influence exercised jointly ([17]). For the same reason, an operation involving the acquisition of joint control of one part of an undertaking and sole control of another part is in principle regarded as two separate concentrations under the Merger Regulation ([18]).

17. The concept of control under the Merger Regulation may be different from that applied in specific areas of legislation concerning, for example, prudential rules, taxation, air transport or the media. In addition, national legislation within a Member State may provide specific rules on the structure of bodies representing the organisation of decision-making within an undertaking, in particular, in relation to the rights of representatives of employees. While such legislation may confer some power of control upon persons other than the shareholders, the concept of control under the Merger Regulation is related only to the means of influence normally enjoyed by the owners of an undertaking. Finally, the prerogatives exercised by a State acting as a public authority rather than as a shareholder, in so far as they are limited to the protection of the public interest, do not constitute control within the meaning of the Merger Regulation to the extent that they have neither the aim nor the effect of enabling the State to exercise a decisive influence over the activity of the undertaking ([19]).

2. Joint control

18. As in the case of sole control, the acquisition of joint control (which includes changes from sole control to joint control) can also be established on a legal or *de facto* basis. There is joint control if the shareholders (the parent companies) must reach agreement on major decisions concerning the controlled undertaking (the joint venture).

19. Joint control exists where two or more undertakings or persons have the possibility of exercising decisive influence over another undertaking. Decisive influence in this sense normally means the power to block actions which determine the strategic commercial behaviour of an undertaking. Unlike sole control, which confers the power upon a specific shareholder to determine the strategic decisions in an undertaking, joint control is characterized by the possibility of a deadlock situation resulting from the power of two or more parent companies to reject proposed strategic decisions. It follows, therefore, that these shareholders must reach a common understanding in determining the commercial policy of the joint venture.

([16]) Judgment in Cafe T 2/93, *Air France* v. *Commission* [1994] ECR II-323.
([17]) This issue is dealt with in paragraphs 30, 31 and 32 of the Notice on the concept of undertakings concerned.
([18]) Case IV/M.409 — ABB/Renault Automation, of 9 March 1994.
([19]) Case IV/M.493 — Tractebel/Distrigaz II, of 1 September 1994.

2.1. Equality in voting rights or appointment to decision-making bodies

20.   The clearest form of joint control exists where there are only two parent companies which share equally the voting rights in the joint venture. In this case, it is not necessary for a formal agreement to exist between them. However, where there is a formal agreement, it must be consistent with the principle of equality between the parent companies, by laying down, for example, that each is entitled to the same number of representatives in the management bodies and that none of the members has a casting vote ([20]). Equality may also be achieved where both parent companies have the right to appoint an equal number of members to the decision-making bodies of the joint venture.

2.2. Veto rights

21.   Joint control may exist even where there is no equality between the two parent companies in votes or in representation in decision-making bodies or where there are more than two parent companies. This is the case where minority shareholders have additional rights which allow them to veto decisions which are essential for the strategic commercial behaviour of the joint venture ([21]). These veto rights may be set out in the statute of the joint venture or conferred by agreement between its parent companies. The veto rights themselves may operate by means of a specific quorum required for decisions taken at the shareholders' meeting or by the board of directors to the extent that the parent companies are represented on this board. It is also possible that strategic decisions are subject to approval by a body, e.g. supervisory board, where the minority shareholders are represented and form part of the quorum needed for such decisions.

22.   These veto rights must be related to strategic decisions on the business policy of the joint venture. They must go beyond the veto rights normally accorded to minority shareholders in order to protect their financial interests as investors in the joint venture. This normal protection of the rights of minority shareholders is related to decisions on the essence of the joint venture, such as changes in the statute, an increase or decrease in the capital or liquidation. A veto right, for example, which prevents the sale or winding-up of the joint venture does not confer joint control on the minority share-holder concerned ([22]).

23.   In contrast, veto rights which confer joint control typically include decisions and issues such as the budget, the business plan, major investments or the appointment of senior management. The acquisition of joint control, however, does not require that the acquirer has the power to exercise decisive influence on the day-to-day running of an undertaking. The crucial element is that the veto rights are sufficient to enable the parent companies to exercise such influence in relation to the strategic business behaviour of the joint venture. Moreover, it is not necessary to establish that an acquirer of joint control of the joint venture will actually make use of its decisive influence. The possibility of exercising such influence and, hence, the mere existence of the veto rights, is sufficient.

24.   In order to acquire joint control, it is not necessary for a minority shareholder to have all the veto rights mentioned above. It may be sufficient that only some, or even

---

([20])   Case IV/M.272 — Matra/CAP Gemini Sogeti, of 17 March 1993.
([21])   Case T 2/93 — Air France v Commission (ibid). Case IV/M.010 — Conagra/Idea, of 3 May 1991.
([22])   Case IV/M.062 — Eridania/ISI, of 30 July 1991.

one such right, exists. Whether or not this is the case depends upon the precise content of the veto right itself and also the importance of this right in the context of the specific business of the joint venture.

Appointment of management and determination of budget

25.   Normally the most important veto rights are those concerning decisions on the appointment of the management and the budget. The power to co-determine the structure of the management confers upon the holder the power to exercise decisive influence on the commercial policy of an undertaking. The same is true with respect to decisions on the budget since the budget determines the precise framework of the activities of the joint venture and, in particular, the investments it may make.

Business plan

26.   The business plan normally provides details of the aims of a company together with the measures to be taken in order to achieve those aims. A veto right over this type of business plan may be sufficient to confer joint control even in the absence of any other veto right. In contrast, where the business plan contains merely general declarations concerning the business aims of the joint venture, the existence of a veto right will be only one element in the general assessment of joint control but will not, on its own, be sufficient to confer joint control.

Investments

27.   In the case of a veto right on investments, the importance of this right depends, first, on the level of investments which are subject to the approval of the parent companies and, secondly, on the extent to which investments constitute an essential feature of the market in which the joint venture is active. In relation to the first criterion, where the level of investments necessitating approval of the parent companies is extremely high, this veto right may be closer to the normal protection of the interests of a minority shareholder than to a right conferring a power of co-determination over the commercial policy of the joint venture. With regard to the second, the investment policy of an undertaking is normally an important element in assessing whether or not there is joint control. However, there may be some markets where investment does not play a significant role in the market behaviour of an undertaking.

Market-specific rights

28.   Apart from the typical veto rights mentioned above, there exist a number of other veto rights related to specific decisions which are important in the context of the particular market of the joint venture. One example is the decision on the technology to be used by the joint venture where technology is a key feature of the joint venture's activities. Another example relates to markets characterised by product differentiation and a significant degree of innovation. In such markets, a veto right over decisions relating to new product lines to be developed by the joint venture may also be an important element in establishing the existence of joint control.

Overall context

29.   In assessing the relative importance of veto rights, where there are a number of them, these rights should not be evaluated in isolation. On the contrary, the determination of whether or not joint control exists is based upon an assessment of these rights as a whole. However, a veto right which does not relate either to commercial policy and strategy or to the budget or business plan cannot be regarded as giving joint control to its owner ([23]).

([23])   Case IV/M.295 — SITA-RPC/SCORI, of 19 March 1993.

2.3. Joint exercise of voting rights

30. Even in the absence of specific veto rights, two or more undertakings acquiring minority shareholdings in another undertaking may obtain joint control. This may be the case where the minority shareholdings together provide the means for controlling the target undertaking. This means that the minority shareholders, together, will have a majority of the voting rights; and they will act together in exercising these voting rights. This can result from a legally binding agreement to this effect, or it may be established on a *de facto* basis.

31. The legal means to ensure the joint exercise of voting rights can be in the form of a holding company to which the minority shareholders transfer their rights, or an agreement by which they undertake to act in the same way (pooling agreement).

32. Very exceptionally, collective action can occur on a *de facto* basis where strong common interests exist between the minority shareholders to the effect that they would not act against each other in exercising their rights in relation to the joint venture.

33. In the case of acquisitions of minority shareholdings, the prior existence of links between the minority shareholders or the acquisition of the shareholdings by means of concerted action will be factors indicating such a common interest.

34. In the case where a new joint venture is established, as opposed to the acquisition of minority shareholdings in a pre-existing company, there is a higher probability that the parent companies are carrying out a deliberate common policy. This is true, in particular, where each parent company provides a contribution to the joint venture which is vital for its operation (e.g. specific technologies, local know-how or supply agreements). In these circumstances, the parent companies may be able to operate the joint venture with full cooperation only with each other's agreement on the most important strategic decisions even if there is no express provision for any veto rights. The greater the number of parent companies involved in such a joint venture, however, the more remote is the likelihood of this situation occurring.

35. In the absence of strong common interests such as those outlined above, the possibility of changing coalitions between minority shareholders will normally exclude the assumption of joint control. Where there is no stable majority in the decision-making procedure and the majority can on each occasion be any of the various combinations possible amongst the minority shareholders, it cannot be assumed that the minority shareholders will jointly control the undertaking. In this context, it is not sufficient that there are agreements between two or more parties having an equal shareholding in the capital of an undertaking which establish identical rights and powers between the parties. For example, in the case of an undertaking where three shareholders each own one-third of the share capital and each elect one-third of the members of the Board of Directors, the shareholders do not have joint control since decisions are required to be taken on the basis of a simple majority. The same considerations also apply in more complex structures, for example, where the capital of an undertaking is equally divided between three shareholders and where the Board of Directors is composed of twelve members, each of the shareholders A, B and C electing two, another two being elected by A, B and C jointly, whilst the remaining four are chosen by the other eight members jointly. In this case also there is no joint control, and hence no control at all within the meaning of the Merger Regulation.

2.4. Other considerations related to joint control

36. Joint control is not incompatible with the fact that one of the parent companies enjoys specific knowledge of and experience in the business of the joint venture. In such

a case, the other parent company can play a modest or even non-existent role in the daily management of the joint venture where its presence is motivated by considerations of a financial, long-term-strategy, brand image or general policy nature. Nevertheless, it must always retain the real possibility of contesting the decisions taken by the other parent company, without which there would be sole control.

37.   For joint control to exist, there should not be a casting vote for one parent company only. However, there can be joint control when this casting vote can be exercised only after a series of stages of arbitration and attempts at reconciliation or in a very limited field ([24]).

2.5.   Joint control for a limited period

38.   Where an operation leads to joint control for a starting-up period ([25]) but, according to legally binding agreements, this joint control will be converted to sole control by one of the shareholders, the whole operation will normally be considered to be an acquisition of sole control.

3.   Control by a single shareholder on the basis of veto rights

39.   An exceptional situation exists where only one shareholder is able to veto strategic decisions in an undertaking, but this shareholder does not have the power, on his own, to impose such decisions. This situation occurs either where one shareholder holds 50% in an undertaking whilst the remaining 50% is held by two or more minority shareholders, or where there is a quorum required for strategic decisions which in fact confers a veto right upon only one minority shareholder ([26]). In these circumstances, a single shareholder possesses the same level of influence as that normally enjoyed by several jointly-controlling shareholders, i.e. the power to block the adoption of strategic decisions. However, this shareholder does not enjoy the powers which are normally conferred on an undertaking with sole control, i.e. the power to impose strategic decisions. Since this shareholder can produce a deadlock situation comparable to that in normal cases of joint control, he acquires decisive influence and therefore control within the meaning of the Merger Regulation ([27]).

4.   Changes in the structure of control

40.   A concentration may also occur where an operation leads to a change in the structure of control. This includes the change from joint control to sole control as well as an increase in the number of shareholders exercising joint control. The principles for determining the existence of a concentration in these circumstances are set out in detail in the Notice on the concept of undertakings concerned ([28]).

([24])   Case IV/M.425 — British Telecom/Banco Santander, of 28 March 1994.
([25])   This starting-up period must not exceed three years. Case IV/M.425 — British Telecom/Banco Santander, *ibid.*
([26])   Case IV/M.258 — CCIE/GTE, of 25 September 1992, where the veto rights of only one shareholder were exercisable through a member of the board appointed by this shareholder.
([27])   Since this shareholder is the only undertaking acquiring a controlling influence, only this shareholder is obliged to submit a notification under the Merger Regulation.
([28])   Paragraphs 30 to 48.

IV. *Exceptions*

41.   Article 3(5) sets out three exceptional situations where the acquisition of a controlling interest does not constitute a concentration under the Merger Regulation.

42.   First, the acquisition of securities by companies whose normal activities include transactions and dealing in securities for their own account or for the account of others is not deemed to constitute a concentration if such an acquisition is made in the framework of these businesses and if the securities are held on only a temporary basis (Article 3(5)(a)). In order to fall within this exception, the following requirements must be fulfilled:

— the acquiring undertaking must be a credit or other financial institution or insurance company the normal activities of which are described above,
— the securities must be acquired with a view to their resale,
— the acquiring undertaking must not exercise the voting rights with a view to determining the strategic commercial behaviour of the target company or must exercise these rights only with a view to preparing the total or partial disposal of the undertaking, its assets or securities,
— the acquiring undertaking must dispose of its controlling interest within one year of the date of the acquisition, that is, it must reduce its shareholding within this one-year period at least to a level which no longer confers control. This period, however, may be extended by the Commission where the acquiring undertaking can show that the disposal was not reasonably possible within the one-year period.

43.   Secondly, there is no change of control, and hence no concentration within the meaning of the Merger Regulation, where control is acquired by an office-holder according to the law of a Member State relating to liquidation, winding-up, insolvency, cessation of payments, compositions or analogous proceedings (Article 3(5)(b));

44.   Thirdly, a concentration does not arise where a financial holding company within the meaning of the Fourth Council Directive 78/660/EEC ([29]) acquires control, provided that this company exercises its voting rights only to maintain the full value of its investment and does not otherwise determine directly or indirectly the strategic commercial conduct of the controlled undertaking.

45.   In the context of the exceptions under Article 3(5), the question may arise whether a rescue operation constitutes a concentration under the Merger Regulation. A rescue operation typically involves the conversion of existing debt into a new company, through which a syndicate of banks may acquire joint control of the company concerned. Where such an operation meets the criteria for joint control, as outlined above, it will normally be considered to be a concentration ([30]). Although the primary intention of the banks is to restructure the financing of the undertaking concerned for its subsequent resale, the exception set out in Article 3(5)(a) is normally not applicable to such an operation. This is because the restructuring programme normally requires the controlling banks to determine the strategic commercial behaviour of the rescued

---

([29])   OJ L 222, 14.8.1978, p. 11, as last amended by the Act of Accession of Austria, Finland and Sweden. Article 5(3) of this Directive defines financial holding companies as 'those companies the sole objective of which is to acquire holdings in other undertakings, and to manage such holdings and turn them to profit, without involving themselves directly or indirectly in the management of those undertakings, the foregoing without prejudice to their rights as shareholders'.

([30])   Case IV/M. 116 — Kelt/American Express, of 28 August 1991.

undertaking. Furthermore, it is not normally a realistic proposition to transform a rescued company into a commercially viable entity and to resell it within the permitted one-year period. Moreover, the length of time needed to achieve this aim may be so uncertain that it would be difficult to grant an extension of the disposal period.

v. *Final*

46.   The Commission's interpretation of Article 3 as set out in this Notice is without Prejudice to the interpretation which may be given by the Court of Justice or the Court of First Instance of the European Communities.

ANNEX 5

COMMISSION NOTICE ON THE CONCEPT OF UNDERTAKINGS CONCERNED UNDER COUNCIL REGULATION (EEC) NO 4064/89 ON THE CONTROL OF CONCENTRATIONS BETWEEN UNDERTAKINGS (98/C 66/03)

(Text with EEC relevance)

I. *Introduction*

1.   The purpose of this notice is to clarify the Commission's interpretation of the term 'undertakings concerned' used in Articles 1 and 5 of Council Regulation (EEC) No 4064/89 ([1]) as last amended by Regulation (EC) No 1310/97 ([2]) (hereinafter referred to as 'the Merger Regulation') and to help identify the undertakings concerned in the most typical situations which have arisen in cases dealt with by the Commission to date. The principles set out in this notice will be followed and further developed by the Commission's practice in individual cases.

This Notice replaces the Notice on the notion of undertakings concerned ([3]).

2.   According to Article 1 of the Merger Regulation, the Regulation only applies to operations that satisfy two conditions. First, several undertakings must merge, or one or more undertakings must acquire control of the whole or part of other undertakings through the proposed operation, which must qualify as a concentration within the meaning of Article 3 of the Regulation. Secondly, those undertakings must meet the turnover thresholds set out in Article 1.

3.   From the point of view of determining jurisdiction, the undertakings concerned are, broadly speaking, the actors in the transaction in so far as they are the merging, or acquiring and acquired parties; in addition, their total aggregate economic size in terms of turnover will be decisive in determining whether the thresholds are met.

4.   The Commission's interpretation of Articles 1 and 5 with respect to the concept of undertakings concerned is without prejudice to the interpretation which may be given by the Court of Justice or by the Court of First Instance of the European Communities.

II. *The concept of undertaking concerned*

5.   Undertakings concerned are the direct participants in a merger or acquisition of control. In this respect, Article 3(1) of the Merger Regulation provides that:
'A concentration shall be deemed to arise where:

   (a)   two or more previously independent undertakings merge, or
   (b)   — one or more persons already controlling at least one undertaking, or
          — one or more undertakings
          acquire, whether by purchase of securities or assets, by contract or by any other means, direct or indirect control of the whole or parts of one or more other undertakings'.

6.   In the case of a merger, the undertakings concerned will be the undertakings that are merging.

7.   In the remaining cases, it is the concept of 'acquiring control' that will determine which are the undertakings concerned. On the acquiring side, there can be one or more companies acquiring sole or joint control. On the acquired side, there can be one or more companies as a whole or parts thereof, when only one of their subsidiaries or

---

([1])   OJ L 395, 30.12.1989, p. 1; corrected version L 257, 21.9.1990, p. 13.
([2])   OJ L 180, 9.7.1997, p. 1.
([3])   OJ C 385, 31.12.1994, p. 12.

some of their assets are the subject of the transaction. As a general rule, each of these companies will be an undertaking concerned within the meaning of the Merger Regulation. However, the particular features of specific transactions require some refinement of this principle, as will be seen below when analysing different possible scenarios.

8.   In concentrations other than mergers or the setting-up of new joint ventures, i.e. in cases of sole or joint acquisition of pre-existing companies or parts of them, there is an important party to the agreement that gives rise to the operation who is to be ignored when identifying the undertakings concerned: the seller. Although it is clear that the operation cannot proceed without his consent, his role ends when the transaction is completed since, by definition, from the moment the seller has relinquished all control over the company, his links with it disappear. Where the seller retains joint control with the acquiring company (or companies), it will be considered to be one of the undertakings concerned.

9.   Once the undertakings concerned have been identified in a given transaction, their turnover for the purposes of determining jurisdiction should be calculated according to the rules set out in Article 5 of the Merger Regulation (⁴). One of the main provisions of Article 5 is that where the undertaking concerned belongs to a group, the turnover of the whole group should be included in the calculation. All references to the turnover of the undertakings concerned in Article 1 should therefore be understood as the turnover of their entire respective groups.

10.   The same can be said with respect to the substantive appraisal of the impact of a concentration in the market place. When Article 2 of the Merger Regulation provides that the Commission is to take into account 'the market position of the undertakings concerned and their economic and financial power', that includes the groups to which they belong.

11.   It is important, when referring to the various undertakings which may be involved in a procedure, not to confuse the concept of 'undertakings concerned' under Articles 1 and 5 with the terminology used in the Merger Regulation and in Commission Regulation (EC) No 447/98 of 1 March 1998 on the notifications, time-limits and hearings provided for in Council Regulation (EEC) No 4064/89 (hereinafter referred to as the 'Implementing Regulation') (⁵) referring to the various undertakings which may be involved in a procedure. This terminology refers to the notifying parties, other involved parties, third parties and parties who may be subject to fines or periodic penalty payments, and they are defined in Chapter III of the Implementing Regulation, along with their respective rights and duties.

III.   *Identifying the undertakings concerned in different types of operations*

1.   **Mergers**

12.   In a merger, several previously independent companies come together to create a new company or, while remaining separate legal entities, to create a single economic unit. As mentioned earlier, the undertakings concerned are each of the merging entities.

(⁴)   The rules for calculating turnover in accordance with Article 5 are detailed in the Commission Notice on calculation of turnover.

(⁵)   OJ L 61, 2.3.1998, p. 1.

2. Acquisition of sole control

2.1. Acquisition of sole control of the whole company

13. Acquisition of sole control of the whole company is the most straightforward case of acquisition of control; the undertakings concerned will be the acquiring company and the acquired or target company.

2.2. Acquisition of sole control of part of a company

14. The first subparagraph of Article 5(2) of the Merger Regulation provides that when the operation concerns the acquisition of parts of one or more undertakings, only those parts which are the subject of the transaction shall be taken into account with regard to the seller. The concept of 'parts' is to be understood as one or more separate legal entities (such as subsidiaries), internal subdivisions within the seller (such as a division or unit), or specific assets which in themselves could constitute a business (e.g. in certain cases brands or licences) to which a market turnover can be clearly attributed. In this case, the undertakings concerned will be the acquirer and the acquired part(s) of the target company.

15. The second subparagraph of Article 5(2) includes a special provision on staggered operations or follow-up deals, whereby if several acquisitions of parts by the same purchaser from the same seller occur within a two-year period, these transactions are to be treated as one and the same operation arising on the date of the last transaction. In this case, the undertakings concerned are the acquirer and the different acquired part(s) of the target company taken as a whole.

2.3. Acquisition of sole control after reduction or enlargement of the target company

16. The undertakings concerned are the acquiring company and the target company or companies, in their configuration at the date of the operation.

17. The Commission bases itself on the configuration of the undertakings concerned at the date of the event triggering the obligation to notify under Article 4(1) of the Merger Regulation, namely the conclusion of the agreement, the announcement of the public bid or the acquisition of a controlling interest. If the target company has divested an entity or closed a business prior to the date of the event triggering notification or where such a divestment or closure is a pre-condition for the operation ([6]), then sales of the divested entity or closed business are not to be included when calculating turnover. Conversely, if the target company has acquired an entity prior to the date of the event triggering notification, the sales of the latter are to be added ([7]).

([6]) See judgment of the Court of First Instance of 24 March 1994 in Case T-3/93 — Air France v Commission [1994] ECR II-21.

([7]) The calculation of turnover in the case of acquisitions or divestments subsequent to the date of the last audited accounts is dealt with in the Commission Notice on calculation of turnover, paragraph 27.

2.4. Acquisition of sole control through a subsidiary of a group

18. Where the target company is acquired by a group through one of its subsidiaries, the undertakings concerned for the purpose of calculating turnover are the target company and the acquiring subsidiary. However, regarding the actual notification, this can be made by the subsidiary concerned or by its parent company.

19. All the companies within a group (parent companies, subsidiaries, etc.) constitute a single economic entity, and therefore there can only be one undertaking concerned within the one group – i.e. the subsidiary and the parent company cannot each be considered as separate undertakings concerned, either for the purposes of ensuring that the threshold requirements are fulfilled (for example, if the target company does not meet the ECU 250 million Community-turnover threshold), or that they are not (for example, if a group was split into two companies each with a Community turnover below ECU 250 million).

20. However, even though there can only be one undertaking concerned within a group, Article 5(4) of the Merger Regulation provides that it is the turnover of the whole group to which the undertaking concerned belongs that shall be included in the threshold calculations ([8]).

3. Acquisition of joint control

3.1. Acquisition of joint control of a newly-created company

21. In the case of acquisition of joint control of a newly-created company, the undertakings concerned are each of the companies acquiring control of the newly set-up joint venture (which, as it does not yet exist, cannot be considered to be an undertaking concerned and moreover, as yet, has no turnover of its own).

3.2. Acquisition of joint control of a pre-existing company

22. In the case of acquisition of joint control of a pre-existing company or business ([9]), the undertakings concerned are each of the companies acquiring joint control on the one hand, and the pre-existing acquired company or business on the other.

23. However, where the pre-existing company was under the sole control of one company and one or several new shareholders acquire joint control while the initial parent company remains, the undertakings concerned are each of the jointly-controlling companies (including this initial shareholder). The target company in this case is not an undertaking concerned, and its turnover is part of the turnover of the initial parent company.

([8]) The calculation of turnover in the case of company groups is dealt with in the Commission Notice on calculation of turnover, paragraphs 36 to 42.

([9]) i.e. two or more companies (companies A, B, etc.) acquire a pre-existing company (company X). For changes in the shareholding in cases of joint control of an existing joint venture, see Section III.6.

3.3. Acquisition of joint control with a view to immediate partition of assets

24.   Where several undertakings come together solely for the purpose of acquiring another company and agree to divide up the acquired assets according to a pre-existing plan immediately upon completion of the transaction, there is no effective concentration of economic power between the acquirers and the target company since the assets acquired are jointly held and controlled for only a 'legal instant'. This type of acquisition with a view to immediate partition of assets will in fact be considered to be several operations, whereby each of the acquiring companies acquires its relevant part of the target company. For each of these operations, the undertakings concerned will therefore be the acquiring company and that part of the target which it is acquiring (just as if there was an acquisition of sole control of part of a company).

25.   This scenario is referred to in recital 24 of Regulation (EEC) No 4064/89, which states that the Regulation applies to agreements whose sole object is to divide up the assets acquired immediately after the acquisition.

4.   Acquisition of control by a joint venture

26.   In transactions where a joint venture acquires control of another company, the question arises whether or not, from the point of view of the acquiring party, the joint venture should be regarded as a single undertaking concerned (the turnover of which would include the turnover of its parent companies), or whether each of its parent companies should individually be regarded as undertakings concerned. In other words, the issue is whether or not to 'lift the corporate veil' of the intermediate undertaking (the vehicle). In principle, the undertaking concerned is the direct participant in the acquisition of control. However, there may be circumstances where companies set up 'shell' companies, which have little or no turnover of their own, or use an existing joint venture which is operating on a different market from that of the target company in order to carry out acquisitions on behalf of the parent companies. Where the acquired or target company has a Community turnover of less than ECU 250 million, the question of determining the undertakings concerned may be decisive for jurisdictional purposes ([10]). In this type of situation, the Commission will look at the economic reality of the operation to determine which are the undertakings concerned.

27.   Where the acquisition is carried out by a full-function joint venture, i.e. a joint venture which has sufficient financial and other resources to operate a business activity on a lasting basis ([11]) and is already operating on a market, the Commission will

---

([10])   The target company hypothetically has an aggregate Community turnover of less than ECU 250 million, and the acquiring parties are two (or more) undertakings, each with a Community turnover exceeding ECU 250 million. If the target is acquired by a 'shell' company set up between the acquiring undertakings, there would only be one company (the 'shell' company) with a Community turnover exceeding ECU 250 million, and thus one of the cumulative threshold conditions for Community jurisdiction would not be fulfilled (namely, the existence of at least two undertakings with a Community turnover exceeding ECU 250 million). Conversely, if instead of acting through a 'shell' company, the acquiring undertakings acquire the target company themselves, then the turnover threshold would be met and the Merger Regulation would apply to this transaction. The same considerations apply to the national turnover thresholds referred to in Article 1(3).

([11])   The criteria determining the full-function nature of a joint venture are contained in the Commission Notice on the concept of full-function joint ventures.

normally consider the joint venture itself and the target company to be the undertakings concerned (and not the joint venture's parent companies).

28.   Conversely, where the joint venture can be regarded as a vehicle for an acquisition by the parent companies, the Commission will consider each of the parent companies themselves to be the undertakings concerned, rather than the joint venture, together with the target company. This is the case in particular where the joint venture is set up especially for the purpose of acquiring the target company, where the joint venture has not yet started to operate, where an existing joint venture has no legal personality or full-function character as referred to above or where the joint venture is an association of undertakings. The same applies where there are elements which demonstrate that the parent companies are in fact the real players behind the operation. These elements may include a significant involvement by the parent companies themselves in the initiation, organisation and financing of the operation. Moreover, where the acquisition leads to a substantial diversification in the nature of the joint venture's activities, this may also indicate that the parent companies are the real players in the operation. This will normally be the case when the joint venture acquires a target company operating on a different product market. In those cases, the parent companies are regarded as undertakings concerned.

29.   In the TNT case ([12]), joint control over a joint venture (JVC) was to be acquired by a joint venture (GD NET BV) between five postal administrations and another acquiring company (TNT Ltd). In this case, the Commission considered that the joint venture GD NET BV was simply a vehicle set up to enable the parent companies (the five postal administrations) to participate in the resulting JVC joint venture in order to facilitate decision-making amongst themselves and to ensure that the parent companies spoke and acted as one; this configuration would ensure that the parent companies could exercise a decisive influence with the other acquiring company, TNT, over the resulting joint venture JVC and would avoid the situation where that other acquirer could exercise sole control because of the postal administrations' inability to reach a unified position on any decision.

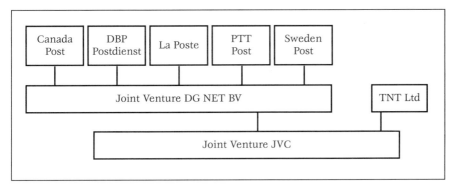

5.   Change from joint control to sale control

30.   In the case of a change from joint control to sole control, one shareholder acquires the stake previously held by the other shareholder(s). In the case of two shareholders,

---

([12])   Case IV/M.102 — TNT/Canada Post, DBP Postdienst, La Poste, PTT Post and Sweden Post, of 2 December 1991.

each of them has joint control over the entire joint venture, and not sole control over 50% of it; hence the sale of all of his shares by one shareholder to the other does not lead the sole remaining shareholder to move from sole control over 50% to sole control over 100% of the joint venture, but rather to move from joint control to sole control of the entire company (which, subsequent to the operation, ceases to be a 'joint' venture).

31.   In this situation, the undertakings concerned are the remaining (acquiring) shareholder and the joint venture. As is the case for any other seller, the 'exiting' shareholder is not an undertaking concerned.

32.   The ICI/Tioxide case ([13]) involved such a change from joint (50/50) control to sole control. The Commission considered that '. . . decisive influence exercised solely is substantially different to decisive influence exercised jointly, since the latter has to take into account the potentially different interests of the other party or parties concerned . . . By changing the quality of decisive influence exercised by ICI on Tioxide, the transaction will bring about a durable change of the structure of the concerned parties . . .'. In this case, the undertakings concerned were held to be ICI (as acquirer) and Tioxide as a whole (as acquiree), but not the seller Cookson.

6.   Change in the shareholding in cases of joint control of an existing joint venture

33.   The decisive element in assessing changes in the shareholding of a company is whether the operation leads to a change in the quality of control. The Commission assesses each operation on a case-by-case basis, but under certain hypotheses, there will be a presumption that the given operation leads, or does not lead, to such a change in the quality of control, and thus constitutes, or does not constitute, a notifiable concentration.

34.   A distinction must be made according to the circumstances of the change in the shareholding; firstly, one or more existing shareholders can exit; secondly, one or more new additional shareholders can enter; and thirdly, one or more existing shareholders can be replaced by one or more new shareholders.

6.1.   Reduction in the number of shareholders leading to a change from joint to sole control

35.   It is not the reduction in the number of shareholders *per se* which is important, but rather the fact that if some shareholders sell their stakes in a given joint venture, these stakes are then acquired by other (new or existing) shareholders, and thus the acquisition of these stakes or additional contractual rights may lead to the acquisition of control or may strengthen an already existing position of control (e.g. additional voting rights or veto rights, additional board members, etc.).

36.   Where the number of shareholders is reduced, there may be a change from joint control to sole control (see also Section III.5.), in which case the remaining shareholder acquires sole control of the company. The undertakings concerned will be the remaining (acquiring) shareholder and the acquired company (previously the joint venture).

([13])   Case IV/M.023 — ICI/Tioxide, of 28 November 1990.

37.   In addition to the shareholder with sole control of the company, there may be other shareholders, for example with minority stakes, but who do not have a controlling interest in the company; these shareholders are not undertakings concerned as they do not exercise control.

6.2.   Reduction in the number of shareholders not leading to a change from joint to sole control

38.   Where the operation involves a reduction in the number of shareholders having joint control, without leading to a change from joint to sole control and without any new entry or substitution of shareholders acquiring control (see Section III.6.3.), the proposed transaction will normally be presumed not to lead to a change in the quality of control and will therefore not be a notifiable concentration. This would be the case where, for example, five shareholders initially have equal stakes of 20% each and where, after the operation, one shareholder exits and the remaining four shareholders each have equal stakes of 25%.

39.   However, this situation would be different where there is a significant change in the quality of control, notably where the reduction in the number of shareholders gives the remaining shareholders additional veto rights or additional board members, resulting in a new acquisition of control by at least one of the shareholders, through the application of either the existing or a new shareholders' agreement. In this case, the undertakings concerned will be each of the remaining shareholders which exercise joint control and the joint venture. In Avesta II ([14]), the fact that the number of major shareholders decreased from four to three led to one of the remaining shareholders acquiring negative veto rights (which it had not previously enjoyed) because of the provisions of the shareholders' agreement which remained in force ([15]). This acquisition of full veto rights was considered by the Commission to represent a change in the quality of control.

6.3.   Any other changes in the composition of the shareholding

40.   Finally, in the case where, following changes in the shareholding, one or more shareholders acquire control, the operation will constitute a notifiable operation as there is a presumption that it will normally lead to a change in the quality of control.

41.   Irrespective of whether the number of shareholders decreases, increases or remains the same subsequent to the operation, this acquisition of control can take any of the following forms:

— entry of one or more new shareholders (change from sole to joint control, or situation of joint control both before and after the operation),
— acquisition of a controlling interest by one or more minority shareholders (change from sole to joint control, or situation of joint control both before and after the operation),

---

([14])   Case IV/M.452 — Avesta II, of 9 June 1994.

([15])   In this case, a shareholder who was a party to the shareholders' agreement sold its stake of approximately 7%. As the exiting shareholder had shared veto rights with another shareholder who remained, and as the shareholders' agreement remained unchanged, the remaining shareholder now acquired full veto rights.

—   substitution of one or more shareholders (situation of joint control both before and after the operation).

42.   The question is whether the undertakings concerned are the joint venture and the new shareholder(s) who would together acquire control of a pre-existing company, or whether all of the shareholders (existing and new) are to be regarded as undertakings concerned acquiring control of a new joint venture. This question is particularly relevant when there is no express agreement between one (or more) of the existing shareholders and the new shareholder(s), who might only have had an agreement with the 'exiting' shareholder(s), i.e. the seller(s).

43.   A change in the shareholding through the entry or substitution of shareholders is considered to lead to a change in the quality of control. This is because the entry of a new parent company, or the substitution of one parent company for another, is not comparable to the simple acquisition of part of a business as it implies a change in the nature and quality of control of the whole joint venture, even when, both before and after the operation, joint control is exercised by a given number of shareholders.

44.   The Commission therefore considers that the undertakings concerned in cases where there are changes in the shareholding are the shareholders (both existing and new) who exercise joint control and the joint venture itself. As mentioned earlier, non-controlling shareholders are not undertakings concerned.

45.   An example of such a change in the shareholding is the Synthomer/Yule Catto case ([16]), in which one of two parent companies with joint control over the pre-existing joint venture was replaced by a new parent company. Both parent companies with joint control (the existing one and the new one) and the joint venture were considered to be undertakings concerned.

7.   'Demergers' and the break-up of companies

46.   When two undertakings merge or set up a joint venture, then subsequently demerge or break up their joint venture, and in particular the assets ([17]) are split between the 'demerging' parties, particularly in a configuration different from the original, there will normally be more than one acquisition of control (see the Annex).

47.   For example, undertakings A and B merge and then subsequently demerge with a new asset configuration. There will be the acquisition by undertaking A of various assets (assets which may previously have been owned by itself or by undertaking B and assets jointly acquired by the entity resulting from the merger), with similar acquisitions by undertaking B. Similarly, a break-up of a joint venture can be deemed to involve a change from joint control over the joint venture's entire assets to sole control over the divided assets ([18]).

48.   A break-up of a company in this way is 'asymmetrical'. For such a demerger, the undertakings concerned (for each break-up operation) will be, on the one hand, the original parties to the merger and, on the other, the assets that each original party is acquiring. For the break-up of a joint venture, the undertakings concerned (for each

---

([16])   Case IV/M.376 — Synthomer/Yule Catto, of 22 October 1993.

([17])   The term 'assets' as used here means specific assets which in themselves could constitute a business (e.g. a subsidiary, a division of a company or, in some cases, brands or licences) to which a market turnover can be clearly attributed.

([18])   IV/M.197 — Solvay-Laporte/Interox, of 30 April 1997.

break-up operation) will be, on the one hand, the original parties to the joint venture, each as acquirer, and, on the other, that part of the joint venture that each original party is acquiring.

8. Exchange of assets

49. In those transactions where two (or more) companies exchange assets, regardless of whether these constitute legal entities or not, each acquisition of control constitutes an independent concentration. Although it is true that both transfers of assets in a swap are usually considered by the parties to be interdependent, that they are often agreed in a single document and that they may even take place simultaneously, the purpose of the Merger Regulation is to assess the impact of the operation resulting from the acquisition of control by each of the companies. The legal or even economic link between those operations is not sufficient for them to qualify as a single concentration.

50. Hence the undertakings concerned will be, for each property transfer, the acquiring companies and the acquired companies or assets.

9. Acquisitions of control by individual persons

51. Article 3(1) of the Merger Regulation specifically provides that a concentration is deemed to arise, *inter alia*, where 'one or more persons already controlling at least one undertaking' acquire control of the whole or parts of one or more undertakings. This provision indicates that acquisitions of control by individuals will bring about a lasting change in the structure of the companies concerned only if those individuals carry out economic activities of their own. The Commission considers that the undertakings concerned are the target company and the individual acquirer (with the turnover of the undertaking(s) controlled by that individual being included in the calculation of the individual's turnover).

52. This was the view taken in the Commission decision in the Asko/Jacobs/Adia case ([19]), where Asko, a German holding company with substantial retailing assets, and Mr Jacobs, a private Swiss investor, acquired joint control of Adia, a Swiss company active mainly in personnel services. Mr Jacobs was considered to be an undertaking concerned because of the economic interests he held in the chocolate, confectionery and coffee sectors.

10. Management buy-outs

53. An acquisition of control of a company by its own managers is also an acquisition by individuals, and what has been said above is therefore also applicable here. However, the management of the company may pool its interests through a 'vehicle company', so that it acts with a single voice and also to facilitate decision-making. Such a vehicle company may be, but is not necessarily, an undertaking concerned. The general rule on acquisitions of control by a joint venture applies here (see Section III.4.).

54. With or without a vehicle company, the management may also look for investors in order to finance the operation. Very often, the rights granted to these investors

---

([19]) Case IV/M.082 — Asko/Jacobs/Adia, of 16 May 1991.

according to their shareholding may be such that control within the meaning of Article 3 of the Merger Regulation will be conferred on them and not on the management itself, which may simply enjoy minority rights. In the CWB/Goldman Sachs/Tarkett decision ([20]), the two companies managing the investment funds taking part in the transaction were those acquiring joint control, and not the managers.

11. Acquisition of control by a State-owned company

55. In those situations where a State-owned company merges with or acquires control of another company controlled by the same State ([21]), the question arises as to whether these transactions really constitute concentrations within the meaning of Article 3 of the Merger Regulation or rather internal restructuring operations of the 'public sector group of companies' ([22]). In this respect, recital 12 of Regulation (EEC) No 4064/89 sets out the principle of non-discrimination between public and private sectors and declares that 'in the public sector, calculation of the turnover of an undertaking concerned in a concentration needs, therefore, to take account of undertakings making up an economic unit with an independent power of decision, irrespective of the way in which their capital is held or of the rules of administrative supervision applicable to them'.

56. A merger or acquisition of control arising between two companies owned by the same State may constitute a concentration and, if so, both of them will qualify as undertakings concerned, since the mere fact that two companies are both owned by the same State does not necessarily mean that they belong to the same 'group'. Indeed, the decisive issue will be whether or not these companies are both part of the same industrial holding and are subject to a coordinated strategy. This was the approach taken in the SGS/Thomson decision ([23]).

([20]) Case IV/M.395 — CWB/Goldman Sachs/Tarkett, of 21 February 1994.

([21]) The term 'State' as used here means any legal public entry, i.e. not only Member States, but also regional or local public entities such as provinces, departments, Länder, etc.

([22]) See also Commission Notice on the concept of concentration, paragraph 8.

([23]) Case IV/M.216 — CEA Industrie/France Telecom/Finmeccanica/SGS-Thomson, of 22 February 1993.

ANNEX: 'DEMERGERS' AND BREAK-UP OF COMPANIES([24])

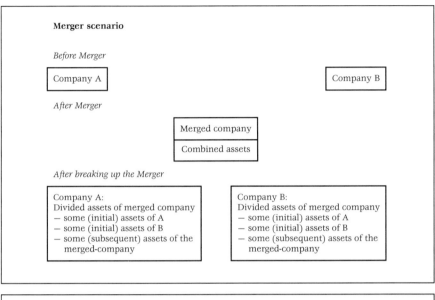

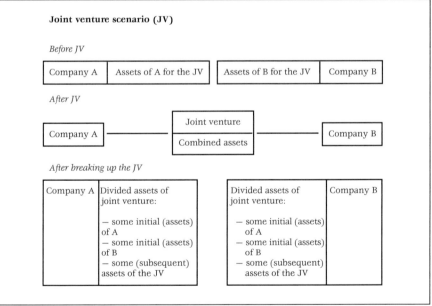

([24]) The term 'assets' as used here means specific assets which in themselves could constitute a business (e.g. a subsidiary, a division of a company or, in some cases, brands or licences) to which a market turnover can be clearly attributed.

Annex 6

COMMISSION NOTICE ON CALCULATION OF TURNOVER UNDER COUNCIL REGULATION (EEC) NO 4064/89 ON THE CONTROL OF CONCENTRATIONS BETWEEN UNDERTAKINGS (98/C 66/04)

(Text with EEA relevance)

1. The purpose of this Notice is to expand upon the text of Articles 1 and 5 of Council Regulation (EEC) No 4064/89 ([1]) as last amended by Council Regulation (EC) No 1310/97 ([2]) (hereinafter referred to as 'the Merger Regulation') and in so doing to elucidate certain procedural and practical questions which have caused doubt or difficulty.

2. This Notice is based on the experience gained by the Commission in applying the Merger Regulation to date. The principles it sets out will be followed and further

---

([1]) OJ L 395, 30.12.1989, p. 1; corrected version OJ L 257, 21.9.1990, p. 13.
([2]) OJ L 180, 9.7.1997, p. 1.

developed by the Commission's practice in individual cases. This Notice replaces the Notice on calculation of turnover (^{3}).

3.   The Merger Regulation has a two fold test for Commission jurisdiction. One test is that the transaction must be a concentration within the meaning of Article 3 (^{4}). The second comprises the turnover thresholds contained in Article 1 and designed to identify those transactions which have an impact upon the Community and can be deemed to be of 'Community interest'. Turnover is used as a proxy for the economic resources being combined in a concentration, and is allocated geographically in order to reflect the geographic distribution of those resources.

Two sets of thresholds are set out in Article 1, in paragraph 2 and paragraph 3 respectively. Article 1(2) sets out the thresholds which must first be checked in order to establish whether the transaction has a Community dimension. In this respect, the worldwide turnover threshold is intended to measure the overall dimension of the undertakings concerned; the Community turnover threshold seek to determine whether the concentration involves a minimum level of activities in the Community; and the two-thirds rule aims to exclude purely domestic transactions from Community juris-diction.

Article 1(3) must only be applied in the event that the thresholds set out in Article 1(2) are not met. This second set of thresholds is designed to tackle those transactions which fall short of achieving Community dimension under Article 1(2), but would need to be notified under national competition rules in at least three Member States (so called 'multiple notifications'). For this purpose, Article 1(3) provides for lower turnover thresholds, both worldwide and Community-wide, to be achieved by the undertakings concerned. A concentration has a Community dimension if these lower thresholds are fulfilled and the undertakings concerned achieve jointly and individually a minimum level of activities in at least three Member States. Article 1(3) also contains a two-thirds rule similar to that of Article 1(2) which aims to identify purely domestic transactions.

4.   The thresholds as such are designed to establish jurisdiction and not to assess the market position of the parties to the concentration nor the impact of the operation. In so doing they include turnover derived from, and thus the resources devoted to, all areas of activity of the parties, and not just those directly involved in the concentration. Article 1 of the Merger Regulation sets out the thresholds to be used to determine a concentra-tion with a 'Community dimension' while Article 5 explains how turnover should be calculated.

5.   The fact that the thresholds of Article 1 of the Merger Regulation are purely quantitative, since they are only based on turnover calculation instead of market share or other criteria, shows that their aim is to provide a simple and objective mechanism that can be easily handled by the companies involved in a merger in order to determine if their transaction has a Community dimension and is therefore notifiable.

6.   The decisive issue for Article 1 of the Merger Regulation is to measure the economic strength of the undertakings concerned as reflected in their respective turnover figures, regardless of the sector where such turnover was achieved and of whether those sectors will be at all affected by the transaction in question. The Merger Regulation has thereby given priority to the determination of the overall economic and financial resources that are being combined through the merger in order to decide whether the latter is of Community interest.

(^{3})   OJ C 385, 31.12,1994, p. 21.

(^{4})   See the Notice on the concept of concentration.

7. In this context, it is clear that turnover should reflect as accurately as possible the economic strength of the undertakings involved in a transaction. This is the purpose of the set of rules contained in Article 5 of the Merger Regulation which are designed to ensure that the resulting figures are a true representation of economic reality.

8. The Commission's interpretation of Articles 1 and 5 with respect to calculation of turnover is without prejudice to the interpretation which may be given by the Court of Justice or the Court of First Instance of the European Communities.

I. *'Accounting' calculation of turnover*

1. Turnover as a reflection of activity

1.1. The concept of turnover

9. The concept of turnover as used in Article 5 of the Merger Regulation refers explicitly to 'the amounts derived from the sale of products and the provision of services'. Sale, as a reflection of the undertaking's activity, is thus the essential criterion for calculating turnover, whether for products or the provision of services. 'Amounts derived from sale' generally appear in company accounts under the heading 'sales'.

10. In the case of products, turnover can be determined without difficulty, namely by identifying each commercial act involving a transfer of ownership.

11. In the case of services, the factors to be taken into account in calculating turnover are much more complex, since the commercial act involves a transfer of 'value'.

12. Generally speaking, the method of calculating turnover in the case of services does not differ from that used in the case of products: the Commission takes into consideration the total amount of sales. Where the service provided is sold directly by the provider to the customer, the turnover of the undertaking concerned consists of the total amount of sales for the provision of services in the last financial year.

13. Because of the complexity of the service sector, this general principle may have to be adapted to the specific conditions of the service provided. Thus, in certain sectors of activity (such as tourism and advertising), the service may be sold through the intermediary of other suppliers. Because of the diversity of such sectors, many different situations may arise. For example, the turnover of a service undertaking which acts as an intermediary may consist solely of the amount of commissions which it receives.

14. Similarly, in a number of areas such as credit, financial services and insurance, technical problems in calculating turnover arise which will be dealt with in Section III.

1.2. Ordinary activities

15. Article 5(1) states that the amounts to be included in the calculation of turnover must correspond to the 'ordinary activities' of the undertakings concerned.

16. With regard to aid granted to undertakings by public bodies, any aid relating to one of the ordinary activities of an undertaking concerned is liable to be included in the

calculation of turnover if the undertaking is itself the recipient of the aid and if the aid is directly linked to the sale of products and the provision of services by the undertaking and is therefore reflected in the price ([5]). For example, aid towards the consumption of a product allows the manufacturer to sell at a higher price than that actually paid by consumers.

17. With regard to services, the Commission looks at the undertaking's ordinary activities involved in establishing the resources required for providing the service. In its Decision in the Accor/Wagons-Lits case ([6]), the Commission decided to take into account the item 'other operating proceeds' included in Wagons-Lits's profit and loss account. The Commission considered that the components of this item which included certain income from its car-hire activities were derived from the sale of products and the provision of services by Wagons-Lits and were part of its ordinary activities.

2. 'Net' turnover

18. The turnover to be taken into account is 'net' turnover, after deduction of a number of components specified in the Regulation. The Commission's aim is to adjust turnover in such a way as to enable it to decide on the real economic weight of the undertaking.

2.1. The deduction of rebates and taxes

19. Article 5(1) provides for the 'deduction of sales rebates and of value added tax and other taxes directly related to turnover'. The deductions thus relate to business components (sales rebates) and tax components (value added tax and other taxes directly related to turnover).

20. 'Sales rebates' should be taken to mean all rebates or discounts which are granted by the undertakings during their business negotiations with their customers and which have a direct influence on the amounts of sales.

21. As regards the deduction of taxes, the Merger Regulation refers to VAT and 'other taxes directly related to turnover'. As far as VAT is concerned, its deduction does not in general pose any problem. The concept of 'taxes directly related to turnover' is a clear reference to indirect taxation since it is directly linked to turnover, such as, for example, taxes on alcoholic beverages.

2.2. The deduction of 'internal' turnover

22. The first subparagraph of Article 5(1) states that 'the aggregate turnover of an undertaking concerned shall not include the sale of products or the provision of services between any of the undertakings referred to in paragraph 4', i.e. those which have links with the undertaking concerned (essentially parent companies or subsidiaries).

([5]) See Case IV/M.156 — Cereol/Continentale Italiana of 27 November 1991. In this case, the Commission excluded Community aid from the calculation of turnover because the aid was not intended to support the sale of products manufactured by one of the undertakings involved in the merger, but the producers of the raw materials (grain) used by the undertaking, which specialized in the crushing of grain.

([6]) Case IV/M.126 — Accor/Wagons-Lits, of 28 April 1992.

23. The aim is to exclude the proceeds of business dealings within a group so as to take account of the real economic weight of each entity. Thus, the 'amounts' taken into account by the Merger Regulation reflect only the transactions which take place between the group of undertakings on the one hand and third parties on the other.

3. Adjustment of turnover calculation rules for the different types of operations

3.1. The general rule

24. According to Article 5(1) of the Merger Regulation, aggregate turnover comprises the amounts derived by the undertakings concerned in the preceding financial year from the sale of products and the provision of services. The basic principle is thus that for each undertaking concerned the turnover to be taken into account is the turnover of the closest financial year to the date of the transaction.

25. This provision shows that since there are usually no audited accounts of the year ending the day before the transaction, the closest representation of a whole year of activity of the company in question is the one given by the turnover figures of the most recent financial year.

26. The Commission seeks to base itself upon the most accurate and reliable figures available. As a general rule therefore, the Commission will refer to audited or other definitive accounts. However, in cases where major differences between the Community's accounting standards and those of a non-member country are observed, the Commission may consider it necessary to restate these accounts in accordance with Community standards in respect of turnover. The Commission is, in any case, reluctant to rely on management or any other form of provisional accounts in any but exceptional circumstances (see the next paragraph). Where a concentration takes place within the first months of the year and audited accounts are not yet available for the most recent financial year, the figures to be taken into account are those relating to the previous year. Where there is a major divergence between the two sets of accounts, and in particular, when the final draft figures for the most recent years are available, the Commission may decide to take those draft figures into account.

27. Notwithstanding paragraph 26, an adjustment must always be made to account for acquisitions or divestments subsequent to the date of the audited accounts. This is necessary if the true resources being concentrated are to be identified. Thus if a company disposes of part of its business at any time before the signature of the final agreement or the announcement of the public bid or the acquisition of a controlling interest bringing about a concentration, or where such a divestment or closure is a pre-condition for the operation (⁷) the part of the turnover to be attributed to that part of the business must be subtracted from the turnover of the notifying party as shown in its last audited accounts. Conversely, the turnover to be attributed to assets of which control has been acquired subsequent to the preparation of the most recent audited accounts must be added to a company s turnover for notification purposes.

28. Other factors that may affect turnover on a temporary basis such as a decrease in orders for the product or a slow-down in the production process within the period prior

---

(⁷) See Judgment of the Court of First Instance in Case T-3/93, Air France v Commission, [1994] ECR II-21.

to the transaction will be ignored for the purposes of calculating turnover. No adjustment to the definitive accounts will be made to incorporate them.

29.   Regarding the geographical allocation of turnover, since audited accounts often do not provide a geographical breakdown of the sort required by the Merger Regulation, the Commission will rely on the best figures available provided by the companies in accordance with the rule laid down in Article 5(1) of the Merger Regulation (see Section II.1).

3.2.   Acquisitions of parts of companies

30.   Article 5(2) of the Merger Regulation provides that 'where the concentration consists in the acquisition of parts, whether or not constituted as legal entities, of one or more undertakings, only the turnover relating to the parts which are the subject of the transaction shall be taken into account with regard to the seller or sellers'.

31.   This provision states that when the acquirer does not purchase an entire group, but only one, or part, of its businesses, whether or not constituted as a subsidiary, only the turnover of the part acquired should be included in the turnover calculation. In fact, although in legal terms the seller as a whole (with all its subsidiaries) is an essential party to the transaction, since the sale-purchase agreement cannot be concluded without him, he plays no role once the agreement has been implemented. The possible impact of the transaction on the market will depend only on the combination of the economic and financial resources that are the subject of a property transfer with those of the acquirer and not on the remaining business of the seller who remains independent.

3.3.   Staggered operations

32.   Sometimes certain successive transactions are only individual steps within a wider strategy between the same parties. Considering each transaction alone, even if only for determining jurisdiction, would imply ignoring economic reality. At the same time, whereas some of these staggered operations may be designed in this fashion because they will better meet the needs of the parties, others could be structured like this in order to circumvent the application of the Merger Regulation.

33.   The Merger Regulation has foreseen these scenarios in Article 5(2), second subparagraph, which provides that 'two or more transactions within the meaning of the first subparagraph which take place within a two-year period between the same persons or undertakings shall be treated as one and the same concentration arising on the date of the last transaction'.

34.   In practical terms, this provision means that if company A buys a subsidiary of company B that represents 50% of the overall activity of B and one year later it acquires the other subsidiary (the remaining 50% of B), both transactions will be taken as one. Assuming that each of the subsidiaries attained a turnover in the Community of only ECU 200 million, the first transaction would not be notifiable unless the operation fulfilled the conditions set out in Article 1(3). However, since the second transaction takes place within the two-year period, both have to be notified as a single transaction when the second occurs.

35.   The importance of the provision is that previous transactions (within two years) become notifiable with the most recent transaction once the thresholds are cumulatively met.

3.4. Turnover of groups

36.   When an undertaking concerned in a concentration within the meaning of Article 1 of the Merger Regulation ([8]) belongs to a group, the turnover of the group as a whole is to be taken into account in order to determine whether the thresholds are met. The aim is again to capture the total volume of the economic resources that are being combined through the operation.

37.   The Merger Regulation does not define the concept of group in abstract terms but focuses on whether the companies have the right to manage the undertaking's affairs as the yardstick to determine which of the companies that have some direct or indirect links with an undertaking concerned should be regarded as part of its group.

38.   Article 5(4) of the Merger Regulation provides the following:

'Without prejudice to paragraph 2 [acquisitions of parts], the aggregate turnover of an undertaking concerned within the meaning of Article 1(2) and (3) shall be calculated by adding together the respective turnovers of the following:

    (a)   the undertaking concerned;
    (b)   those undertakings in which the undertaking concerned directly or indirectly:
        —   owns more than half the capital or business assets, or
        —   has the power to exercise more than half the voting rights, or
        —   has the power to appoint more than half the members of the supervisory board, the administrative board or bodies legally representing the undertakings, or
        —   has the right to manage the undertaking's affairs;
    (c)   those undertakings which have in an undertaking concerned the rights or powers listed in (b);
    (d)   those undertakings in which an undertaking as referred to in (c) has the rights or powers listed in (b);
    (e)   those undertakings in which two or more undertakings as referred to in (a) to (d) jointly have the rights or powers listed in (b).'

This means that the turnover of the company directly involved in the transaction (point (a)) should include its subsidiaries (point (b)), its parent companies (point (c)), the other subsidiaries of its parent companies (point (d)) and any other undertaking jointly controlled by two or more of the companies belonging to the group (point (e)). A graphic example is as follows:

([8])   See the Commission Notice on the concept of undertakings concerned.

The undertaking concerned and its group:

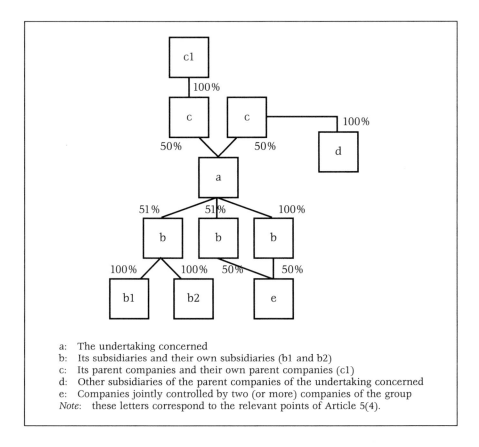

a: The undertaking concerned
b: Its subsidiaries and their own subsidiaries (b1 and b2)
c: Its parent companies and their own parent companies (c1)
d: Other subsidiaries of the parent companies of the undertaking concerned
e: Companies jointly controlled by two (or more) companies of the group
Note: these letters correspond to the relevant points of Article 5(4).

Several remarks can be made from this chart:

1. As long as the test of control of point (b) is fulfilled, the whole turnover of the subsidiary in question will be taken into account regardless of the actual shareholding of the controlling company. In the example, the whole turnover of the three subsidiaries (called b) of the undertaking concerned (a) will be included.

2. When any of the companies identified as belonging to the group also controls others, these should also be incorporated into the calculation. In the example, one of the subsidiaries of a (called b) has in turn its own subsidiaries b1 and b2.

3. When two or more companies jointly control the undertaking concerned (a) in the sense that the agreement of each and all of them is needed in order to manage the undertaking affairs, the turnover of all of them should be included ([9]). In the example, the two parent companies (c) of the undertaking concerned (a) would be taken into account as well as their own parent companies (c1 in the example). Although the

---

([9]) See Commission Notice on the concept of undertakings concerned (paragraphs 26–29).

Merger Regulation does not explicitly mention this rule for those cases where the undertaking concerned is in fact a joint venture, it is inferred from the text of Article 5(4)(c), which uses the plural when referring to the parent companies. This interpretation has been consistently applied by the Commission.

4. Any intra-group sale should be subtracted from the turnover of the group (see paragraph 22).

39. The Merger Regulation also deals with the specific scenario that arises when two or more undertakings concerned in a transaction exercise joint control of another company. Pursuant to point (a) of Article 5(5), the turnover resulting from the sale of products or the provision of services between the joint venture and each of the undertakings concerned or any other company connected with any one of them in the sense of Article 5(4) should be excluded. The purpose of such a rule is to avoid double counting. With regard to the turnover of the joint venture generated from activities with third parties, point (b) of Article 5(5) provides that it should be apportioned equally amongst the undertakings concerned, to reflect the joint control ([10]).

40. Following the principle of point (b) of Article 5(5) by analogy, in the case of joint ventures between undertakings concerned and third parties, the Commission's practice has been to allocate to each of the undertakings concerned the turnover shared equally by all the controlling companies in the joint venture. In all these cases, however, joint control has to be demonstrated.

The practice shows that it is impossible to cover in the present Notice the whole range of scenarios which could arise in respect of turnover calculation of joint venture companies or joint control cases. Whenever ambiguities arise, an assessment should always give priority to the general principles of avoiding double counting and of reflecting as accurately as possible the economic strength of the undertakings involved in the transaction ([11]).

41. It should be noted that Article 5(4) refers only to the groups that already exist at the time of the transaction, i.e. the group of each of the undertakings concerned in an operation, and not to the new structures created as a result of the concentration. For example, if companies A and B, together with their respective subsidiaries, are going to merge, it is A and B, and not the new entity, that qualify as undertakings concerned, which implies that the turnover of each of the two groups should be calculated independently.

42. Since the aim of this provision is simply to identify the companies belonging to the existing groups for the purposes of turnover calculation, the test of having the right to manage the undertaking's affairs in Article 5(4) ([12]) is somewhat different from the test of control set out in Article 3(3), which refers to the acquisition of control carried out by means of the transaction subject to examination. Whereas the former is simpler and easier to prove on the basis of factual evidence, the latter is more demanding because in the absence of an acquisition of control no concentration arises.

([10])   For example, company A and company B set up a joint Venture C. These two parent companies exercise at the same time joint control of company D, although A has 60% and B 40% of the capital. When calculating the turnover of A and B at the time they set up the new joint venture C, the turnover of D with third parties is attributed in equal parts to A and B.

([11])   See for example Case IV/M.806 — BA/TAT, of 26 August 1996.

([12])   See for example Case IV/M.126 — Accor/Wagons-Lits, of 28 April 1992, and Case lV/M.940 — UBS/Mister Minit, of 9 July 1997.

3.5. Turnover of State-owned companies

43. While Article 5(4) sets out the method for determining the economic grouping to which an undertaking concerned belongs for the purpose of calculating turnover, it should be read in conjunction with recital 12 to Regulation (EEC) No 4064/89 in respect of State-owned enterprises. This recital states that in order to avoid discrimination between the public and private sector, account should be taken 'of undertakings making up an economic unit with an independent power of decision, irrespective of the way in which their capital is held or of the rules of administrative supervision applicable to them'. Thus the mere fact that two companies are both State-owned should not automatically lead to the conclusion that they are part of a group for the purposes of Article 5. Rather, it should be considered whether there are grounds to consider that each company constitutes an independent economic unit.

44. Thus where a State-owned company is not part of an overall industrial holding company and is not subject to any coordination with other State-controlled holdings, it should be treated as an independent group for the purposes of Article 5, and the turnover of other companies owned by that State should not be taken into account. Where, however, a Member State's interests are grouped together in holding companies, or are managed together, or where for other reasons it is clear that State-owned companies form part of an 'economic unit with an independent power of decision', then the turnover of those businesses should be considered part of the group of the undertaking concerned's for the purposes of Article 5.

II. *Geographical allocation of turnover*

1. General rule

45. The thresholds other than those set by Article 1(2)(a) and Article 1(3)(a) select cases which have sufficient turnover within the Community in order to be of Community interest and which are primarily cross-border in nature. They require turnover to be allocated geographically to achieve this. The second subparagraph of Article 5(1) provides that the location of turnover is determined by the location of the customer at the time of the transaction:

'Turnover, in the Community or in a Member State, shall comprise products sold and services provided to undertakings or consumers, in the Community or in that Member State as the case may be.'

46. The reference to 'products sold' and 'services provided' is not intended to discriminate between goods and services by focusing on where the sale takes place in the case of goods but the place where a service is provided (which might be different from where the service was sold) in the case of services. In both cases, turnover should be attributed to the place where the customer is located because that is, in most circumstances, where a deal was made, where the turnover for the supplier in question was generated and where competition with alternative suppliers took place ([13]). The second subparagraph of Article 5(1) does not focus on where a goal or service is enjoyed or the benefit of the good or service derived. In the case of a mobile good, a motor car may well be driven across Europe by its purchaser but it was purchased at only one place — Paris, Berlin or

---

([13]) If the place where the customer was located when purchasing the goods or service and the place where the billing was subsequently made are different, turnover should be allocated to the former.

Madrid say. This is also true in the case of those services where it is possible to separate the purchase of a service from its delivery. Thus in the case of package holidays, competition for the sale of holidays through travel agents takes place locally, as with retail shopping, even though the service may be provided in a number of distant locations. This turnover is, however, earned locally and not at the site of an eventual holiday.

47. This applies even where a multinational corporation has a Community buying strategy and sources all its requirements for a good or service from one location. The fact that the components are subsequently used in ten different plants in a variety of Member States does not alter the fact that the transaction with a company outside the group occurred in only one country. The subsequent distribution to other sites is purely an internal question for the company concerned.

48. Certain sectors do, however, pose very particular problems with regard to the geographical allocation of turnover (see Section III).

2. Conversion of turnover into ecu

49. When converting turnover figures into ecu great care should be taken with the exchange rate used. The annual turnover of a company should be converted at the average rate for the twelve months concerned. This average can be obtained from the Commission. The audited annual turnover figures should not be broken down into component quarterly, monthly, or weekly sales figures which are converted individually at the corresponding average quarterly, monthly or weekly rates, with the ecu figures then added to give a total for the year.

50. When a company has sales in a range of currencies, the procedure is no different. The total turnover given in the consolidated audited accounts and in that company's reporting currency is converted into ecu at the average rate for the twelve months. Local currency sales should not be converted directly into ecu since these figures are not from the consolidated audited accounts of the company.

III. *Credit and other financial institutions and insurance undertakings*

1. Definitions

51. The specific nature of banking and insurance activities is formally recognized by the Merger Regulation which includes specific provisions dealing with the calculation of turnover for these sectors ([14]). Although the Merger Regulation does not provide a definition of the terms, 'credit institutions and other financial institutions' within the meaning of point (a) of Article 5(3), the Commission in its practice has consistently adopted the definitions provided in the First and Second Banking Directives:

— 'Credit institution means an undertaking whose business is to receive deposits or other repayable funds from the public and to grant credits for its own account ([15])'.

([14]) See Article 5(3) of the Merger Regulation.
([15]) Article 1 of First Council Directive 77/780/EEC of 12 December 1977 on the coordination of laws, regulations and administrative provisions relating to the taking up and pursuit of the business of credit institutions (OJ L 322, 17.12.1977, p. 30).

— 'Financial institution shall mean an undertaking other than a credit institution, the principal activity of which is to acquire holdings or to carry one or more of the activities listed in points 2 to 12 in the Annex ([16])'.

52. From the definition of 'financial institution' given above, it is clear that on the one hand holding companies must be regarded as financial institutions and, on the other hand, that undertakings which perform on a regular basis as a principal activity one or more activities expressly mentioned in points 2 to 12 of the abovementioned Annex must also be regarded as financial institutions within the meaning of point (a) of Article 5(3) of the Merger Regulation. These activities include:

— lending (*inter alia*, consumer credit, mortgage credit, factoring, . . .),
— financial leasing,
— money transmission services,
— issuing and managing instruments of payment (credit cards, travellers' cheques and bankers' drafts),
— guarantees and commitments,
— trading on own account or on account of customers in money market instruments, foreign exchange, financial futures and options, exchange and interest rate instruments, and transferable securities,
— participation in share issues and the provision of services related to such issues,
— advice to undertakings on capital structure, industrial strategy and related questions and advice and services relating to mergers and the purchase of undertakings,
— money broking,
— portfolio management and advice,
— safekeeping and administration of securities.

2. Calculation of turnover

53. The methods of calculation of turnover for credit and other financial institutions and for insurance undertakings are described in Article 5(3) of the Merger Regulation. The purpose of this Section is to provide an answer to supplementary questions related to turnover calculation for the abovementioned types of undertakings which were raised during the first years of the application of the Merger Regulation.

2.1. Credit and financial institutions (other than financial holding companies)

2.1.1. General

54. There are normally no particular difficulties in applying the banking income criterion for the definition of the worldwide turnover to credit institutions and other kinds of financial institutions. Difficulties may arise for determining turnover within the Community and also within individual Member States. For this purpose, the appropriate criterion is that of the residence of the branch or division, as provided by Article 5(3)(a)(v), second subparagraph, of the Merger Regulation.

([16]) Article 1(6) of Second Council Directive 89/646/EEC of 15 December 1989 on the coordination of laws, regulations and administrative provisions relating to the taking up and pursuit of the business of credit institutions (OJ L 386, 30.12.1989, p. 1).

2.1.2. Turnover of leasing companies

55. There is a fundamental distinction to be made between financial leases and operating leases. Basically, financial leases are made for longer periods than operating leases and ownership is generally transferred to the lessee at the end of the lease term by means of a purchase option included in the lease contract. Under an operating lease, on the contrary, ownership is not transferred to the lessee at the end of the lease term and the costs of maintenance, repair and insurance of the leased equipment are included in the lease payments. A financial lease therefore functions as a loan by the lessor to enable the lessee to purchase a given asset. A financial leasing company is thus a financial institution within the meaning of point (a) of Article 5(3) and its turnover has to be calculated by applying the specific rules related to the calculation of turnover for credit and other financial institutions. Given that operational leasing activities do not have this lending function, they are not considered as carried out by financial institutions, at least as primary activities, and therefore the general turnover calculation rules of Article 5(1) should apply ([17]).

2.2. Insurance undertakings

2.2.1. Gross premiums written

56. The application of the concept of gross premiums written as a measure of turnover for insurance undertakings has raised supplementary questions notwithstanding the definition provided in point (b) of Article 5(3) of the Merger Regulation. The following clarifications are appropriate:

— 'gross' premiums written are the sum of received premiums (which may include received reinsurance premiums if the undertaking concerned has activities, in the field of reinsurance). Outgoing or outward reinsurance premiums, i.e. all amounts paid and payable by the undertaking concerned to get reinsurance cover, are already included in the gross premiums written within the meaning of the Merger Regulation,

— wherever the word 'premiums' is used (gross premiums, net (earned) premiums, outgoing reinsurance premiums, etc.), these premiums are related not only to new insurance contracts made during the accounting year being considered but also to all premiums related to contracts made in previous years which remain in force during the period taken into consideration.

2.2.2. Investments of insurance undertakings

57. In order to constitute appropriate reserves allowing for the payment of claims, insurance undertakings, which are also considered as institutional investors, usually hold a huge portfolio of investments in shares, interest-bearing securities, land and property and other assets which provide an annual revenue which is not considered as turnover for insurance undertakings.

58. With regard to the application of the Merger Regulation, a major distinction should be made between pure financial investments, in which the insurance undertaking is not

---

([17])   See Case IV/M.234 — GECC/Avis Lease, 15 July 1992.

involved in the management of the undertakings where the investments have been made, and those investments leading to the acquisition of an interest giving control in a given undertaking thus allowing the insurance undertaking to exert a decisive influence on the business conduct of the subsidiary or affiliated company concerned. In such cases Article 5(4) of the Merger Regulation would apply, and the turnover of the subsidiary or affiliated company should be added to the turnover of the insurance undertaking for the determination of the thresholds laid down in the Merger Regulation ([18]).

2.3. Financial holding companies ([19])

59. A financial holding company is a financial institution and therefore the calculation of its turnover should follow the criteria established in point (a) of Article 5(3) for the calculation of turnover for credit and other financial institutions. However, since the main purpose of a financial holding is to acquire and manage participation in other undertakings, Article 5(4) also applies, (as for insurance undertakings), with regard to those participations allowing the financial holding company to exercise a decisive influence on the business conduct of the undertakings in question. Thus, the turnover of a financial holding is basically to be calculated according to Article 5(3), but it may be necessary to add turnover of undertakings falling within the categories set out in Article 5(4) ('Article 5(4) companies').

In practice, the turnover of the financial holding company (non-consolidated) must first be taken into account. Then the turnover of the Article 5(4) companies must be added, whilst taking care to deduct dividends and other income distributed by those companies to the financial holdings. The following provides an example for this kind of calculation:

		ECU million
1.	Turnover related to financial activities (from non-consolidated P&L)	3 000
2.	Turnover related to insurance Article 5(4) companies (gross premiums written)	300
3.	Turnover of industrial Article 5(4) companies	2 000
4.	Deduct dividends and other income derived from Article 5(4) companies 2 and 3	(200)
5.	Total turnover financial holding and its group	5 100

60. In such calculations different accounting rules, in particular those related to the preparation of consolidated accounts, which are to some extent harmonised but not identical within the Community, may need to be taken into consideration. Whilst this consideration applies to any type of undertaking concerned by the Merger Regulation, it is particularly important in the case of financial holding companies ([20]) where the number and the diversity of enterprises controlled and the degree of control the holding holds on its subsidiaries, affiliated companies and other companies in which it has shareholding requires careful examination.

61. Turnover calculation for financial holding companies as described above may in practice prove onerous. Therefore a strict and detailed application of this method will be

---

([18]) See Case IV/M.018 — AG/AMEV, of 21 November 1990.

([19]) The principles set out in this paragraph for financial holdings may to a certain extent be applied to fund management companies.

([20]) See for example Case IV/M.166 — Torras/Sarrió, of 24 February 1992, Case IV/M.213 — Hong Kong and Shanghai Bank/Midland, of 21 May 1992, IV/M.192 — Banesto/Totta, of 14 April 1992.

necessary only in cases where it seems that the turnover of a financial holding company is likely to be close to the Merger Regulation thresholds; in other cases it may well be obvious that the turnover is far from the thresholds of the Merger Regulation, and therefore the published accounts are adequate for the establishment of jurisdiction.

ANNEX 7

COMMISSION NOTICE CONCERNING ALIGNMENT OF PROCEDURES FOR PROCESSING MERGERS UNDER THE ECSC AND EC TREATIES (98/C 66/05)

(Text with EEA relevance)

I. *Introduction*

1. The following provisions relate to mergers governed by the ECSC Treaty. They are designed to increase transparency and improve compliance with the rights of the defence in connection with the examination of such mergers and to expedite decisions making. To this end, they are based on an alignment of certain rules with those governing mergers covered by Council Regulation (EEC) No 4064/89 of 21 December 1989 on the control of concentrations between undertakings ([1]).

2. The Commission hopes, in this context, to meet the expectations of undertakings, in particular as regards merger operations which are covered by the ECSC and EC Treaties at the same time. This notice should also be seen as an attempt at simplification, albeit within the limits imposed by having two separate treaties. The rules thus introduced should make it possible for ECSC undertakings to familiarise themselves with the procedures of law against the background of the forthcoming expiry of the ECSC Treaty.

II. *Main procedural changes envisaged with regard to merger control pursuant to the ECSC treaty*

Publication of the fact of notification

3. The Commission will from now on publish in the *Official Journal of the European Communities* the fact of notification in the case of mergers covered by the ECSC Treaty. It will state in particular the names of the interested parties, the nature of the merger operation and the economic sectors concerned. Publication will take account of the legitimate interest of undertakings in not having their business secrets divulged.

([1]) OJ L 395, 30.12.1989, p. 1; corrected version: OJ L 257, 21.9.1990, p. 14.

Statement of objections where the Commission plans to subject the authorisation of a merger to conditions or even to prohibit an operation

4.   The sending of a statement of objections prior to the conditional authorisation or prohibition of a merger does not appear explicitly in Article 66 of the ECSC Treaty. It is provided for only in the event of a pecuniary sanction (Article 36 of the ECSC Treaty) or of a decision requiring a demerger or other measures designed to restore effective competition where a merger has already been carried out (second paragraph of Article 66(5) of the ECSC Treaty). The Commission believes, however, that it can commit itself to sending such a statement in pursuance of the general principle of the protection of the rights of the defence, which is recognised by the Court as a general principle of Community law. It will therefore base its decisions only on those objections on which the interested parties have been able to express their views.

Of course, this does not prevent the Commission from allowing undertakings to alter their merger proposals on their own initiative, thus making it unnecessary to send a statement of objections, in particular where the competition problem perceived is easily identifiable, limited in scope and easy to resolve, as currently happens in the Community field.

Access to the file and possibility of making oral observations (hearing)

5.   The possibility of access to the Commission file and making oral observations (at a hearing) when a statement of objections has been sent is the logical consequence of such a statement. Accordingly, the Commission confirms that it will give such an opportunity to interested natural or legal persons. It will apply in this context, and by analogy, the rules in Articles 14 to 16 of Commission Regulation (EC) No 3384/94 of 21 December 1994 on the notification, time-limits and hearings provided for in Council Regulation (EEC) No 4064/89 on the control of concentrations between undertakings ([2]), which is an implementing regulation, and in accordance with Commission Decision 94/810/ECSC, EC of 12 December 1994 on the terms of reference of hearing officers in competition procedures before the Commission ([3]) and the Commission notice on the internal rules of procedure for processing requests for access to the file in cases pursuant to Articles 85 and 86 of the EC Treaty, Articles 65 and 66 of the ECSC Treaty and Council Regulation (EEC) No 4064/89 ([4]).

Publication in the *Official Journal of the European Communities* of the final decisions adopted after communication of the objections, and the public nature of all authorisation decisions

6.   Final decisions adopted after the objections have been communicated will be systematically published in the *Official Journal of the European Communities*. Similarly, all authorisation decisions will be made public. Publication will respect business secrecy in accordance with Article 47 of the ECSC Treaty.

([2])   OJ L 377, 31.12.1994, p. 1.
([3])   OJ L 330, 21.12.1994, p. 67.
([4])   OJ C 23, 23.1.1997, p. 3.

Time-limits

7.   A statement of objections will be sent at the latest within ten weeks of notification of the merger operation. The final decision, where a statement of objections has been sent, will be taken at the latest within five months of notification. These time-limits presuppose that undertakings use form CO annexed to Regulation (EC) No 3384/94 and supply the Commission with five copies of the notification. Where the Commission considers it unnecessary to send a statement of objections, it will endeavour to adopt its decision within one month of notification.

8.   As regards the effective date of notification, the Commission will apply by analogy the provisions of Article 4 of the abovementioned Regulation (EC) No 3384/94. As far as the application of paragraph 5 of that Article is concerned, the terms 'pursuant to Article 4(3) of Regulation (EEC) No 4064/89' are to be read as 'pursuant to point 3 of this notice'. As regards the time-limits of ten weeks and five months mentioned at point 7 above, these will start to run on the working day following that on which the notification becomes effective. The time-limit of ten weeks will end on the same weekday as that on which it commenced. The time-limit of five months will end on the same numerical date as that of its commencement: where no such date occurs in that month, the time-limit will end with the expiry of the last day of the month. Where the last day is not a working day, the time-limit will end with the expiry of the first working day which follows. Working days are taken into account in the time-limits, in accordance with the rules laid down in Article 8 of the abovementioned Regulation (EC) No 3384/94 and are defined in the same way as in Article 22 of that Regulation.

9.   The Commission will give favourable consideration to requests for dispensation from supplying certain information required in the form CO where those requests are submitted to it in a prenotification, limiting the information required to that which is strictly necessary for examining the cases.

III.   *Implementation*

10.   The Commission will apply the above rules, where they are not already in force, to notified mergers from 1 March 1998.

ANNEX 8

INFORMATION ON THE ASSESSMENT OF FULL-FUNCTION JOINT VENTURES PURSUANT TO THE COMPETITION RULES OF THE EUROPEAN COMMUNITY (98/C 66/06)

(Text with EEA relevance)

By Council Regulation (EC) No 1310/97 of 30 June 1997, which amended Regulation (EEC) No 4064/89 on the control of concentrations between undertakings (¹), all full-function joint ventures which have a Community dimension and have as their object or effect the coordination of the competitive behaviour of undertakings that remain independent were included in the scope of the latter Regulation. Consequently, such joint ventures will no longer fall under the provisions of Council Regulations No 17 (²), (EEC) No 1017/68 (³), (EEC) No 4056/86 (⁴) and (EEC) No 3975/87 (⁵). Hence, the regulations that the Commission adopted for the implementation of those Council Regulations, namely Regulations (EC) No 3385/94 (⁶), No 99/63/EEC (⁷), (EEC) No 1629/69 (⁸), (EEC) No 1630/69 (⁹), (EEC) No 4260/88 (¹⁰) and (EEC) No 4261/88 (¹¹), and in particular their provisions concerning communications, complaints, applications and notifications, also cease to be applicable to these joint ventures. Forms A/B, I, II and III, MAR as well as AER will be adapted to the new legal situation.

There is no change in the provisions applicable to joint ventures other than those described above, namely those full-function joint ventures which do not have a Community dimension within the meaning of the amended Regulation (EEC) No 4046/89 and which have as their object or effect the coordination of the competitive behaviour of undertakings that remain independent, as well as non-full-function joint ventures.

(¹)   OJ L 180, 9.7.1997, p. 1.
(²)   OJ 13, 20.2.1962, p. 204/62 (Special Edition 1959–62, p. 87).
(³)   OJ L 175, 23.7.1968, p. 1 (Special Edition. 1968 1, p. 302).
(⁴)   OJ L 378, 31.12.1986, p. 4.
(⁵)   OJ L 374, 31.12.1987, p. 1.
(⁶)   OJ L 377, 31.12.1994, p. 28.
(⁷)   OJ 127, 20.8.1963, p. 2268/63 (Special Edition 1963–64, p. 47).
(⁸)   OJ L 209, 21.8.1969, p. 1 (Special Edition 1969 II, p. 371).
(⁹)   OJ L 209, 21.8.1969, p. 11 (Special Edition 1969 II, p. 381).
(¹⁰) OJ L 376, 31.12.1988, p. 1.
(¹¹) OJ L 376, 31.12.1988, p. 10.

ANNEX 9

COMMISSION NOTICE REGARDING RESTRICTIONS ANCILLARY TO CONCENTRATIONS (90/C 203/05)

I. Introduction

1.   Council Regulation (EEC) No 4064/89 of 21 December 1989 on the control of concentrations between undertakings ('the Regulation') (^{1}) states in its 25th recital that its application is not excluded where the undertakings concerned accept restrictions which are directly related and necessary to the implementation of the concentration, hereinafter referred to as 'ancillary restrictions'. In the scheme of the Regulation, such restrictions are to be assessed together with the concentration itself. It follows, as confirmed by Article 8(2), second subparagraph, last sentence of the Regulation, that a decision declaring the concentration compatible also covers these restrictions. In this situation, under the provisions of Article 22, paragraphs 1 and 2, the Regulation is solely applicable, to the exclusion of Regulation No 17 (^{2}) as well as Regulations (EEC) No 1017/68 (^{3}), (EEC) No 4056/86 (^{4}) and (EEC) No 3975/87 (^{5}). This avoids parallel Commission proceedings, one concerned with the assessment of the concentration under the Regulation, and the other aimed at the application of Articles 85 and 86 to the restrictions which are ancillary to the concentration.

2.   In this notice, the Commission sets out to indicate the interpretation it gives to the notion of 'restrictions directly related and necessary to the implementation of the concentration'. Under the Regulation such restrictions must be assessed in relation to the concentration, whatever their treatment might be under Articles 85 and 86 if they were to be considered in isolation or in a different economic context. The Commission endeavours, within the limits set by the Regulation, to take the greatest account of business practice and of the conditions necessary for the implementation of concentrations.

This notice is without prejudice to the interpretation which may be given by the Court of Justice of the European Communities.

(^{1})   OJ No L 395, 30. 12. 1989, p. 1.
(^{2})   OJ No 13, 21. 2. 1962, p. 204/62.
(^{3})   OJ No L 175, 23. 7. 1968, p. 1.
(^{4})   OJ No L 378, 31. 12. 1986, p. 4.
(^{5})   OJ No L 374, 31. 12. 1987, p. 1.

II. Principles of evaluation

3.   The 'restrictions' meant are those agreed on between the parties to the concentration which limit their own freedom of action in the market. They do not include restrictions to the detriment of third parties. If such restrictions are the inevitable consequence of the concentration itself, they must be assessed together with it under the provisions of Article 2 of the Regulation. If, on the contrary, such restrictive effects on third parties are separable from the concentration they may, if appropriate, be the subject of an assessment of compatibility with Articles 85 and 86 of the EEC Treaty.

4.   For restrictions to be considered 'directly related' they must be ancillary to the implementation of the concentration, that is to say subordinate in importance to the main object of the concentration. They cannot be substantial restrictions wholly different in nature from those which result from the concentration itself. Neither are they contractual arrangements which are among the elements constituting the concentration, such as those establishing economic unity between previously independent parties, or organizing joint control by two undertakings of another undertaking. As integral parts of the concentration, the latter arrangements constitute the very subject matter of the evaluation to be carried out under the Regulation.

Also excluded, for concentrations which are carried out in stages, are the contractual arrangements relating to the stages before the establishment of control within the meaning of Article 3, paragraphs 1 and 3 of the Regulation. For these, Articles 85 and 86 remain applicable as long as the conditions set out in Article 3 are not fulfilled.

The notion of directly related restrictions likewise excludes from the application of the Regulation additional restrictions agreed at the same time which have no direct link with the concentration. It is not enough that the additional restrictions exist in the same context as the concentration.

5.   The restrictions must likewise be 'necessary to the implementation of the concentration', which means that in their absence the concentration could not be implemented or could only be implemented under more uncertain conditions, at substantially higher cost, over an appreciably longer period or with considerably less probability of success. This must be judged on an objective basis.

6.   The question of whether a restriction meets these conditions cannot be answered in general terms. In particular as concerns the necessity of the restriction, it is proper not only to take account of its nature, but equally to ensure, in applying the rule of proportionality, that its duration and subject matter, and geographic field of application, do not exceed what the implementation of the concentration reasonably requires. If alternatives are available for the attainment of the legitimate aim pursued, the undertakings must choose the one which is objectively the least restrictive of competition.

These principles will be followed and further developed by the Commission's practice in individual cases. However, it is already possible, on the basis of past experience, to indicate the attitude the Commission will take to those restrictions most commonly encountered in relation to the transfer of undertakings or parts of undertakings, the division of undertakings or of their assets following a joint acquisition of control, or the creation of concentrative joint ventures.

III. Evaluation of common ancillary restrictions in cases of the transfer of an undertaking

A. Non-competition cases

1.   Among the ancillary restrictions which meet the criteria set out in the Regulation are contractual prohibitions on competition which are imposed on the vendor in the context of a concentration achieved by the transfer of an undertaking or part of an undertaking. Such prohibitions guarantee the transfer to the acquirer of the full value of the assets transferred, which in general include both physical assets and intangible assets such as the goodwill which the vendor has accumulated or the know-how he has developed. These are not only directly related to the concentration, but are also necessary for its implementation because, in their absence, there would be reasonable grounds to expect that the sale of the undertaking or part of an undertaking could not be accomplished satisfactorily. In order to take over fully the value of the assets transferred, the acquirer must be able to benefit from some protection against competitive acts of the vendor in order to gain the loyalty of customers and to assimilate and exploit the know-how. Such protection cannot generally be considered necessary when *de facto* the transfer is limited to physical assets (such as land, buildings or machinery) or to exclusive industrial and commercial property rights (the holders of which could immediately take action against infringements by the transferor of such rights).

However, such a prohibition on competition is justified by the legitimate objective sought of implementing the concentration only when its duration, its geographical field of application, its subject matter and the persons subject to it do not exceed what is reasonably necessary to that end.

2.   With regard to the acceptable duration of a prohibition on competition, a period of five years has been recognized as appropriate when the transfer of the undertaking includes the goodwill and know-how, and a period of two years when it includes only the goodwill. However, these are not absolute rules; they do not preclude a prohibition of longer duration in particular circumstances, where for example the parties can demonstrate that customer loyalty will persist for a period longer than two years or that the economic life cycle of the products concerned is longer than five years and should be taken into account.

3.   The geographic scope of the non-competition clause must be limited to the area where the vendor had established the products or services before the transfer. It does not appear objectively necessary that the acquirer be protected from competition by the vendor in territories which the vendor had not previously penetrated.

4.   In the same manner, the non-competition clause must be limited to products and services which form the economic activity of the undertaking transferred. In particular, in the case of a partial transfer of assets, it does not appear that the acquirer needs to be protected from the competition of the vendor in the products or services which constitute the activities which the vendor retains after the transfer.

5.   The vendor may bind himself, his subsidiaries and commercial agents. However, an obligation to impose similar restrictions on others would not qualify as an ancillary restriction. This applies in particular to clauses which would restrict the scope for resellers or users to import or export.

6.   Any protection of the vendor is not normally an ancillary restriction and is therefore to be examined under Articles 85 and 86 of the EEC Treaty.

B.   Licences of industrial and commercial property rights and of know-how

1.   The implementation of a transfer of an undertaking or part of an undertaking generally includes the transfer to the acquirer, with a view to the full exploitation of the assets transferred, of rights to industrial or commercial property or know-how. However, the vendor may remain the owner of the rights in order to exploit them for activities other than those transferred. In these cases, the usual means for ensuring that the acquirer will have the full use of the assets transferred is to conclude licensing agreements in his favour.

2.   Simple or exclusive licences of patents, similar rights or existing know-how can be accepted as necessary for the completion of the transaction, and likewise agreements to grant such licences. They may be limited to certain fields of use, to the extent that they correspond to the activities of the undertaking transferred. Normally it will not be necessary for such licences to include territorial limitations on manufacture which reflect the territory of the activity transferred. Licences may be granted for the whole duration of the patent or similar rights or the duration of the normal economic life of the know-how. As such licences are economically equivalent to a partial transfer of rights, they need not be limited in time.

3.   Restrictions in licence agreements, going beyond what is provided above, fall outside the scope of the Regulation. They must be assessed on their merits according to Article 85(1) and (3). Accordingly, where they fulfil the conditions required, they may benefit from the block exemptions provided for by Regulation (EEC) No 2349/84 on patent licences ([6]) or Regulation (EEC) No 559/89 on know-how licences ([7]).

4.   The same principles are to be applied by analogy in the case of licences of trademarks, business names or similar rights. There may be situations where the vendor wishes to remain the owner of such rights in relation to activities retained, but the acquirer needs the rights to use them to market the products constituting the object of the activity of the undertaking or part of an undertaking transferred.

In such circumstances, the conclusion of agreements for the purpose of avoiding confusion between trademarks may be necessary.

C.   Purchase and supply agreements

1.   In many cases, the transfer of an undertaking or part of an undertaking can entail the disruption of traditional lines of internal procurement and supply resulting from the previous integration of activities within the economic entity of the vendor. To make possible the break up of the economic unity of the vendor and the partial transfer of the assets to the acquirer under reasonable conditions, it is often necessary to maintain, at least for a transitional period, similar links between the vendor and the acquirer. This objective is normally attained by the conclusion of purchase and supply agreements between the vendor and the acquirer of the undertaking or part of an undertaking. Taking account of the particular situation resulting from the break up of the economic unity of the vendor such obligations, which may lead to restrictions of competition, can be recognized as ancillary. They may be in favour of the vendor as well as the acquirer.

([6])   OJ No L 219, 16. 8. 1984, p. 15.
([7])   OJ No L 61, 4. 3. 1989, p. 1.

2.   The legitimate aim of such obligations may be to ensure the continuity of supply to one or other of the parties of products necessary to the activities retained (for the vendor) or taken over (for the acquirer). Thus, there are grounds for recognizing, for a transitional period, the need for supply obligations aimed at guaranteeing the quantities previously supplied within the vendor's integrated business or enabling their adjustment in accordance with the development of the market.

Their aim may also be to provide continuity of outlets for one or the other of the parties, as they were previously assured within the single economic entity. For the same reason, obligations providing for fixed quantities, possibly with a variation clause, may be recognized as necessary.

3.   However, there does not appear to be a general justification for exclusive purchase or supply obligations. Save in exceptional circumstances, for example resulting from the absence of a market or the specificity of products, such exclusivity is not objectively necessary to permit the implementation of a concentration in the form of a transfer of an undertaking or part of an undertaking.

In any event, in accordance with the principle of proportionality, the undertakings concerned are bound to consider whether there are no alternative means to the ends pursued, such as agreements for fixed quantities, which are less restrictive than exclusivity.

4.   As for the duration of procurement and supply obligations, this must be limited to a period necessary for the replacement of the relationship of dependency by autonomy in market. The duration of such a period must be objectively justified.

IV.   Evaluation of ancillary restrictions in the case of a joint acquisition

1.   As set out in the 24th recital, the Regulation is applicable when two or more undertakings agree to acquire jointly the control of one or more other undertakings, in particular by means of a public tender offer, where the object or effect is the division among themselves of the undertakings or their assets. This is a concentration implemented in two successive stages; the common strategy is limited to the acquisition of control. For the transaction to be concentrative, the joint acquisition must be followed by a clear separation of the undertakings or assets concerned.

2.   For this purpose, an agreement by the joint acquirers of an undertaking to abstain from making separate competing offers for the same undertaking, or otherwise acquiring control, may be considered an ancillary restriction.

3.   Restrictions limited to putting the division into effect are to be considered directly related and necessary to the implementation of the concentration. This will apply to arrangements made between the parties for the joint acquisition of control in order to divide among themselves the production facilities or the distribution networks together with the existing trademarks of the undertaking acquired in common. The implementation of this division may not in any circumstances lead to the coordination of the future behaviour of the acquiring undertakings.

4.   To the extent that such a division involves the break up of a pre-existing economic entity, arrangements that make the break up possible under reasonable conditions must be considered ancillary. In this regard, the principles explained above in relation to purchase and supply arrangements over a transitional period in cases of transfer of undertakings should be applied by analogy.

V. Evaluation of ancillary restrictions in cases of concentrative joint ventures within the meaning of Article 3(2) subparagraph 2 of the Regulation

This evaluation must take account of the characteristics peculiar to concentrative joint ventures, the constituent elements of which are the creation of an autonomous economic entity exercising on a long-term basis all the functions of an undertaking, and the absence of coordination of competitive behaviour between the parent undertakings and between them and the joint venture. This condition implies in principle the withdrawal of the parent undertakings from the market assigned to the joint venture and, therefore, their disappearance as actual or potential competitors of the new entity.

A. Non-competition obligations

To the extent that a prohibition on the parent undertakings competing with the joint venture aims at expressing the reality of the lasting withdrawal of the parents from the market assigned to the joint venture, it will be recognized as an integral part of the concentration.

B. Licences for industrial and commercial property rights and know-how

The creation of a new autonomous economic entity usually involves the transfer of the technology necessary for carrying on the activities assigned to it, in the form of a transfer of rights and related know-how. Where the parent undertakings intend nonetheless to retain the property rights, particularly with the aim of exploitation in other fields of use, the transfer of technology to the joint venture may be accomplished by means of licences. Such licences may be exclusive, without having to be limited in duration or territory, for they serve only as a substitute for the transfer of property rights. They must therefore be considered necessary to the implementation of the concentration.

C. Purchase and supply obligations

If the parent undertakings remain present in a market upstream or downstream of that of the joint venture, any purchase and supply agreements are to be examined in accordance with the principles applicable in the case of the transfer of an undertaking.

ANNEX 10

MERGER: BEST PRACTICE GUIDELINES

One of the fundamental principles underlying the EC Merger Regulation is that in all cases that do not involve «serious doubts», a clearance decision is taken by the Commission within one month from notification. The confidence of European industry and of legal practitioners in the Commission's regulation of mergers is dependent on the Commission being able to process the majority of cases that do not raise competition issues within the one month period.

Declarations of incompleteness under Article 4(2) of the Implementing Regulation have only been made in a few cases (17 cases out of a total of 172 notifications in 1997 and 17 cases out of a total of 196 notifications until 13.11.1998).

However there has been a certain increase in declarations of incompleteness in recent years. Members of the ECLF Committee have had an open discussion with the Merger Task Force with a view to coming to a better understanding of the reasons for these declarations.

We have been informed that declarations according to Article 4(2) are still only made in exceptional circumstances. The Merger Task Force has explained that notifications have been declared incomplete for principally the following reasons:

- In some cases it was not technically possible to accept a notification. These cases include for example notifications made by two parties while they should have been made by three or more parties, or notifications made before there were sufficiently clear legally binding agreements.
- A number of notifications have been poor in terms of the drafting and adequacy of the information provided.
- In some cases the Merger Task Force has identified late during the one month period potential affected markets that should have been identified by the notifying parties in good faith during the pre-notification stage and in the notification itself.

As a more general point, it was explained that in a number of cases in which the notification has been declared incomplete the notification was not preceded by a pre-notification contact, or such contact has been very limited. The consequence of this is that in the absence of any pre-notification discussions there is a higher risk of a declaration of incompleteness.

It is in the interests of the Commission, European business and the legal community to ensure that declarations of incompleteness are kept to the minimum. With this in mind, we have developed the following best practice guidelines in consultation with the

Merger Task Force. We recognise that it will not be possible for notifying parties to follow these guidelines in all circumstances.

Guidelines

- It is always appropriate even in straightforward cases to have pre-notification contacts with the Merger Task Force case team. Notifying parties should submit a briefing memorandum at least three working days before a first meeting. This first meeting should take place preferably at least one or two weeks before the expected date of notification. In more difficult cases, a more protracted pre-notification period may well be appropriate.
  Following this first meeting, the parties should provide before notification the Merger Task Force with a substantially complete draft Form CO. The Merger Task Force should be given in general one week to review the draft before a further meeting or being asked to comment on the phone on the adequacy of the draft.
- At pre-notification meetings, a discussion should take place on what should and what should not be included in the notification. Indeed, it may not be necessary to provide all information specified in *Form CO*. However all requests to omit any part of the information specified should be discussed in detail and agreed with the Merger Task Force beforehand.
- Potentially affected markets should be openly discussed with the case team in good faith, even if the notifying parties take a different view on market definition. Furthermore, wherever there may be uncertainty or differences of view over market definitions, it will be more prudent to produce market shares on one or more alternative basis — e.g. by national markets as well as by an EU-wide-one.
- Notifying parties and their advisers should take care to ensure that the information contained in Form CO has been carefully prepared and verified. Contact details for customers and competitors should be carefully checked to ensure that the Merger Task Force's investigations are not delayed.
- At meetings in general (both at the pre-notification stage and during notification), it is preferable that cases are discussed with both legal advisers and business representatives who have a good understanding of the relevant markets.

Provided these guidelines are complied with, the Merger Task Force case team will in principle be prepared to confirm informally the adequacy of a draft notification at the pre-notification stage or, if appropriate to identify in what specific respects it is incomplete.

Despite these guidelines, we recognise that it will not be possible for the Merger Task Force to exclude the fact that it may have to declare a notification incomplete in appropriate cases.

Annex 11

NATIONAL AUTHORITIES DEALING WITH MERGERS

Austria:

Oberlandesgericht Wien als Kartellgericht
Justizpalast
Schmerlingplatz 11
1016 Vienna
Austria
Tel: +43 1 52152 3566
Fax: +43 1 52152 3690
(President: Eckhart Hermann)

Belgium:

Conseil de la Concurrence
North Gate III
Boulevard Emile Jacqmain 154
Brussels 1000
Belgium
Tel: +32 2 206 5227
Fax: +32 2 206 5773
(President: Christine Schurmans)

Denmark:

Konkurrencertyreltyrelsen
Nørregade 49
1165 Copenhagen
Denmark
Tel: +45 33 177 000
Fax: +45 33 326 144
(Director General: Finn Lauritzen

Finland:

Kilpailuvirasto
Pitkansillanranta 3
PO Box 332
00530 Helsinki
Finland
Tel: +358 9 73141
Fax: +358 9 73143328
(Director General: Matti Purasjoki)

France:

Ministere de l'Economie, des Finances et de l'Industrie
DGCCRF, Bureau B3 Teledoc 031 59
Bld Vincent-Auriol
75703 Paris cedex 13
France
Tel: +33 1 44972333
Fax: +33 1 44973467
(Director Général: Jérome Gallot)

Germany:

Bundeskartellamt
Kaiser-Friedrich-Strasse 16
53113 Bonn
Germany
Tel: +49-228-913980
Fax: +49-228-9139868
(President: Dr. Ulf Böge)

Greece:

Competition Committee
Building of Ministry of Commerce (5th floor)
10 Kaningos Square
GR - 10181 Athens
Greece
Tel: +30-1-382990
Fax: +30-1-3829654
(President: St. Argyropoulos)

Ireland:

Department of Enterprise, Trade and Employment
South Frederick Street
Dublin 2
Ireland
Tel: +353 1 6312240
Fax: +353 1 6312820
(Assistant Secretary: Brian Whitney)

210

Italy:

Autorita Garante della Concorrenza e del Mercato
Via Liguria 26
00187 Rome
Italy
Tel: +39 06 481 621
Fax: +39 06 481 622 56
(President: Guiseppe Tesauro)

Luxembourg:

Ministere de l'Economie
Case Postale 97
19–21 Boulevard Royal
2914 Luxembourg
Luxembourg
Tel: +352 47 84172
Fax: +352 221 607
(Attache de Government: Pierre Rauchs)

Netherlands:

Nederlandse Mededingingsautoriteit
107 Johanna Westerdijkplein
Postbus 16326
2500 BH The Hague - N
Tel: +31 70 330 3392
Fax: +31 70 330 3390
(Director General: Anne Willem Kist)

Portugal:

Direccao-Geral da Comercio da Concorrencia
Avenida Visconde Valmor 72
1069–041 Lisbon
Portugal
Tel: +351 1 791 9100
Fax: +351 1 791 9260
(Director-Geral: Dr. Jose Cortez)

Spain:

Servicio de Defensa de la Competencia
Calle Alcala 9
4 planta
28071 Madrid
Spain
Tel: +34 91 595 8000/ +34 91 595 8263
Fax: +34 91 595 8787/ +34 91 595 8261
(Director General: Luis de Guindos)

Sweden:

Konkurrensverket
Malmskillnadsgatan 32
10385 Stockholm
Sweden
Tel: +46 8 700 1600
Fax: +46 8 245 543/+46 8 796 9608
(Director General: Anne-Christine Nykvist)

United Kingdom:

The Office of Fair Trading
Fleetbank House
2–6 Salisbury Square
London EC4Y 8JX
UK
Tel: +44 171 211 8902
Fax: +44 171 211 8800
(Director General: John Bridgeman)